TEN DAYS
IN MAY
MANCHESTER UNITED THE CLASS OF 63

Published by
Legends Publishing

E-mail david@legendspublishing.net
Website www.legendspublishing.net

Copyright 2021

THIS BOOK IS DEDICATED TO THE MEMORIES OF HARRY GREGG,
TONY DUNNE, MAURICE SETTERS, NOBBY STILES & ALBERT QUIXALL.
FIVE PLAYERS WHO PLAYED TOGETHER DURING THE 1962-63 SEASON
AND WHO ALL PASSED AWAY DURING 2020, AS WELL AS TO
PHIL CHISNALL WHO DIED IN 2021.

THANKS TO LESLIE MILLMAN, JAMES THOMAS, GARY CAPLAN,
TONY PARKS AND SIMON RUMSEY FOR THE USE OF ITEMS FROM
THEIR COLLECTIONS.

CONTENTS

INTRODUCTION

Mention 'Ten Days In May' to the majority of Manchester United supporters and they will undoubtedly go misty eyed and drift back to 1999, when the 16th of that month saw a dramatic fight back at Old Trafford, on a nail-biting Sunday afternoon, when Tottenham Hotspur took a 1-0 lead in a game that United had to win to clinch the Premier League title.

A David Beckham goal, two minutes before the interval, clawed United back into the game, then a mere three minutes into the second half, Andy Cole scored what was to be the winner and the championship was won.

Six days later, it was off to Wembley, with Newcastle United standing between Alex Ferguson's side and the double. Below the twin towers, the north-east side were never in the hunt and, despite an injury to Roy Keane, goals from Teddy Sheringham and Paul Scholes ensured victory.

The travelling Red Army celebrated, but many did not head for home. They had made their plans in the weeks and days leading up to that Wembley final as United chased not simply the Premier League title and the FA Cup, but also the Champions League crown – an unprecedented treble, and Barcelona was their destination.

At the Camp Nou on May 26th Bayern Munich took the lead via a Basler free-kick in the sixth minute – it was an advantage they hung onto throughout the next eighty-four. It looked to be a step too far for United and, in any case, two out of three wasn't too bad.

A mere three minutes stoppage time remained. United won a corner. David Beckham swung it into the Bayern goalmouth, as United goalkeeper Peter Schmeichel caused a distraction. The ball was partly cleared, only as far as Ryan Giggs who quickly returned it goalward. Substitute Teddy Sheringham stuck out a foot, scuffed a shot, whatever, the ball slipped inside the post and into the net. Extra-time beckoned.

It was never to materialise as, with stoppage time edging to an end, United had won yet another corner. There was no Schmeichel this time, but there was Solskjaer, who got onto to the end of Sheringham's header to angle the ball into the roof of the Bayern Munich net, thus bringing ten, never to be forgotten days to a magnificent close.

Back in May 1963, there was no treble shining on the horizon, just black clouds, as relegation threatened. That there was also an F.A. Cup Final to play was of minor importance. Securing the club's First Division future was more of a priority.

But having retained their place in the English top flight, thanks to an Alex Quixall penalty at Maine Road in a 1-1 draw, a result that nudged neighbours City towards the Second Division instead, Matt Busby marched his players to Wembley ten days later to face Leicester City.

United players hold Fergie aloft after completing a remarkable treble

United were the underdogs on the day as Leicester City had finished fourth behind Champions Everton, but United turned the form book on its head and lifted the famous old trophy with a 3-1 win.

It wasn't simply an F.A. Cup victory. It was much more than that, as the victory went a huge way to nudge the horrors of Munich to one side, whilst also kick-starting a memorable decade in the club's history which saw them claim the First Division title on two occasions – 1964-65 and 1966-67 – as well as winning the supreme accolade of the European Cup in 1968.

This is the story of not simply those ten days in May, but the trials and tribulations the club endured since that Thursday afternoon in 1958. It is also a tribute to five members of that 1962-63 United squad – Harry Gregg, Tony Dunne, Nobby Stiles, Albert Quixall and Maurice Setters who all died within a short period of each other in 2020.

CHAPTER ONE
MUNICH AND THE AFTERMATH

Munich. The word wasn't exactly taboo within the confines of Old Trafford, it was simply never mentioned, it didn't fall into the Manchester United vocabulary in the early sixties.

It had been just over five years since that fateful Thursday afternoon in Germany, such a short period of time, the length span between giving birth and that same child going to school. You could remember those first tentative steps, that first word, while those who supported Manchester United could also recall, just as easily, the colossus that was Duncan Edwards, the deceptive body-swerve of Eddie Colman and the dark head of hair above the seemingly constant smile of Tommy Taylor.

Although the Munich disaster brought a premature end to a chapter in the history of Manchester United, one that would surely have gone on to see countless honours bestowed upon it, it was not the death knell of the club itself. The tough talking, chain-smoking Welshman that was Jimmy Murphy, spared the journey to Belgrade through international duties with Wales, grabbed the club by the scruff of its neck, cajoled the youngsters, who were already well versed in Murphy's ways, into becoming men, and more than capable first team footballers overnight. They gave the grief-stricken club hope for the future.

Thirteen days after the disaster Murphy's depleted side, augmented with the veteran Ernie Taylor, signed from Blackpool and a last gasp addition in Stan Crowther from Aston Villa, whose signing as the minutes ticked away towards kick-off against Sheffield Wednesday had to be given special clearance by the Football Association to play as he had already appeared for Villa in the competition [it was against the rules to play for two teams in the same season], had to cast all thoughts of what had occurred a mere couple of weeks previously to the back of their minds and concentrate on what was an F.A. Cup fifth round tie against the Yorkshire side.

Bill Foulkes leads out United for that first game after Munich

Sheffield Wednesday would have preferred to have been any-where but Old Trafford on the evening of February 19th, but they had no choice in the matter. What was said in that visitors dressing room, or what thoughts went through the minds of those Wednesday play-ers as they drove, arguably silently, towards Old Trafford is anyone's guess. Their minds may well have been as blank as the United team in the match programme.

The game was to be written into Manchester United folklore, with the two goals from twenty-year-old debutant Shay Brennan and another from eighteen-year-old Alex Dawson enough to secure vic-tory. Wednesday were beaten by boyish enthusiasm, coupled with grit and determination and perhaps with the help of one or two ghosts.

Had the remainder United's 1957-58 season been simply F.A. Cup ties, then it was without doubt that they would have lifted the famous old trophy below the twin towers at the beginning of May, but they were caught up in a whirlwind of fixtures – eight in March [including four cup-ties] and nine in April, enough to subdue the best of teams, but they games that were to leave Murphy's players exhausted and they were to win only one league game following the disaster, a 2-1 success at Sunderland. They also failed to score in seven of those four-teen fixtures that followed. Their attempt at maintaining an assault upon leaders Wolves, and clinching a third successive First Division title lay in tatters. They finished ninth.

At Wembley, near neighbours Bolton Wanderers showed little mercy, not that it was expected, but their 2-0 victory was achieved in dubious circumstances and on another day, their second goal would have been disallowed as Nat Lofthouse bundled Harry Gregg and the ball over the line to the disgust of many.

It was a step too far, something that was only too obvious to the diminutive Ernie Taylor who was to say: "I knew we hadn't a chance. The night before the game, while the youngsters were feting and fuming and wondering what Wembley was going to be like, I took myself away for a couple of quiet beers. "It's up to you, the old man", I told myself. This was one I wanted to win more than any other match – and not because it would have meant a third Wembley winners medal for me.

"But the more I thought the game over, the more I decided we hadn't a snowball in hell's chance of stopping Bolton. Mind you, I still think we were unlucky to lose 2-0, because I'm sure that Nat Loft-house fouled Harry Gregg in scoring Bolton's second goal.

"Manchester United rose above themselves before the Final."

Even when that final whistle echoed around the north London sta-dium, United's season, their agony, was still not over as they had to face AC Milan in the semi-final of the European Cup, a trophy that many simply wanted to give to United without them having to take any further part in the competition.

A 2-1 victory in the first-leg at Old Trafford was not enough to ensure a place in the final, as the Italians romped through with a 4-0 victory on their home soil.

The season, one that had seemingly stretched forever and had taken Manchester United Football Club from the verge of greatest to hell and back, was finally over. Enough tears to have had an effect on a rain forest had been shed, but it was now time to move on. The past would never be forgotten, but it was without a shadow of doubt, time to look towards the future, not the past. There was nothing to be gained from standing still and August, and a new season would be upon them soon enough.

The summer of 1958 gave United some breathing space and for Matt Busby to make something of a recovery from his, at one time, life threatening injuries. Many clubs, having been affected in the way United had been would, if finances permitted, would have spent the close season replenishing their playing staff. But United had lost players of immense quality, irreplaceable individuals, and although there had been immediate offers of help following the disaster, those helping hands were no longer reaching out to the club and they now had to stand on their own feet and simply get on with it.

Reinforcements were undoubtedly required, as Busby had, since the early Fifties, built not one but two Manchester United first elevens, and when one individual was missing through injury or international call-ups, his position could be filled by a more than capable replacement.

Between the sticks, if Harry Gregg wasn't available, then Ray Wood could step in. At full-back, it was Bill Foulkes and Roger Byrne who claimed the numbers two and three shirts as their own, but waiting in the wings were Ian Greaves and Geoff Bent. The half-back line would normally see Eddie Colman, Mark Jones and Duncan Edwards, but there was the back-up of Jackie Blanchflower, Wilf McGuinness and Freddie Goodwin. Up front it was Johnny Berry, Liam Whelan, Tommy Taylor, Dennis Violet and David Pegg or you could see Albert Scanlon, Alex Dawson, Colin Webster and Bobby Charlton thrown into the mix.

Certainly, half of those mentioned were still at the club, although Berry and Blanchflower would never play again, but those who remained were simply the supporting cast, the stars had all gone, leaving many of the games observers with the expectation that having taken stock of the situation at hand, there would be headlines aplenty during the summer of 1958 as Manchester United set about re-building for the future.

Those headlines, however, were never to materialise for one reason or another. There were certainly a handful of talented youngsters at the club, kids such as Johnny Giles, Frank Haydock, Nobby Stiles, Phil Chisnall and Jimmy Nicholson, but for them, first team football was still nothing more than an ambition, as it had been for those like Mark Pearson and Shay Brennan who were thrown in at the deep end in the aftermath of Munich.

The only transfer activity was to centre around one of that afore-mentioned 'supporting cast', Welsh international Colin Webster. Something of a utility forward who had filled all forward positions for the club during the previous season and played every game following the crash, Webster had everything to look forward to and had hoped secure a regular place at the start of the 1958-59 season. This, however, failed to materialise and although having played in the recent World Cup Finals in Sweden, he was to find himself on the United transfer list.

It was a strange decision, as Webster was a more than capable individual and, as mentioned, United were not exactly brimming with quality within their ranks at this particular time.

Were there no players of the quality that Busby and Murphy required? Possibly, but there would certainly have been the odd seasoned professional out there who could have arrived in Manchester and done a creditable job in the short term if the need arose. Money wasn't exactly a problem as a profit of £97,987 had been made the previous season, but from a media point of view, without any new summer signings, United would be one of the teams who would find themselves at the wrong end of the table.

The pre-season of 1958-59, somewhat surprisingly, saw United not only back in Germany, but in Munich, the journey taken overland by train, with Matt Busby stating: "When I was recovering in hospital it became my wish to bring United to play here to try and repay some of the debt of gratitude, we owe the people of Munich."

In the first of the two fixtures in Germany, six of those who had experienced the horrors of the previous February - Harry Gregg, Bill Foulkes, Kenny Morgans, Dennis Viollet, Bobby Charlton and Albert Scanlon were all included in the team that lost 4-3 to a Munich select side, while all but Scanlon took part in the second of the two friendlies, a 2-0 defeat at the hands of Hamburg.

What the 1958-59 First Division campaign would bring was a matter of debate around the public houses of Manchester and beyond. "Some of our finest players together with some of the most experienced members of our staff are no longer with us. As Matt Busby regains his strength, the team you cheer today is about to start one of the most testing seasons in the history of the club" wrote Chairman Harold Hardman in the first issue of the club programme for the opening match against Chelsea, a game that was to see United get off to the perfect start with a 5-2 victory, curtesy of a Charlton hat-trick and a Dawson double, sending the majority of the 52,362 crowd home happy.

A 3-0 victory at Nottingham Forest four days later confirmed it wasn't simply a one-off and, despite a 2-1 defeat at Bloomfield Road Blackpool, United remained in second place following a 1-1 draw in the return fixture against Forest and an emphatic 6-1 hammering of Blackburn Rovers at Old Trafford, a team who had not simply travelled through rural Lancashire having conceded only two goals in their four games to date, but sat at the top of First Division prior to kick-off.

Three points from the following three fixtures maintained the momentum, keeping United in the leading pack and things continued to look more than promising in mid-September when Busby at last took the cheque book out of his desk drawer and paid Sheffield Wednesday £37,500 or even £45,000 depending on whatever paper you cared to read, for their twenty-four- year-old forward Albert Quixall.

Quixall, who had captained Sheffield Wednesday in that first game following the Munich disaster at Old Trafford, was once hailed as the golden boy of English football and had asked the Sheffield club to put him on the transfer list. Twelve hours after his request had been granted, he was a Manchester United player.

"As you know we have been team building since our unfortunate accident" said Busby. "I have always been a great admirer of this boy and I am delighted he has signed for us. He will be a great asset." Quixall was to add: "I am glad it is all over and I am happy to be joining Manchester United."

This was seen as only the start, with more additions to come, sooner rather than later. Brian Clough and Joe Baker were considered possible targets, along with a much needed outside-right and a left-back. Suddenly the press was bubbling with numerous names as regards possible signings, from Stokes City's nineteen-year-old defender Tony Allen to the currently unhappy Preston North End veteran Tom Finney.

It was perhaps rather ironic that the arrival of Albert Quixall was to coincide with the early season momentum stutter. Goals were often at a premium, Quixall himself would only score once in nine games and from dropping only eight points in the opening ten games, United would pick up three in the next eight outings. The 6-3 defeat at Bolton on November 15th leaving them fifteenth in the table, on fifteen points. It was a swift, rapid fall, with many outside of Manchester being of the opinion that it had been expected.

What wasn't expected though was United not simply shrugging off that mauling by their near neighbours, but by some manner of means, taking the First Division by the scruff of the neck, attacking all and sundry as if in a maniacal frenzy and by February 21st, following a 2-1 victory over leaders and current champions Wolves, finding themselves not just in second place, but level on points with the Midlands club.

Had it not been for Munich, there would have been further games on the United fixture list in the European Cup, possibly as European

Quixall joined United in September 1958 for a British record fee of £45,000

champions, if not, perhaps as League champions. Magical nights under the Old Trafford floodlights.

The events at Munich had touched the hearts of many, not just on home shores, but also abroad, so much so with the latter that an invitation had landed on the Old Trafford doormat in early June from Dr. E. Schwarz, president of the European Football Union, asking the club if it would like to participate in the 1958-59 European Cup competition.

The invite from the Executive Committee said that it had decided that in view of the loss suffered by United in the Munich disaster, the invitation might be helpful to them and their young players to become re-established in the football world. It was an invite, not simply made out of sympathy, but one that had also been taken with financial consideration in mind, as United would obviously have to dip into their bank balance at some point in the weeks and months ahead, in order to rebuild the team to a similar standard to what it was before the crash.

Clubs competing in the European Cup could be expected to earn around £20,000 from the first-round ties, with the sum increasing as progress was made. Such a sum was not to be brushed aside, as the opportunity of making vast amounts of cash through the game in the late 1950's was few and far between. A look at the club accounts from this time reveal £100,701 in the Deposit Account and £12,051 in the Current Account, not exactly vast sums of money, although the profit of £97,957 was a record for a football club at that time. The income from a few European Cup ties in the months ahead, however, would certainly have been more than welcome.

There was obviously a positive response when the invitation arrived at Old Trafford, but they were unable to say "yes" right away as competing in the competition had to be sanctioned by both the Football Association and the Football League. As they had done when United were first invited to take part in the European Cup back in 1956 the Football Association responded positively, but their Football League counterparts once again stood firm and said that United would not be allowed to take part.

Matt Busby, as he had done in the summer of 1956, advised his board of directors that they should accept such a generous invitation and a letter was sent to UEFA to that effect. Despite the huge debate surrounding the matter on home soil, the name of Manchester United was included in the draw for the opening round of the competition when they were paired with Young Boys of Berne in Group Two, along with the likes of Juventus, Schalke and Wiener Sports Club.

Despite this positive step, correspondence continued to be exchanged almost daily between United, the Football League and the Football Association and at the United board meeting on July 8th a letter from the Football League was read out which refused to give the club permission to participate in the forthcoming seasons European Cup competition. It was a callous decision which angered the board.

Seven days later the board made the decision to appeal against the Football League's decision, with a letter sent to the Management Committee and on July 29th it was reported that the appeal had been upheld with the decision of the Board of Appeal as follows:- "The Board of Appeal has come to the conclusion that whatever the intention of the Football League was, they have not the power under League Regulation 33 to refuse permission to the Manchester United Football Club to compete in the European Champion Clubs Cup Competition for season 1958/59. In these circumstances the Board of Appeal has decided to allow the appeal and the Appeal fee will, therefore, be returned."

Any thoughts, however, that Manchester United had secured yet another famous victory were soon thrown into disarray as on August 8th, a statement was released from Mr. J. Richards of the Football League, which read: "The position is that Manchester United have made and won their appeal and naturally so far as they are concerned, the matter is at an end. The Management Committee has decided to pursue the questions, but there is nothing to say on that point at this stage. We have certainly not inferred that United are about to be expelled from the League."

The matter dragged on and on, with the Football League sticking to their guns, with the Football Association eventually doing a complete reversal and siding with the League. The decision had been made, there was no possibility of it being reversed and the proposed European Cup ties became friendlies instead.

Goals were never a problem. They only failed to score in one game between October 8th and April 11th and during that remarkable run between the defeat at Bolton and the 0-0 draw at Luton that April afternoon they always managed to score two or more in each game.

Bobby Charlton was without doubt the main man, finishing the season on twenty-nine from thirty-eight outings. Dennis Viollet chipped in with twenty-one, but perhaps the biggest contribution came from Warren Bradley, a complete unknown, who only arrived in Manchester, along with Bishop Auckland team mates Derek Lewin and Bob Hardisty in order to bolster the depleted ranks following Munich.

Promoted to the first team, five days after signing professional forms for the first time, Bradley made his debut in that 6-3 defeat by Bolton, but went on to played two dozen games, scoring twelve goals.

That meteoric surge up the table might never have happened but for two things. One was a Third Round 3-0 F.A. Cup defeat at the hands of Norwich City, while the other was that body of faceless men who seldom met, but had the power to make decisions on any important and urgent matters, denying United the opportunity to play in the European Cup.

That shock F.A. Cup defeat displayed the fragility of the Manchester United of this period. The week before they had beaten Blackpool at home 3-1, while the next four fixtures saw them draw 4-4 with Newcastle United at home, then defeat Tottenham Hotspur away 3-1, Manchester City at home 4-1 and beat Wolves at home 2-1. Sixteen goals in five games, yet they couldn't score against, nor defeat a Second Division side.

So, with no mid-week distractions of additional unwanted fixtures, all focus was on the improbable vision of the First Division title.

A 3-2 defeat at Arsenal propelled the Gunners into first place, whilst another reversal at the end of March, 4-2 at Burnley, left United a point behind Wolves, but they had played two games more, with only five remaining.

Wolves dropped a point at Burnley and again at Bolton as United won at home against Bolton and drew at Luton, but it was the two games in hand that were to edge Wolves to the title, finishing six points ahead of United who were to lose at Leicester City on the last day of the season, exhausted but certainly not disgraced.

No-one could have guessed that Manchester United would have come so close to being crowned First Division champions with the anguish of Munich being just over twelve months in the past. In all honesty, many had United down as relegation favourites, the reality of what they had suffered recoiling back to hit them hard.

Rebuilding was still very much an ongoing thing and it would be a matter of years, not months, before Busby's team would show any resemblance to what had gone before.

CHAPTER TWO
FROM THE ASHES

Prior to the start of the 1959-60 season United were back in Germany, defeating Bayern Munich 2-1, but losing by the same score line to Hamburg SV. The line-up showed little in the way of change to the one that seen out the previous campaign. There was plenty of goodwill off the field, but on it was an entirely different business with Albert Quixall and Joe Carolan both sent-off against Bayern.

The domestic season kicked off with a visit to West Bromwich Albion where Dennis Viollet scored twice in a 3-2 defeat. Unperturbed by a second defeat 1-0 at home against Chelsea four days later, United sent out a message of intent by winning three of their next four games, drawing the other, scoring sixteen goals in the process. Newcastle United were beaten 3-2, revenge was secured against Chelsea in 6-3 win, while Leeds United were also hit for six without reply. Only a 1-1 draw at Birmingham City blotted the copybook. Dennis Viollett added to his opening day double with a further five.

Were United going to be challenging for that title once again? Many certainly thought so, but that was soon to change to more than likely not, as they failed to win any of their next four games, scoring only thrice, two of the games leaving the goals for column blank.

A 5-1 hammering at home against Tottenham Hotspur was a clear indication that there could be problems ahead, especially in defence, but Busby insisted that there would be no panic buying and, in any case, he considered that there was no-one available. Or perhaps more to the point, the Old Trafford coffers were not exactly bulging at the seams.

In his "Matt Busby Talking" column in the 'United Review', the manager wrote: "With only eight points from our first ten games, we have made a very disappointing start to the season that on paper, held high promise of sweet success in view of our performances last term. I make no excuses for saying here that in the last few weeks we have not had 'the run of the green'. We've had a little luck in the past – and we will get our share in the future, particularly when the boys break out of the recent poor patch that has brought a crop of "wrong" results.

"What I would like to make clear is that we are not sitting back Micawber-like and 'waiting for something to turn up'. That there are weaknesses I am fully aware – but good players are not often available for transfer in these days as many other clubs in addition to United have found out recently."

In the 'Daily Mirror' following the Tottenham debacle, Frank McGhee was to pen: "The patient voice of Matt Busby sounded a bit tired yesterday – tired of trying to provide a reasonable answer to the semi-hysterical scream that he must buy to bolster up his defence, that he must buy BIG and buy SOON. He knows the defence is suspect. He makes it clear that as soon as a top-class defender who can meet his standards of skill and strength comes on to the market Manchester United will be the financial pace-makers in the race to sign a star."

Following a 2-2 draw with Leeds, who they had defeated 6-0 only the week before, United lost 3-0 at Manchester City and 4-0 at Preston North End, but there was still little in the way of concern, "Just because we lose a couple of early games there's no need to think the world's come to an end. We have got to give the lads who finished second in the League last season a fair chance" said Busby. He was, however, far from convincing, putting on a strong front as when questioned further as to whether he would buy top-class players if and when they became available, he replied: "That is something the club and myself would have to consider. The younger material in the club is very encouraging and I think time will show United will be alright. Viollet, Quixall and Charlton made a fine goal producing trio, but I knew in my heart that this high place (finishing second in the League last season) was false. We were just not that good. The players were going all out, but the leaks were beginning to show. We had to buy. We couldn't wait now for youth, though our youth policy was going on. The players of the quality we needed were not in the quantity we needed."

But United bounced back and if they were going to mount a championship challenge then it was going to be on the back of Dennis Viollet's goals.

Viollet had only played twice at the tail end of the 1957-58 season following Munich, but had missed only five games during 1958-59, scoring twenty-one goals. By mid-December 1959 he had scored twenty-three – two hat-tricks, half a dozen doubles and five singles. His last fifteen had come in eleven outings, but only six of those had resulted in United victories, there were three draws and two defeats. Despite this, the First Division table showed United occupying a mid-table position, seven points behind leaders Tottenham.

Such a position was of little concern to those who pulled the strings within the Old Trafford set-up. They knew that they were perhaps fortunate to be even a member of the English games top flight following Munich and that reaching the level that they had achieved prior to February 1958 was going to take time. The question was, however, would it be achieved with Matt Busby at the helm?

There had been an indirect approach from an unnamed Scottish club, offering him a salary of £4,000

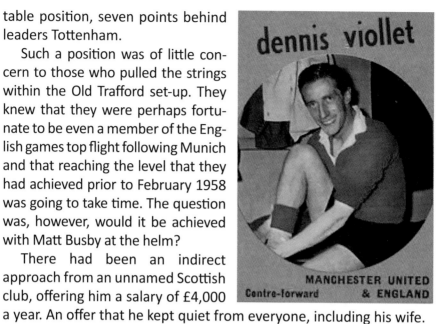

dennis viollet

MANCHESTER UNITED
Centre-forward   & ENGLAND

a year. An offer that he kept quiet from everyone, including his wife.

"Yes, there was an approach" Busby later confirmed, "but it was an indirect approach, which I never even hesitated about. My life is with Manchester United and there it is going to remain. I told them: "I have no desire to leave. Manchester United have always been very good to me, so as far as I am concerned, they are the only club I shall ever be with.""

There was never a mention as to who the club were, but at a guess, it could be narrowed down to two – Celtic or Hibs. It matters little as Matt Busby remained in Manchester.

Up front, United looked fairly solid, it was in defence there appeared to be a problem, or perhaps it would be better to say a weakness. Looking for suitable individuals to strengthen the United rear guard, Busby's interest centred around Glasgow Rangers full-back Eric Caldow, an established Scottish internationalist, but one who had lost his place in the Ibrox first team line up.

But here was an individual who add some stability to the lacklustre United defence and it was somewhat ironic that Busby had him watched in a Rangers reserve fixture the same afternoon that United conceded four without reply against Preston at Deepdale.

Caldow's wife was apparently unsettled in Glasgow, hankering on a return to her native north-east, but despite this, the two clubs agreed a fee of around £28,000. The Rangers man, however, stalled for time, as it was rumoured that Newcastle United were contemplating a

move. Busby was unmoved by the attempted hijack and was confident that the transfer would go through.

A meeting in Manchester, with the couple shown houses, looked to have sealed the deal, but having asked for a further twenty-four hours to 'think about it', Caldow announced he was staying put.

No sooner had Caldow 'aborted' his move and Busby had discarded the unsolicited approach for his services than Liverpool were reported as to be wanting Jimmy Murphy as their next manager, offering a salary of £2,500. Old Trafford was becoming akin to a soap opera.

Countless names were being linked with the club – Knapp of Leicester City, Allen of Stoke City, Armfield and Gratix of Blackpool, Charlton of Leeds, but it wasn't until April that Busby eventually managed to bring a defender to the club and even then, it was an untried eighteen-year-old Irishman called Tony Dunne [pictured], signed from Shelbourne for a fee of around £2,500.

Following Dennis Viollet's avalanche of goals, it was back to normality, or was it mediocrity, as the results in the second half of December 1959 up to the beginning of March 1960 was like being on a fairground big-dipper. Two other results, friendlies against Real Madrid, could also be thrown into the mix, losing 6-1 at Old Trafford, but almost turning things around in Spain and only losing by the odd goal in eleven!

In the First Division, it was beating Nottingham Forest 5-1 at the City Ground one Saturday, then losing 3-2 at home to West Bromwich Albion the next. Beating Burnley away 4-1, then losing to Newcastle United away 7-3. Winning 6-0 at Blackpool, losing 2-0 at home to Wolves, then beating Nottingham Forest at home 3-1. Unpredictable didn't even come into it!

It was all down to nothing more than indifferent form. The only bad luck that came into it was for Wilf McGuinness. Dropped for the visit of Blackpool to Old Trafford on December 5th, he was to break his leg the following weekend when playing against Stoke City reserves at Old Trafford. An injury that was in effect to bring an end to his playing career.

The injury was a blow to not just the player himself, but to the club. Shay Brennan stepped into the void and filled the position admirably until the end of the season. Strangely, Brennan, alongside Ronnie Cope and Bill Foulkes, were the only players to play in all the remaining league fixtures.

Knowing that he needed some muscle in the defence, Busby finally got the chequebook out in January, signing half-back Maurice Setters from West Bromwich Albion. He had denied any interest in the player a matter of days earlier, but with neighbours City also sniffing around, willing to pay Albion's asking price of £25,000, he stepped in with an offer of £30,000 and secured his signature. Having lost some of the steel in the heart of the defence by selling Stan Crowther last season, Setters was a ready-made replacement.

After signing for United, Setters said: "This is a wonderful day for me. I have had some sleepless nights since I asked Albion for a move – and it was a damned sight worse when I read that Manchester United were not interested in my future."

"I am not a rebel or a trouble maker. I've tried to do my job as skipper by acting as spokesman for others with a grievance and because of that, I have been carpeted and for that alone acquired a reputation."

Having paid out around £30,000, Matt Busby was given the opportunity of recouping his outlay less than a fortnight later, whilst adding a further £90,000 to the Old Trafford coffers. This was the era of the 'Lure of the Lira'; when household names such as Denis Law and Jimmy Greaves were tempted by the wages offered for plying their trade in Italian football.

Today, the possibility of cashing on an 'asset' such as Bobby Charlton might have created much in the way of debate around the corridors of Old Trafford, but the £90,000 offered by six Italian clubs did little to persuade Matt Busby to part with United's golden boy. "I do not want to leave Manchester United" said Charlton, "but when you hear of the fantastic cash inducements overseas, you have to think twice about your future. Footballers have only a short life, but I will accept whatever decision the club. My future wife does not want to live abroad. We'll be satisfied with any success we can find here."

Munich was never far from the thoughts of many and a dismal wet Thursday morning, just over two years since the tragedy, around two hundred and fifty people, including parents, relatives and friends gathered along with the current playing staff, outside the main entrance at Old Trafford for the unveiling of the Munich Memorial.

Clearly moved by the occasion, Matt Busby made a brief speech after pulling back the drapes, saying: "I know that those who are

MAURICE SETTERS (Manchester United)

near and dear have a memorial in their hearts which will last for all time. But now our many friends will also have an everlasting memorial here to the lads who helped make this such a great club."

Mr. Dan Marsden, chairman of the Ground Committee, unveiled a clock, which was situated at the Warwick Road end of the ground, high up on the wall and inscribed above and below the two-faced dial – February 6th 1958, Munich. Inside the stadium, a bronze plaque in the press box, bearing the names of the eight journalists who died was unveiled by the only surviving journalist, Mr. Frank Taylor.

On the playing front, Viollet's goals dried up following that glorious early season burst, although to be fair he did miss seven of the final ten games through injury. Thankfully, Bobby Charlton and Alex Dawson took on the mantle, scoring seven and eleven goals respectively in those final ten fixtures. Viollet weighed in with three.

Of those final ten games, seven were won and some twenty-nine goals were scored. Had it not been for the indifferent from between late December and March then that final position of seventh would undoubtedly have been improved upon.

United were still a long way away from returning to the consistent form that would once again make them a team to be reckoned with.

SEASON 1960-61

Finishing seventh was certainly creditable, slightly disappointing perhaps, but a position that many of United's rivals would have looked upon with envy. Manchester United, however, continued to be very much a work in progress and Matt Busby would undoubtedly have tossed and turned at night debating the merits of countless individuals and how they might help aid the re-building of his team.

The close season was to see no additions to the playing staff, with the Old Trafford coffers only opened to secure the raw materials required to make improvements to the stadium.

Two games into the 1960-61 season, the defeats, 3-1 at home to Blackburn Rovers and 4-0 away at Everton, saw United occupy bottom place in the First Division. True to recent form, Everton were then beaten 4-0 at Old Trafford, before they once again conceded four, scoring one in reply, at Tottenham. The following Saturday they lost again in London, 2-1 at West Ham, but when the Upton Park side made the journey to Old Trafford nine days later, United won 6-1. Inconsistency certainly reigned in those early days of the new season, but even that was to disappear and it was nothing but poor performances as winter approached. Between September and November only four games were won, three drawn and eight lost. The 3-0 defeat at Cardiff City on November 26th left United sixth from the foot of the First Division on thirteen points, two above bottom side Nottingham Forest.

Matt Busby, although not a man to panic, knew he had to do something to ensure that his team climbed the table, and fast, not wanting to be involved in any relegation dog fight come April. He confessed that even he did not think the poor patch would be as bad as it had been and that it all boiled down to the fact that the team as a whole were playing badly, or to be more exact, there were too many players off form at the same time. "This is something that has been visualised because we lost the services of ten great players in that awful Munich disaster and I only signed two as replacements. Whatever patching up was done after that black day, it was obvious that it would leave some impression eventually.

"In a way I consider it unfortunate that we had so much artificial success immediately after the crash. Had we slumped to the Second Division, people would have only nodded their heads in sympathy, as such a fall was expected. But instead, we continued with success that on the cards looked impossible to get."

Back Row: Setters, Foulkes, Brennan, Gregg, Cantwell, Nicholson.
Front Row: Quixall, Stiles, Dawson, Pearson, Charlton.

Back he went to Ibrox to see if Mrs. Caldow would change her mind about moving south. He eyed Ray Wilson at Huddersfield Town, George Thomson at Heart of Midlothian, Ron Yeats at Dundee United and Mel Nurse at Swansea Town.

A move for Nurse looked a distinct possibility, although £20,000 did little to persuade the Welsh club's directors to sell. What might have tipped the scales was throwing Alex Dawson into the mix, but Busby, although well aware that he needed to strengthen his defence, was equally aware that if his team were going to leak goals then they had to combat that by scoring them and Dawson, on his day, was as good as any.

Nurse came nowhere near to moving to Manchester, despite the Welsh connection with Jimmy Murphy and Busby was criticised for not only failing to use Dawson as part of the bait in order to secure a player he obviously wanted, but for also attempting to dictate the terms of the transfer. He was to explain that with injuries playing as much a part in the current predicament as poor form, he felt that selling the bustling centre-forward was a gamble that he just could not take, as any further injuries to his forward line following any transfer of Dawson, would simply mean that he had to go out and buy yet another replacement.

What is worth noting is the fact that of the players United showed an interest in, three of them eventually moved and became important individuals at their new clubs. Nurse moved to Middlesbrough, Wilson

to Everton and Yeats to Liverpool. Many asked the question as to why did they not end up at Old Trafford when there was interest there? There was still the conveyor belt from reserves to first team, but it did not have the constant flow of old. Johnny Giles had emerged at the end of the previous season and continued in the side this season until a broken leg set him back.

Jimmy Nicholson [pictured] came in against Everton in only the second game of the season and progressed to the Northern Ireland international set-up, while Frank Haydock was another who appeared on the first team scene, but was part of the insecure defence and soon disappeared from view. Mark Pearson, one of the hero of that post-Munich Sheffield Wednesday cup tie, was another who made a re-appearance in the first team following only fleeting outings in the previous campaign and became a regular.

If that Norwich City F.A. Cup defeat of the 1958-59 season was a telling factor in where Manchester United found themselves in those post-Munich days, then early November 1960 produced what could be classed as the definitive result of United in the early sixties.

Involved in the Football League Cup for the first time, they struggled to draw 1-1 away at Fourth Division Exeter City. Just over 15,000 bothered to turn up at Old Trafford for the replay, which United won 4-1, giving them another away tie at Bradford City. Against the Third Division side, and despite taking the lead, the Yorkshire side went on to win 2-1. It was a defeat that took three games to recover from and one that forced Busby into finally making a move into the transfer market.

Prior to the visit of Bayern Munich for yet another of those hopeful money-making friendlies, terms were agreed for the transfer of Noel Cantwell from West Ham United, with an estimated £25,000 changing hands. Some of that Cantwell transfer fee was recouped from the sale of Munich survivor Albert Scanlon to Newcastle United for £15,000. Scanlon had started the previous campaign in fine form, but in the closing weeks of the season, rarely featured.

NOEL CANTWELL
LEFT-BACK
MANCHESTER UNITED & EIRE

If Cantwell was happy enough to move from the East End of London, he was taken aback by what he was confronted with in Manchester. Accustomed to the in-depth tactical awareness of the Hammers school of soccer where games were analysed and digested, often using sugar and salt pots and ketchup bottles on a café table top near to the Hammers ground, he was taken aback by the distinct lack of any tactical planning at his new club, with training bordering on the basic.

Dennis Viollet's goals had arguably saved United's 1959-60 season from completely falling apart, but there was little hope of player who was born within the shadows of Maine Road from doing likewise this season, as he was to suffer a broken collar bone in the 3-0 defeat by Cardiff City, an injury that was to rule him out from the end of November until the beginning of April.

Despite losing 6-0 at Leicester City in late January and 5-1 at Sheffield Wednesday towards the end of March, United managed to maintain a mid-table placing, which could be considered surprising due to the indifferent displays. But it was still obvious to all, that despite the final four games of the 1960-61 season producing four straight wins and a draw, along with seventeen goals, shared between only five players – Charlton [4], Quixall [4], Viollet [4], Setters [3] and Pearson [2], there was still much work to be done.

Many of the understudies were not up to scratch and the strength in depth was reduced by the sales during the season of Ian Greaves to Lincoln City, Joe Carolan to Brighton and Hove Albion and Kenny Morgans to Swansea.

The abolition of the maximum wage had now also put pressure on Manchester United with their reluctance to pay high wages, along with their on-field failings making the competition to sign players now even greater. Matt Busby certainly had his work cut out, with the club's overall strategy requiring much examination.

SEASON 1961-62

"It was certainly disappointing being a Manchester United supporter during this period" recalled Walter Johnston, "worrying too if I am completely honest, as it was not something that myself, and the friends I stood alongside on United Road, were really used to.

"Back in the immediate post-war years we had a really solid side. Strong in defence with an attack that was the envy of others. Yes, of course there were ups and downs as the players who won the Cup in 1948 and lifted the league in 1952 began to age and be replaced, but the transition went smoothly, the odd change here and there, and suddenly a new team was there. Of course, we watched the reserves and the youth team, so we were aware of what was waiting in the wings, but all that has changed.

"Personally, I think Munich took more out of Matt Busby than people, and perhaps even himself, realise and it is taking him a while to get back into the swing of things. Ok, Jimmy Murphy is there, but Munich must have taken a hell of a lot out of him as well as what you have got to remember is that he spent more time with the reserves and the kids than Busby did and losing Duncan Edwards, Eddie Colman, David Pegg and Liam Whelan must have been akin to losing a son. Losing one would be bad enough, but four... Season 1958-59 was a fluke and perhaps did little to help the couple of seasons that have followed, but the worrying thing was not just the heavy defeats and the inconsistency, but the threat from other clubs. At the time of Munich, it was just Wolves really who made us look over our shoulder, but then there were a number of teams who looked threatening, Tottenham Hotspur, Burnley, Everton, even Leicester City. These clubs are also not afraid to splash the cash, something that United appeared to be reluctant to do. Buying success, or even your way out of trouble, perhaps wasn't the United way, but they could never think that the name alone would keep them amongst the front runners."

Not only were those other teams a threat on the field, they were even more so off it, as many were paying higher wages than United. It took a meeting with the manager for the players to secure a pay rise of a fiver, plus another fiver appearance money, giving them £35 and £10 respectively, along with rewritten contracts now included a crowd bonus scheme, which guaranteed £1 per thousand between 37,000 and 45,000 and then £2 per thousand over 45,000. The ground capacity at this time was 65,000. There was also a win bonus of £4 and incentive

David Herd moved to Manchester United in July 1961 for £38,000

pay determined by the team's actual League position. A far cry from the maximum £20 per week! Others, however, were earning more.

If the United defence were going to leak goals then Busby was going to go with the old adage that if you scored one more than your opponent you won, confirmed by the signing of David Herd from Arsenal for a fee of around £38,000 in late July. Busby had initially shown an interest in the player nine months previously, but at the time the London club were reluctant to let him go and it took an additional £5,000 this time around to secure his signature.

Partnering either Alex Dawson or Dennis Viollet, with Albert Quix-all and Bobby Charlton for company would surely see Herd and United amongst the goals, but despite three in his first three games, he didn't find the net again until late November. Had Busby wasted his money?

Despite the lack of David Herd goals, United lost only one of their opening nine games, 2-0 at Chelsea at the end of August, with the 3-2 victory against Manchester City on September 23rd seeing them in second spot in the first Division, three points behind leaders Burn-ley with a game in hand. A look at the opposite end could have been considered as something of a warning to Busby's team as it showed recent champions Wolves propping up the table.

But on par with recent form, they drew two and lost eight of the next ten games, which included two 5-1 and two 4-1 defeats. The second of those 5-1 reversals, against Everton on December 2nd, saw United occupy fourth bottom, a point above bottom club Chelsea. They had neighbours City down there with them, level on points, for company. The only plus point was the name of Herd appearing, at last, on the score sheet.

Following the 4-1 defeat against leaders Burnley at the end of November the wrath of the press-box was upon them, with the 'Man-chester Guardian' proclaiming – "Manchester United Pushed Further into the Basement' and their correspondent writing: "What can one say of United that has not been said already? The old sparkle and art-istry have gone. A month away from football would do the whole side good, but that of course is impossible. One step towards improve-ment might be the inclusion of two capable inside-forwards with the physique of Herd. Giles and Quixall, against Burnley's well-built defenders, looked far too small for the task confronting them."

Alex Dawson, who certainly had the necessary physique, but had only featured on four occasions, left for Preston North End, as Busby continued to look for something as near to a winning formula as pos-sible and by the beginning of December, he had used twenty-two players in nineteen games. It was little wonder that results were so varied and performances inconsistent.

Charlton, Herd and Giles could be considered as the only regulars in the front line as Dennis Viollet was out of favour and was eventually sold to Stoke City in January 1962, having failed to appear in the first team since mid-November. His relationship with Busby had soured and his eventual transfer came completely out of the blue.

Attendances fell as results yo-yoed, but surprisingly the F.A. Cup brought something in the way of relief and before they knew it, they were off on a cup run that would take them to the semi-final stage, albeit after replays against Sheffield Wednesday and Preston North End. But there was to be no Wembley appearance as they were outplayed by Tottenham Hotspur at Hillsborough, losing 3-1. "We looked young and raw at times" said a disappointed Matt Busby, "Spurs beat us 3-1, but I saw the pieces of the jigsaw beginning to fit. I felt we were getting within reach of the great Spurs. But one vital item was missing. We had plenty of the ball and used it well, except when it came to the final thrust. There was no end product in the penalty box."

The jigsaw must have been one that the United manager had attempted on countless occasions, as following the semi-final defeat, they were to win only three of their remaining nine games. The form was reflected in the attendances which ranged from 24,000 to 30,000, leaving those pay packets considerably lighter. Strangely, one of that trio of victories was a 5-0 thumping of Ipswich Town who were to be crowned First Division champions! United finished fourteen places behind, but what must be taken into consideration was the fact the Ipswich had only been promoted at the end of the previous season, springing from nowhere while United struggled.

If the supporters had shown with their non-appearance on the Old Trafford terraces that they did not like what was being played out in front of them, they were even more aggrieved to learn that the directors were putting the admission prices up for the following season, a decision based on the fact that since the minimum wage had been abolished, there had been an increase in the Old Trafford wage bill. The money to pay for this had to be found from somewhere and it was decided that it would be the supporters who would foot the difference.

Home performances over the past season had been far from impressive, losing eight of their twenty-one fixtures. Only third bottom Fulham had lost more – ten. If goals were scored were also taken into consideration, there were nine clubs who had scored more than United's tally of forty-four. Only seven had conceded more. But there was nothing those disenchanted supporters could do, except stay away.

Overall, finishing fifteenth was not a position that Manchester United expected to fill, but it was undoubtedly the position that their performances warranted. The thirty-nine points were seventeen less than that of champions Ipswich Town and, with no disrespect to the two Sheffield clubs, United and Wednesday, who finished in fifth and sixth respectively, the name of Manchester United should have featured in a higher position than either of the two.

They were worrying times, as a work in progress could only continue for so long.

CHAPTER THREE
THE ARRIVAL
OF ROYALTY

The 1961-62 season had barely drawn to a close and football should have been put on the back-burner for a few weeks at least, allowing everyone to recharge the batteries, but life at a football club seldom, if ever, stops. Certainly not at Manchester United.

While Matt Busby was hot on the trail of Denis Law, a player he had given his international debut to against Wales in October 1958, his assistant, Jimmy Murphy, although in Switzerland with the United youth team, who were participating in the Blue Stars Tournament, was planning to meet up with fellow Welshman John Charles, who was rumoured to be ready to leave Italian giants Juventus.

Charles, who played for Wales under Murphy, considered the United assistant manager as a friend and mentor, had revealed that he had been offered £12,000 to remain in Italy for another year, but was determined to return to Britain and it was rumoured that United were in secret discussions to lure him to Old Trafford.

It was a move that was never to get near to "just sign here", as his former club Leeds United not only moved into prime position to entice Charles to Elland Road, but secured his signature as others stood by and watched.

Had Busby been determined to build his third Manchester United team using an Identikit of his previous models, then Charles, although twenty-nine years of age, would have been a like-for-like replacement for Duncan Edwards. He was of a similar build and was more than comfortable playing either as a centre-half, his preferred position, or centre-forward.

Age and the transfer fee would have put Busby off signing the Welshman as going over the £50,000 mark for a twenty-nine-year-old could well have been seen as a gamble when you were looking

Dennis Law lines up with his Torino team

towards the long-term future. As it was, Charles returned to Leeds United with the Yorkshire side paying out a club record £53,000 to bring him back to Elland Road.

As it turned out, Busby was proved correct, as Charles found it difficult to re-adjust in Yorkshire, away from sun-kissed Italy, and was to play only eleven games for Leeds before they recouped their outlay, and more, by selling him to Roma for £70,000, where again his career floundered.

But while there were stories circulating as to regards to the arrival of John Charles, these were countered by similar conversations regarding the departure of Bobby Charlton – £300,000 was the figure quoted that Barcelona were willing to pay to take the England international to Spain.

Such had been Charlton's performances in the white of England during the recent World Cup in Chile that Barcelona manager Ladislav Kubala had told his club president: "We MUST sign this man." Such interest wasn't completely dismissed by Charlton, who would only say when asked about the possible transfer: "I'm quite happy with United."

Any possibility of a move was taken out of Charlton's hands a couple of weeks later when he was forced to undergo a hernia operation that would keep him out of the game for a period of two or three months, forcing him to miss the opening weeks of the coming season.

One individual who looked as though he was leaving Old Trafford was trainer Jack Crompton. The former United goalkeeper had returned to United from Luton Town in the wake of the Munich air disaster, but with the managers post at Luton becoming available following the departure of Sam Bartram and interest shown in the United trainer as a replacement, the club felt obliged to release him as a form of 'thank you' to the 'Hatters' for their good turn back in 1958.

Within a week of accepting the post, Crompton had a change of mind and notified Luton that he would not be accepting the job, but remaining at Old Trafford, rejecting the offer for 'personal reasons', that in turn were revealed to be on the advice of his doctor who advised that the stress of management could aggravate his duodenal ulcer trouble.

Although Charlton was missing from the United line-up, there would be no shortage of firepower with the arrival of Denis Law, the long and drawn-out transfer finally being dragged over the line, with United paying Turin £115,000 to bring the Aberdonian back to Britain. It hadn't simply been a matter of weeks of effort for Matt Busby in negotiating the often-complicated transfer, it had been a six-year wait to secure Law's signature.

Busby had first set eyes on the diminutive frame of Law on a rain soaked rough and ready pitch in the West Riding village of Heckmondwike on October 29th 1956, "We were playing Huddersfield in an early round of the youth cup. It was supposed to be just a formality as we had a strong side. But it didn't turn out as easy as we expected.

"At half time we were two down and every time I tried to analyse why and how, I kept coming back to this kid playing inside-right for them.

"He seemed to be as thin as my finger and looked about as strong as a glass of water. He was sixteen and looked fourteen – he skimmed over the mud without any effort. He already looked a mature player, reading the game brilliantly and devastating in attack. I thought we'd had it.

"But he still had something to learn – for he made the mistake of going into defence instead of keeping after us, so our own attack got back into the game and we won 4-2.

"But before I left, I made it my business to check who he was, and where he came from, and over the next few seasons I kept looking out for him."

Busby did keep his eye on him and whilst manager of the Scottish national side, gave the eighteen-year-old his international debut. "By then I was convinced that he would be one of the great players of the era."

Joining Torino in the summer of 1961 in a £100,000 transfer from Manchester City, it was always going to be a step into the unknown for the Aberdonian and the Italians other new signing Joe Baker, but with the promises of an untold fortune in wages, the dark side of the Italian game was not given a second thought, until he arrived in the country. City were prepared to offer Law £100 per week to stay, but with a signing on fee of around £20,000 heading into Law's bank account, plus a similar wage in Italy, money won.

The transfer was covered in controversy before the ink had dried on the contract, as Law admitted that he had actually signed two contracts, a "sort of agreement" with Inter Milan and a final transfer contract with Torino. "It's a rather complicated case" he was to say. "I signed a sort of agreement with Internationale about three weeks ago. As far as I can remember now, it did not envisage any sort of priority for them as far as I was concerned. I do not remember all its terms now.

"Anyway, the contract with Torino was signed by my Manchester City officials and myself, whilst the agreement with Internationale was singed only by me. Manchester City did not even know that I had signed that agreement."

Forgetting the money side of things, life in Italy was far from rosy. He was fined 12,000 Lire [slightly less than £7] for 'incorrect behaviour' during a league match in October 1961, endured further suspensions and rows over appearances for Scotland and trips back home. "It's getting so bad that I am frightened to lift up a paper or answer the phone" he was to comment. Things continued on a downward spiral and almost came to a fatal conclusion in February when along with Joe Baker, he was involved in a car crash which left both players badly injured.

Back in action a couple of months later, things continued to deteriorate and he was removed from the pitch at the trainers request during an Italian cup-tie against Napoli. Having picked up the ball in order to take throw-in, the Torino trainer took the ball from him and told him to: "Get up the filed like a centre-forward should." Law consequently ignored him, but the trainer quickly shouted to the Torino captain to have Law removed from the field, something that was allowed in the Italian game.

Due to the seemingly ever-increasing problematic situation Roma made an inquiry as regards acquiring his signature, while it also saw the possibility of a return to English football moving a step nearer, as following that latest episode, Matt Busby was to throw his hat into the ring a declare a definite interest in bringing his fellow Scot to Old Trafford, saying: "I am ready to fly at a moment's notice to Italy if Torino agrees to sell him. This is the boy we want."

So, no sooner had middle man Gigi Peronace strode out of Manchester City's Maine Road ground having paid the final instalment of Denis Law's transfer fee of the previous summer, than he was heading across Manchester to meet up with Matt Busby to ask if he was indeed interested in signing Law.

Despite his problems in Italy, Juventus were reportedly keen to have Law on their books, with a figure of £150,000 plus a player on loan having been mentioned. It was a figure that United would not meet.

The Juventus interest quickly disappeared, as Law declared that he would not remain in Italy, which left the door wide open for Busby to step in if a fee could be agreed and, with United on something of a close season Mediterranean tour, taking in games in Majorca and Valencia, it was agreed to meet Torino officials in Lausanne, Switzerland were the Italians were currently playing.

Hoping that the meeting would not be too prolonged and a successful outcome could be reached, Matt Busby, chairman Harold Hardman and club director Louis Edwards headed to the Alps for talks with their Italian counterparts. Their journey, however, was to be a wasted one, as the United trio stormed out of the meeting in disgust.

"We have taken this step because we are absolutely fed up with all the intrigue and deceit. It is all over as far as we are concerned. We will be leaving Turin for Amsterdam to tie up with the rest of our own tour party.

"It has been six weeks of hell and had it gone on much longer I'm sure I'd have had a nervous breakdown. We are all disgusted and that is all I want to say at the moment."

But suddenly, Juventus were back on the scene, declaring that they had signed a valid agreement for Law's contract, at a fee of £160,000 and a player on loan, with the move ninety-nine-percent certain of going through. Unlike before, Law had signed nothing.

Twenty-four hours later, however, Torino had climbed down and were back in contact with United, cap in hand, and were apparently prepared to do business, even although supporters demonstrated outside the club's ground against the decision to sell the player. United, however, remained cautious, with chairman Harold Hardman saying

Back Row: Setters, Nicholson, Gaskell, Brennan, Pearson, Cantwell.
Middle Row: Matt Busby, Foulkes, McMillan, Dunne, Stiles, Lawton, Jack
Crompton. Front Row: Giles, Quixall, Herd, Law, Charlton.

that Law, who had returned home to Aberdeen, had to sort out his own problems as he had broken his agreement with the Italians. "Yes, we are interested" he confirmed, "Turin know what we consider Law is worth and we will not increase that figure by one penny. We have never divulged that figure and so far, everyone has been wide of the mark."

The on-off, where will he go, transfer was becoming something of a soap opera and had its regular column inches in every newspaper, with even more being added when it became known that Real Madrid were interested and willing to pay £150,000, although that was most probably nothing more than a smoke screen, as Torino had agreed to pay the Spanish club £300,000 for Del Sol and were struggling to find the money, hence their ploy at attempting to an even higher fee for Law. It had gone from April to June, from Lausanne to Manchester without a conclusion, but it was within the wood panelled walls of the United boardroom that a chink of light finally managed to appear through the curtained windows.

A five-hour meeting between Matt Busby and Gigi Peronace, although not conclusive, looked at last to have made something of dent in the proceedings and although Law, along with Joe Baker, had been recalled by Turin for pre-season training, it looked as though a deal might be close, allowing him to join United.

If Torino didn't hold all the aces, they certainly had the best hand should the deal continue to progress. Law, being the commodity that everyone wanted, might have thought that whatever hand the Italians produced he could not simply match it, but trump it. He was wrong. But the true ace in the pack was neither the club or the player, it was the afore-mentioned Gigi Peronace.

Peronace had been behind taking Law and Baker to Italy, as he had John Charles a few years earlier. Now he had the task of bring Law and Baker back home. "Law was the best player, considering his age, who ever came to Italy" said the Italian. "Better than the great South American's Sivori or Schiaffino, or even the magnificent John Charles.

"When the club for which I bought him, Torino, came to sell him, Denis could have made a fortune – if he hadn't been homesick. If he had stayed here in Italy to play for John Charles's old club, Juventus, he would have got a signing-on fee of nearly £20,000, spread over two years. And Torino, who were selling him, would have given him nearly as much to go."

The Italian go-between went on to say that United had been made aware of Torino's willingness to part company with Law and Baker, as far back as March, although he was not party to this, nor were the two players.

Somewhat surprisingly, Peronace went on to say: "Law was certainly quite happy at the thought of playing a second year for Torino when he left my flat – the English boys both usually ate at my place – to fly home to play for Scotland against England in April.

"He played what I understand you English call a "blinder". But the Denis Law I met at the airport on his return was a vastly different boy from the one I had seen off. He had become homesick almost overnight!

"He told me that he had written from his home in Aberdeen to our president, Signor Angelo Fillipone, asking for a transfer."

Peronace, fed up with the way things had developed with Law and with United as well, walked away from Torino, but was called back due to the mess that the Italians had got themselves into and told to finalise the negotiations that would see both Law and Baker sold to English clubs, although he was to admit that he did try and convince both players that they still had a future in Italy.

When Law confirmed that he had no desire to remain with Torino, or any other Italian side for that matter, Peronace then revealed that he had the authority to sell Law to United and had four clubs interested in signing Joe Baker.

On July 10th, Law travelled to Manchester and met up with Peronace and, the following day, the pair were driven to Old Trafford by journalist Peter Slingsby where the transfer was finally brought to a close with United paying £115,000 to get their man. "It has always been my ambition to play for this club" said Law after signing on the dotted line.

Initially, United offered Torino £110,000, plus the gate receipts from two friendlies between the clubs, but this hit a brick wall when the Italians couldn't find suitable dates, so the fee with upped to £115,000.

With a British record fee having been paid, and another piece of the United jigsaw added, Busby was now edging towards having a team that he considered capable or restoring the club to its former glories. Perhaps the strength in depth of that pre-Munich side wasn't there, but if his team could remain relatively clear of injuries, not to mention suspensions as there were more than the odd short-tempered individual within the ranks, then who knows what the season ahead might bring.

There was however, one unanswered question. If Busby was so certain that Denis Law [pictured above] had every ingredient to become a top player, why did he not sign him in March 1960 when he was available for the sum of £60,000, almost half of what he had just paid?

"At that time, it seemed that the inside forward was the one position that didn't need strengthening", answered Busby, an opinion that suddenly changed following the F.A. Cup semi-final defeat at the hands of Tottenham Hotspur the previous season.

Law's return to home shores wasn't exactly greeted with the fanfare of trumpets and media frenzy that would accompany such a transfer today, but he was certainly acknowledged as one of the top players in the game, with Peter Lorenzo of the 'Daily Herald' going as far as to place him at "No.2 in my world hit parade".

Lorenzo, a highly respected journalist was to write; "In the last few crowded months I've had the good fortune and opportunity to see all the leading inside-forwards in the world of football. Brazil's Pele, Didi and Amarildo, Spain's Puskas and Suarez and Del Sol. Yugoslavia's Sekularac. Italy's Sivori and Rivera, Chile's Toro ... Czechoslovakia's Scherer ... Portugal's Eusebio. The greatest in my book is Pele. He does everything that makes a football sit up and beg.

"But No.2 in my world hit parade, just a bootlace behind in effectiveness and ability, is British based and British produced. I refer, of course, to Denis Law, late of Aberdeen, Huddersfield, Maine Road and Torino, but now thankfully back home to weave his £115,000 magic over Manchester United.

"I saw Pele last May. I saw Law on Saturday and there's so little to choose between the top two today.

"Denis didn't score against Arsenal. He didn't have a foot in any of the three goals. Yet there couldn't have been one of the 62,308 at Highbury who would dispute that Law is the most complete all-round inside-forward in the country today.

"He may not be quite so devastating in finishing as Greaves or Puskas. He may not pass or distribute so accurately as Haynes or Sivori. Or move with the same silky smoothness as John White or Suarez. But combine all his assets and qualities and he emerges so clearly as Britain's and Europe's No. 1 inside-forward.

"Matt Busby, not unnaturally, thinks he's the greatest: "I have seen them all. Alex James, Carter, Doherty and Mannion. But Denis is the tops. He has such amazing stamina, gives so much to the team and to the game. He's the finest I have ever seen."

Lorenzo was also to tip United to lift the F.A. Cup and Tottenham to win the League.

The burden had already been placed upon those scrawny shoulders, so much so, that many were of the expectation that Law, and Law alone, was going to take Manchester United to untold greatness. They were going to have their patience severely tested.

With Denis Law entrenched at Old Trafford, there was now considerable competition for places and one player who has concerns as regards being in contention for a first team place was Mark Pearson, one of the youngsters thrown in at the deep end following Munich. A number of clubs had been watching the Old Trafford merry-go-round with interest and Aston Villa manager Joe Mercer had already considered a £30,000 bid for the former England youth international. Southampton were also interested, but the actual fee was considered something of a stumbling block.

As the dawn of the new season approached, many were of the opinion that Manchester United would be one of the clubs, along with Tottenham Hotspur, Arsenal and Burnley, who would be challenging for the top honours in the English game.

CHAPTER FOUR
THE BIG FREEZE

August 8th saw Manchester United back in action in preparation for the 1962-63 season, with a friendly at Hampden Park against a strong Glasgow Select side – five players from each of Rangers and Celtic plus Niven of Partick Thistle in goal. If the 80,000 crowd were expecting a grand entrance from United's new signing, back on familiar turf having been one of the stars of the Scottish international side who had defeated England 2-0 the previous April, then they were to be disappointed as it was his fellow Aberdonian Ian Moir who was to earn the plaudits with two goals in the 4-2 victory.

With the kick-off delayed as the crowds swarmed around the Hampden turnstiles, it was the white-shirted Glasgow side who took the lead through Divers in the 23rd minute, having had a goal stroked off six minutes earlier for offside. Two minutes from the interval, Ian Moir put United level.

Within minutes of the re-start, MacKay had cleared a Setters drive off the line, but it was the home side who were to take the lead when Crerand got the better of Quixall to present McMillan with the opportunity.

It looked all over for United when Caldow blasted a penalty past Gaskell, but as the trainer of the Select side was still on the pitch, a re-take was ordered, which was saved by Gaskell. This seemed to give United the nudge required to step up a gear and a twenty-five-yard drive by Setters levelled the scoring. David Herd added a third, with Ian Moir rounding things off with a fourth. The nearest Law came to scoring was a shot that cannoned off the crossbar.

A sun-kissed Old Trafford on Saturday August 18th welcomed Law and his team mates back for a new season, as season of expectancy, something that was echoed by both manager Matt Busby and his chairman H.P. Hardman. In his regular column in the 'United Review', the club match-day programme, Busby was to write: "Once again we are on the threshold of a new and challenging season and I feel very confident in forecasting that 1962-63 will see Manchester United emerge as one of the game's most successful sides.

"I do not think one can overstress that injury problems last term did much to disrupt our playing plans and one has to admit that the loss of Bobby Charlton's services for two or three months at the start of this season is a bitter blow." He added: "Overall, I feel our playing strength now approaches what it was a few years ago and we have excellent reserve cover for every position – and competition for first team places is an essential ingredient in building for a successful future."

Hardman, whilst not exactly extolling the confidence of his manager, was quick to get the sometimes-fickle support onside, writing: "I would like to say a word of thanks to you for the support you have given us over the years, and to assure you that it is our intention to deserve your continued attendance in the future. As you will know, we have during the close season obtained the services of Denis Law from A.C. Torino of Italy. This, and other previous signings, is a continuation of the club's policy to provide the very best possible entertainment for our spectators. We hope our efforts will be repaid by renewed and additional interest in our team and improved results in our matches.

"The close season has been a very busy period for all of the staff. Some of their work will be readily seen when looking at the playing pitch, which is indeed a picture, and reflects great credit on our groundsman, Mr. Joe Royals, and his staff. The outer buildings have been repainted and look spick and span and there have been the usual repairs and replacements around the ground.

"The Development Association has installed seating behind the Stretford goal, the cost of which has been met from proceeds of their Football Pool. The Board are most grateful to the Committee, Agents and members for their interest and practical support which has made possible this welcome improvement in the amenities of the ground."

The season, however, did not get off to the best of starts as confirmed by not just the 2-2 score line, but by the correspondent of the 'Times' who witnessed the opening day encounter. "The rich, warm glow of anticipation which Old Trafford basked on Saturday had curdled into grey disappointment long before the end. The image in 50,000 minds of a quick and certain rise by Manchester United to new glories, equally illustrious to those of the past, had blurred – if, perhaps, only temporarily." He was to continue: "The harbinger of all these rosy visions was, of course. Law, the talented and costly repatriate from Italy. Indeed, it is almost certain that all but a handful of those on the terraces were firmly convinced that here at last was the golden key to rapid restoration of Manchester's fortune. Seasoned critics, even,

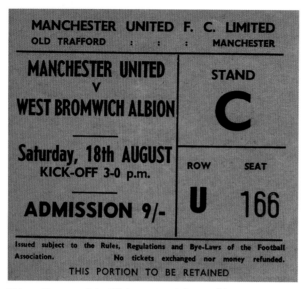

were heard to aver that with so powerful an attack any frailties in United's defence could safely be overlooked." They would soon be proved wrong, very wrong, with their latter assessment.

As for Law, it was his header in the sixth minute that gave United the early 2-0 advantage over West Bromwich Albion, David Herd having given United the lead within a minute of the start. A third 'goal' by Giles three minutes after the superb Herd strike was disallowed for offside.

Confidence rippled through the team; the crowd bayed their encouragement murmuring to their terracing companion "how many will we score?"

Shaken, but not stirred, Albion weathered the storm as United dropped down a gear, happy to cruise along as the momentum decreased and so it continued, with the now somewhat bored crowd longing for the final whistle, although fifteen minutes still remained, content with the 2-0 score line and two points in the bag.

The mood, however, was suddenly to change, although that final whistle was still wanting to be heard, as Albion pulled a goal back through Vernon with just under quarter of an hour to go. United were shaken and found it difficult to regain that early momentum, having virtually switched off. Albion on the other hand were of the opinion that there was now an opportunity to snatch a point, at least.

With six minutes remaining, that equaliser arrived. A rather casual back pass from Setters towards Gaskell in the United goal was under-hit, allowing Smith to nip in and slip the ball into the net as the two United players waited for each other to clear the lines. It was an early lesson in over-confidence, but one that would not be heeded.

Four days, a short journey down the East Lancs Road, there was no confidence of any description to be seen at Goodison Park, although a blond-headed Scot certainly deserved the man-of-the-match award.

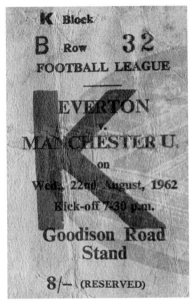

It wasn't, however, the recent addition to the Old Trafford ranks, but Everton's Alex Young, whose two goals in his team's 3-1 victory were more than enough to leave United in complete disarray.

They were booed and slow-hand-clapped by the home support in the 69,501 Merseyside crowd for such an inept performance that could have seen a more emphatic result at the end of the ninety minutes. It was suggested that if Busby had any money left in the coffers then he should be looking to invest it in a defender, or perhaps even two.

For Young's first in the twelfth minute, four United defenders followed the Evertonian as if he was a reincarnation of the pied-piper, but after he had picked out Stevens, they simply forgot about him and when Stevens returned the ball into the middle, Young rose majestically above Foulkes to head firmly past Gaskell.

Gaining possession immediately after the re-start, the blue shirts again surged forward and from Bingham corner, Young sent a looping header over Gaskell and into the net. By half-time it was 3-0. Another Bingham corner was only half cleared, Setter's back pass hitting the post, and up strode Parker to drive home from twenty-five yards.

United, to their credit, invigorated by Busby and Murphy's half time chat over a cup of tea, saw Everton put on the back foot for most of the forty-five minutes, hammering some fifteen shots towards the Everton goal. Only one, however, was to count when Moir picked out Giles whose shot was only parried by West in the Everton goal, allowing Moir to run in and blast the ball high into the roof of the net. Although there was still twenty-six minutes remaining, there was no dramatic come-back. United were not West Bromwich Albion.

The season was still in its infancy, but one point from the opening two fixtures was not the start Matt Busby or the United support either wanted or expected and following the 3-1 defeat at Goodison Park against Everton, Busby made his feelings known in dramatic fashion. "Busby Sacks Skipper Setters" screamed the headlines on the eve of the trip to north London to face Arsenal.

43

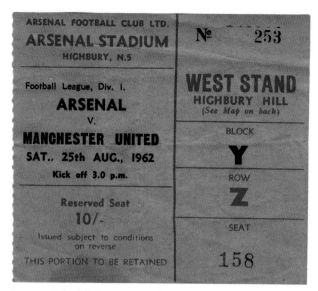

Maurice Setters was not the only head to roll, following the dismal display on Merseyside, as his wing-half partner Nobby Stiles and inside-forward Mark Pearson were also to see their names feature in the reserve side for the Central league fixture against West Bromwich Albion instead of making the journey south to the capital. Setters, although disappointed at losing his place, took it on the chin and simply commented: "If Mr Busby feels that I am not up to expectations and wants me to have a run in the reserves, then he is the boss... and that's it."

The United captain's performance was certainly not be any stretch of the imagination the worst at Goodison, but it was considered strange by some that he was dropped by Busby, while Foulkes, who had endured a far from comfortable night on Merseyside, not only remained in the team, but took over the captaincy.

"We have got to get things sorted out one way or the other" uttered a disappointed Busby. "We have played more than just two League matches. We have also played practice games and these players have not performed as well as they can", he continued.

It was obvious that Denis Law was not going to win games on his own and although the player who received top-billing, he needed the supporting cast to ensure that the overall performance achieved was what the paying public demanded, be they Old Trafford regulars or supporters on the terraces of other clubs around the country who had turned up just to see what all the fuss was about and if the outlay justified the product.

For those who flocked to Arsenal's north London ground on Saturday August 25th they were certainly given their money's worth. They did not see the Manchester United of the past seven days, but they did witness an artist at work. An individual who wove a colourful tap-

estry across the High-bury turf and guided United to their first victory of the 1962-63 season.

In one instance, he could be found on the edge of his own penalty area, dribbling around three bemused opponents, before cheekily back-heeling the ball into the hands of David Gaskell. With seconds, and with the ball transferred to the opposite end of the ground, he appeared as if from nowhere to hit the ball wide of the outstretched hand of McKechnie in the Arsenal goal but into the side netting.

There were no goals for Law to claim, he missed a sitter with the score-line blank, and it was down to former Arsenal player David Herd to deliver the goods, notching a double. Phil Chisnall weighed in with another to deliver the two points, but few, if any, cared that Law had not found the net. United had that first victory under their belt.

The victory, however, was not considered down to the Aberdonian, who was given a standing ovation at the end, although one or two considered his display to be more theatrical than team productive, but to Johnny Giles who roamed wide on the right. The diminutive outside-right being the creative force behind all three goals.

But it was not to be the start of the gold-rush, far from it, although the Mancunian public appeared to think it was, as some twelve thousand more converged on Trafford Park for the visit of Everton, compared with the attendance on the opening day of the season. Although entertained, they were to head towards home, or the pub, to deliberate United's 1-0 defeat.

Derek Potter of the 'Daily Express' was to write: "Hollywood never produced an epic to equal the 90-minute Soccer spectacular of thrills, drama and action-packed value for money. "It rates five stars only because we don't give six." He was to add: "The only thing wrong was the ending … a tragedy for Manchester United."

The first forty-five minutes left the second half playing catch-up. A goal-bound shot cannoned of West in the Everton goal; Law cleared off the line from Bingham; Harris crashed a sot against the United cross-bar; Gaskell did well to save from Stevens after he ghosted past four United defenders. The ten-minute break was required by player and spectator alike.

United looked more likely of the two to gain the advantage as the second half got underway. Moir saw his shot blocked by West three minutes after the re-start. Labone got in the way of a Chisnall goal-bound drive, before both Herd and Moir fired narrowly over from twenty-five yards. At the opposite end, Gaskell was tested more by a Nicholson back-pass than of anything sent his way by the Everton front line.

Eleven minutes remained when the outcome was decided. Morrissey jinked into the United penalty area, Shay Brennan tackled and down went the Everton winger. The referee pointed to the spot, a decision that no-one, not even the most blinkered United supporter, could complain about. From the spot, Vernon blasted the ball past Gaskell, a goal that was enough to seal victory and maintain Everton's unbeaten start to the season.

Glowing press reports, near misses and bad luck did not win you games, nor did it tempt the paying public to part with their hard-earned cash. With only one win in that opening quartet of fixtures, the near full-house that had saw the mid-week defeat against Everton had dwindled by around 14,000 for the visit of Birmingham City on September 1st.

Busby stuck with the eleven who had lost to Everton and was rewarded with a 2-0 victory, although the man on the terraces was not rewarded with a performance akin to that of three days previously. The polished performance was tarnished, although the result was positive and that, at the end of the day was what mattered most.

Although it was a victory by result, it certainly wasn't a victory by performance as there were long periods when United looked to be going nowhere. Short, mind-numbing passes, random shots at goal that were never going to beat Schofield in the Birmingham goal.

If the goal drought that accompanied Denis Law was being used as one of the excuses for United's poor start, the omission of Bobby Charlton from the starting line-ups was certainly another, as his overall contribution rather than his goals – his twenty-one of season 1960-61, followed last season by a meagre eight, was what was missed more. That, however, was not to take anything away from his replace-

ment, Ian Moir, who had played well considering his lack of first team experience. Charlton continued to be side lined due to his hernia operation back in July and it would be mid-October before he was ready to return.

Another United player to go 'under the knife' was Maurice Setters who had already endured something of a stop-start season. Having claimed the number six shirt as his own since his arrival from West Bromwich Albion in January 1960 for a fee of £30,000, he found himself dropped following the 3-1 defeat at Goodison Park. He had been replaced by Nobby Lawton who, although not having the physical attributes of Setters, he had managed to keep him out of the side, therefore allowing Setters to have the necessary operation.

The victory against Birmingham City, although pleasing and much of a relief, was not one that was to kick-start the season, as four days later, a short journey to Bolton's Burnden Park was enough to convince the most sceptical amongst the United following that there was indeed a jinx when it came to playing their Lancashire rivals on their own soil.

The failure to defeat Bolton on September 5th fell solely at the feet of the United defence, who failed in their duties. With only six minutes played, Gaskell and Foulkes got into a tangle as they attempted to deal with a Holden centre and this allowed Davies to poke the ball into the unguarded net.

Although United had their moments, a Moir header cleared off the line by Hartle, they found themselves 2-0 down when Brennan fouled Pilkington in the area and following treatment, the Burnley man placed the ball beyond the reach of Gaskell from the penalty spot.

Ten minutes after the break, United were reduced to ten men. Giles collided with McGarry and left the field with a suspected fractured shoulder. It mattered little, as the game was already lost, although to their credit, United did enjoy a period of pressure during that second forty-five minutes, but there was little to actually concern the home defence.

With thirteen minutes remaining, Holden's through pass found Hill who took the ball in his stride and hammered it past Gaskell from twenty yards to make it 3-0.

As the dejected United players walked off the pitch, heads hung low, and the Bolton supporters headed for home, one Wanderers fans jubilation was to turn to despair as he arrived home to find that his wallet, containing £200 was missing. Following a sleepless night, he returned to the ground early the following morning and made his way to where he had stood enjoying United's humiliation. There, amongst the rubbish of the night before was his wallet with the £200 intact!

United could well have done with a share of some of that good fortune, but their disastrous start to the season continued as the journey to London to face fellow strugglers Leyton Orient produced yet another defeat, although the headlines went to goalkeeper David Gaskell, his performance alone keeping the score down to a respectable 1-0.

Orient, managed by former United captain Johnny Carey, with former player Eddie Lewis in their line-up, having stepped up from the Second Division at the end of the previous season, were the choice of many to immediately drop back into the lower tier. If this indeed was to be the case, then they were at least going to go down fighting and earn a few plaudits along the way.

Gaskell had almost given away a goal in the opening minute, but redeemed himself over the course of the next eighty-nine, dealing comfortably with everything that came his way. Up front, with Setters returning to the fray at inside-right, Law tricked and teased, but it wasn't enough to break down the resolute Orient defence.

Having shaken off that initial fear of facing the country's top sides week in week out, Orient looked more confident than they had done in the opening weeks of the season. The ball pinged from end to end with much regularity, but a goal was not forthcoming and it looked as if the spoils would be shared, a point that the London side would have gladly have accepted prior to kick-off, but with one minute remaining the decisive strike came.

A swerving through pass from Eddie Lewis found outside-left Terry McDonald and, as the United defence stood rooted to the spot, the scrawny winger ran onto the ball and his shot from the edge of the penalty area soared high into the roof of the net with Gaskell helpless. Onto the pitch surged the crowd as the United heads drooped. It was to be yet another long journey back to Manchester.

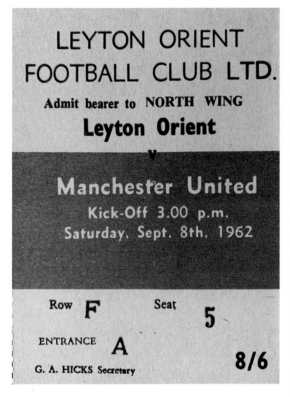

LEYTON ORIENT
FOOTBALL CLUB LTD.

Admit bearer to NORTH WING

Leyton Orient

v

Manchester United

Kick-Off 3.00 p.m.
Saturday, Sept. 8th, 1962

Row **F**   Seat **5**

ENTRANCE **A**

G. A. HICKS Secretary   **8/6**

United's early season performances had been the cause of much concern, more so due to the lack of goals. Many had expected the arrival of Law to herald an avalanche, but goals do not simply appear out of nothing, but are crafted and created and are the work of more than one individual. But that creativeness was missing from United's game, the hardworking inside-forwards and half-backs had been negligent in their field of employment and individuals had paid the price.

One of those relied upon creators was Albert Quixall, the one-time golden boy of English football and a player who Busby had paid out £45,000 for, in the wake of the Munich disaster. The former Sheffield Wednesday star was now a regular in the Central League side rather than finding himself performing on the First Division stage.

Feelings around Old Trafford were now running high. "I want a transfer" uttered Albert Quixall, who wasn't simply downhearted by the recent results, he was disillusioned and disappointed at being omitted from the starting line-up, having made only two appearances all season. "I think it would be the best thing for me and the club if I were transferred. I dislike playing reserve team football and the way things have gone this season I have been very disappointed.

"But I am not at war with the world or anything like that, because I have been dropped a couple of times. It is not true I have demanded a move, but I am concerned about my future, which seems pretty bleak at the moment."

Once the news leaked, there was obviously considerable interest in Quixall, who was far from being past his best and, within days, it looked as though a move to Stoke City was on the cards, with the two clubs agreeing terms. Quixall, however, wanted time to consider the move. This decision to think things over and not to rush into leaving United was to prove decisive, as he was soon to find himself not simply back in favour, but becoming a regular in the side for the remainder of the season.

There was little time to draw breath as the early season games came thick and fast, a good thing perhaps as it did not allow much time to brood over defeats, whilst keeping the match fitness at a considerably high level. There was, however, a greater risk of injury, whilst leaving little time between fixtures for those little, annoying, niggles to disappear allowing a strong fully fit eleven to take the field.

Four days after the last gasp defeat at Brisbane Road against Leyton Orient, United were running out at Old Trafford against Bolton Wanderers, a team who took much pleasure in defeating their near neighbours on the own patch and would often return home on the back of a victory.

On this particular occasion, with three reserves in the side, there was no repeat of their 3-0 home win the previous week, they were to struggle, conceding three without reply, in a dull, lacklustre ninety minutes. "If there be such a man as a connoisseur of soccer, this was no match for him" wrote R. H. Williams in his report for the 'Daily Telegraph'.

The extent of United's dismal start to the season and indeed the lack of strength in depth, not to mention quality, was apparent when the Bolton and United teams were announced over the loudspeaker system, bringing gaps of astonishment, not to mention groans, when the name 'Cantwell' was read out last. Surely that can't be right was the general murmur around the ground, as Noel Cantwell was certainly no outside-left. A full-back or centre-half certainly, but he was no nimble-footed winger with a turn of speed and exquisite crossing ability. Those doubters were, however, soon to be left open-mouthed, as Cantwell not only scored in United's 3-0 victory, but was without doubt the man of the match.

"Noel Cantwell, full-back playing on the left wing for the first time to solve one of Manchester United's many problems, won this match of honest toil last night. And I am convinced it was an accident. Either that or Noel has been hiding considerable forward talent for a long time." wrote Alan Thomson in his match report for the 'Daily Express'. He added: "Cantwell scored in the 32nd minute. To make things more than a little awkward for him, he happened to be standing with his back to towards the Bolton goal – so he scored with a sort of back heel

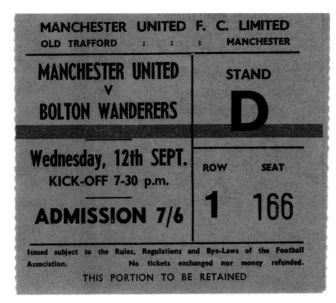

MANCHESTER UNITED F. C. LIMITED
OLD TRAFFORD : : : MANCHESTER

MANCHESTER UNITED
v
BOLTON WANDERERS

STAND

D

Wednesday, 12th SEPT.
KICK-OFF 7-30 p.m.

ROW   SEAT

ADMISSION 7/6

1   166

Issued subject to the Rules, Regulations and Bye-Laws of the Football
Association.   No tickets exchanged nor money refunded.
THIS PORTION TO BE RETAINED

flick." The 'Daily Telegraph' correspondent saw it as being more of a deflection from a Nobby Stiles shot.

Nevertheless, it counted, United were in front and it was a lead they didn't surrender, with David Herd going on to score two more, one in the 69th minute, the other as the crowd were edging towards the exit gates as the clock ticked towards full-time.

The ninety-minutes were more crash than class, but for United it was a much-needed victory, a rare two points from a season of disarray and disappointment and once again it was hoped that it could be a launching pad towards a more favourable run of results.

No one could have imagined that the performances to date would have been such a mixed bag. "I must admit we set out with high hopes that this season we would really do something, and in terms of results I am afraid we have not obtained all we were hoping for" declared trainer Jack Crompton. "But don't write us off yet awhile. I think we may still show the soccer world a thing or two."

The Old Trafford terraces and stands were swept, the pitch rolled and the markings given a new coat of whitewash as the action remained down beside the banks of the Ship Canal three days later when neighbours City came to visit.

Dawn would break on 'derby' day bringing with it that sense of excitement, an edge of expectancy, a head-to-head ninety minutes that more than any other on the fixture list you wanted your team to win. The first meeting between the two old rivals in the 1962-63 season was, perhaps, more meaningful than many that had gone before. Certainly, in the case of Manchester City, who found themselves propping up the First Division table with four points from their eight games, having won only once and drawn twice. United were three points better off, but then again, only three points separated the bottom thirteen clubs. Defeat or victory could mean so much for either club.

There was only the one change in the United line-up to the one that had taken those two most welcome points from Bolton in mid-week and that was Jimmy Nicholson coming in for the hospitalised Maurice Setters, who had gone under the knife for an appendicitis operation. Cantwell, retained his place at outside-left!

It was to be a dismal afternoon for the red half of Manchester as United never really settled as City, a side already written off by many as dead certs to be heading for the Second Division, swept forward in a seemingly constant stream.

With seventeen minutes gone, City were in front. Foulkes handling the ball in the penalty area and Dobing scoring from the spot. Six minutes later, it was 2-0. Harley passed to Dobing, who in turn found Hayes. Although closely marked, the City inside-forward managed to turn and send the ball crashing past Gaskell.

As the half progressed, the tempo increased, with Law seemingly adopting a gung-ho attitude, making more than the odd questionable challenge on his former team-mates. So much so, that he left the referee with little option than to take his name.

Within a minute of the second half getting underway, Law was in the thick of things once again, but on this occasion, there was no reprimand from the match official, just the adoration of the United supporters. A back-heel from Herd saw him run onto the ball and he slipped it, almost casually, past Trautmann in the City goal. A decisive goal at a decisive time.

It was Law again who put United level, but it was a goal gifted by Trautmann, with the United number ten pouncing on the ball after the City 'keeper had dropped a Giles cross, to send it high into the roof of the net. All square.

Law was unfortunate in not claiming his hat-trick as he saw a shot rattle the City bar, while Dobing did likewise at the opposite end. The minutes ticked away and it began to look as if the points would be shared. More so as the hands on the clock moved slowly and closer towards full time.

United forced yet another corner, but on this occasion, there was no butter-fingered slip from Trautmann, the City custodian clutching the ball to his chest before throwing it out to Kennedy, who in turn sent it down the middle. Off went Alex Harley like a greyhound chas-

MANCHESTER UNITED F. C. LIMITED

OLD TRAFFORD : : : MANCHESTER

MANCHESTER UNITED
v
MANCHESTER CITY

STAND

D

Saturday, 15th SEPT.

KICK-OFF 3-0 p.m.

ROW   SEAT

1   181

ADMISSION 7/6

Issued subject to the Rules, Regulations and Bye-Laws of the Football Association.   No tickets exchanged nor money refunded.

THIS PORTION TO BE RETAINED

ing a hare as Foulkes tried desperately to catch him. Into the United penalty area the City man sped as Gaskell ran from his goal, but to no avail, the ball flashed past him and into the net.

The City support roared in acclaim, while referee Les Tirebuck didn't even bother with restarting the game, so close that winner was too full-time. It was City's first Old Trafford win in seven seasons, but it was their most important for many a long day, if ever.

Pitting his wits against the cream of the European clubs had been on Matt Busby's agenda for a considerable time and was behind his determination to take on not just the Spaniards, Italians and others, but also the Football League in his determination to have his team play on that ever-evolving European stage.

Since that traumatic 1957-58 season, when United's world crumbled around them on a cold afternoon in Germany, Busby had to content himself with nothing more than friendly fixtures. Hamburg, Bayern Munich, Young Boys of Berne, Wiener Sports Club, Torino, AS Roma and Valencia, amongst others, had filled that competitive void against the continent's best, but there was one other club who featured more than any other when a friendly fixture was sought and that was Real Madrid.

Old foes and friends since they first locked horns in the semi-final of the 1956-57 European Cup, the Spanish giants had stretched out that hand of friendship in those often-dark post-Munich days, waiving their usually high appearance fee in order to help United.

October 1959 saw the first of those lucrative post-Munich meetings when the Spaniards strode into Old Trafford and handed out a footballing lesson, and an evening of entertainment to the 63,500 packed into the ground, notching up a 6-1 victory. Just over a month later, United travelled to Madrid for the return meeting and again

conceded six, but on this occasion, they were far from outplayed and fielding the same eleven, impressing the 80,000 in the Bernabeu by scoring five in reply. One year down the line, Real Madrid were back in Manchester, winning a close encounter by the odd goal in five, while December 13th 1961 saw United triumph at last, beating their by now familiar, opponents 3-1.

Despite the rather full early season fixture list, Busby once again sought European opposition and lined up fixtures against First Vienna, Portuguese side Benfica the European Cup winners for the past two seasons, while the invitation to Madrid was again on his desk and it was there that United found themselves on September 19th 1962.

Current league form could be forgotten underneath the warm Spanish sky and it was, as United became the first English side defeat Madrid on their home turf. This was no fluke, no own goal, scrambled effort or otherwise, it was a victory on merit against Di Stefano, Gento and co.

Following a goal less first forty-five minutes, the game turned on its axis three minutes after the interval. Mark Pearson collected the ball on the edge of the Madrid penalty area and sent it hard and low towards goal. Vincente, although having the shot covered, allowed it to squirm from his grasp and trickle into the corner of the net.

Twelve minutes later, United scored a second. Law sent Giles scurrying down the wing, he in turn dummied Casada before crossing to an unmarked David Herd who headed home. Try as they could, Madrid found no way through the steadfast United defence, with the home side soundly booed off the pitch at the end, whilst the triumphant red shirted players were afforded warm applause by the often-partisan crowd.

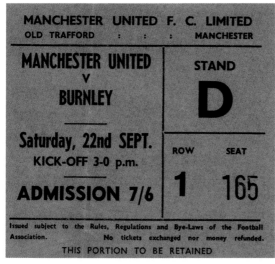

MANCHESTER UNITED F. C. LIMITED
OLD TRAFFORD : : : MANCHESTER

MANCHESTER UNITED
v
BURNLEY

STAND
D

Saturday, 22nd SEPT.
KICK-OFF 3-0 p.m.

ROW   SEAT
1   165

ADMISSION 7/6

Issued subject to the Rules, Regulations and Bye-Laws of the Football
Association.   No tickets exchanged nor money refunded.
THIS PORTION TO BE RETAINED

So, United could beat the Spaniards at ease, but struggle against the likes of Leyton Orient and City. There was no logic behind the season to date, but if any result was going to radiate belief and see performances move up a gear or two, then the ninety minutes in Madrid was it. Or at least it most certainly should have.

Buoyant by the result in Spain, United looked forward to playing host to Lancastrian neighbours Burnley three days later and getting their league programme back on track. The Turf Moor side, First Division champions in 1959-60, and runners-up in both the League and FA Cup the following season, were a far cry from being Real Madrid, but they were to show more grit and determination than the white shirted Spaniards over the course of the ninety minutes.

What materialised that Saturday afternoon at Old Trafford was one of the worst defensive performances ever seen at the ground, certainly the ineptest since those relegation haunted days of the 1930's. Every time Burnley surged forward, it seemed as if they would score, such was the fragility of the red rear guard.

As early as the first minute Burnley threatened, Tony Dunne giving John Connelly too much space and the wingers shot flew narrowly past, but the score line wasn't blank for long as Andy Lochhead, who was to lead Bill Foulkes a merry dance for the majority of the afternoon, gave the visitors the lead after five minutes. Half an hour later it was 2-0, Connelly, after several attempts, finally getting his name on the scoresheet.

At 2-0 United were presented with the opportunity to get back into the game when Angus handled inside the area, but Blacklaw dived to his left to deny Brennan the opportunity to edge United back into the game. The miss was punished by McIlroy who added a third for Burnley three minutes before the interval.

Although the second forty-five minutes saw United's attempt to claw themselves back into the game severely hampered by an injury to David Herd, which left him little more than a passenger out on the wing, they pulled a goal back on the hour. Nobby Stiles running on to a through pass from Law, just as the slow hand claps began to echo around the ground. Those roles were then reversed six minutes later when Stiles set up Law to reduce the arrears further.

There was now a buzz of anticipation around the ground, but it was Burnley, however, who were more invigorated by the United goal. Reacting to the impudence of United in trying to deny them victory, John Connelly not simply added a fourth in the 66th minute, but claimed his hat-trick, and Burnley's fifth and final goal twenty minutes later.

Needless to say, the men in the press-box were far from kind in their reporting of the game. "United looked just what they are – a struggling, unhappy outfit" wrote Leslie Duxbury in the 'Sunday Express', while the un-named correspondent writing for the 'Guardian' penned "Assuming that the first duty of a defence is to tackle and dispossess opponents, Manchester United were more or less defenceless. The tackling of their half-backs was inefficient because it was usually late, quite often appeared vicious, and frequently succeeded only in holding up play while the trainer intruded or an opponent prepared to take a free kick."

The erratic shooting of the United forwards during that 5-2 home defeat by Burnley on September 22nd was not simply costly in the loss of another two, much needed points, but it was also to prove costly to two teenage United supporters – James Judge and Anthony Moore, who were fined for stealing the match ball after it had been kicked into the crowd.

Following its disappearance into the crowd, it wasn't returned to the pitch and the pair were spotted with the ball by a policeman at half-time. "We were going to take it home and play with it" said Moore as he pleaded guilty along with his friend. The ball was valued at £8 10/- [£8.50p] and the two local teenagers were each fined £2.

"Manchester United's Liking for Foreign Opposition – A spirit not seen in League matches" was the headline on page fourteen of the 'Guardian' on the morning of September 26th, following a 2-2 draw with Portuguese side Benfica, the current European Cup holders.

Having defeated Real Madrid the previous week, this was yet another favourable result, but one that left the United support, and those who followed football in general, wondering as to how Busby's team could produce two rather exceptional performances against top class opposition, but yet stutter along against their more familiar, but less talented, First Division stablemates.

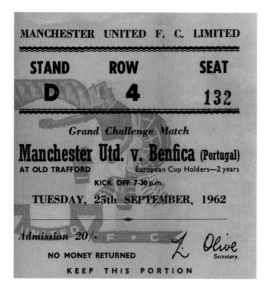

The 5-2 defeat by Burnley was the straw that broke the camel's back, or perhaps that should read, the defeat that forced manager Matt Busby to suddenly decide that enough was enough and that he had to make changes, and the visit of Benfica allowed him to do so and to see how those given the opportunity accepted the challenge handed to them. Harry Gregg, who was warmly welcomed by the 47,532 crowd, was given his first start since the previous November, the Irishman having returned to his place between the sticks in the Central League fixture against Manchester City at Maine Road following injury, a game that the United second string won 5-0. Albert Quixall also returned to the fold at centre-forward, as did Phil Chisnall in the number ten shirt, with Sammy McMillan getting a run out as partner on the left flank. Benfica on the other hand included seven of the players who had beaten Real Madrid in the European Cup Final at the end of the previous season.

In an all-white strip, the Old Trafford floodlights gave the United players a completely different appearance, while those same players managed to cast the dismal performances of late from the minds of the near 50,000 crowd and help produce a magical night of football. Ninety minutes that saw United match the European champions stride by stride and goal for goal.

In the red of Benfica, Eusebio stood out from the first minute to the last, as one would have expected, but like to two sides, his performance was matched by that of Denis Law. The only difference between the two being their supporting cast, giving the former something of an advantage.

United's early forages towards the Benfica goal could have been considered enthusiastic rather than dangerous, but there was more than the solitary instance when the Portuguese defenders were simply content to clear the ball with feet, head and body as long as it was away from the danger area.

A Eusebio free-kick some thirty-yards from goal flew narrowly past, while another effort from the Benfica danger man went narrowly over after he had flummoxed Law twice, leaving the Scot sprawled out on the turf. Gregg earned warm applause with two fine saves from Aguas and Eusebio.

As the half-hour mark approached, United took the lead. They had threatened only minutes earlier when Law shot over, but on this occasion, he took a pass from McMillan before firing past Barroca. It was, however, a lead that United held for a mere sixty seconds as Benfica surged forward from the re-start. Foulkes and Stiles failed to clear the immediate danger thus allowing Eusebio time to pick his spot after gliding past the advancing Gregg and side-foot the ball home.

Five minutes prior to the interval United were handed the opportunity to take the lead. Humberto fell on the ball in the penalty area and the referee, amid a storm of complaints from the Benfica players, pointed to the penalty spot following a brief conversation with his linesman. Quixall made no mistake with his kick.

The United defence stood firm in the second half amid much pressure as the red shirts surged forward time and time again, but fifteen minutes from the end Eusebio was there again to equalise. Flicking the ball out to Simoes, he moved forward to take the return pass which he duly despatched past Gregg.

At the full-time whistle, the United players stood on the touch line and applauded their opponents off the pitch, as did the appreciative crowd, as the players returned handshakes. A fitting finale for those present and it made a worthwhile spectacle for those who decided that a later bedtime than normal would do little harm and tuned into Granada TV at 11.25pm to watch half an hour's highlights.

A draw against Benfica and a victory against Real Madrid should have raised the confidence level by a notch or two and the performance against the former saw Busby decide to stick with the same eleven who started against the Portuguese side for the trip across the Pennines to face Sheffield Wednesday.

There was certainly no Yorkshire-Lancashire rivalry, no war of the roses, it was a tedious ninety minutes. That it produced only one goal was down to the brilliance of Harry Gregg, back to his pre-Munich best, denying Wednesday on three occasions with excellent saves. Plus, had it not been for the home sides inadequacy when attacking the always suspect United defence, it could have been a few more.

It was a defeat that left United firmly in the relegation zone, sitting alongside neighbours City, Fulham and Birmingham City on seven points. It was also a defeat that produced several questions that needed to be answered, the main one being, how can a team which includes the brilliance of Denis Law be so lacklustre and poor so often?

Perhaps too much was expected of the Aberdonian, his team mates looking to him for not just the goals, but the inspiration to guide them to victory, like an army with their backs to the wall seeking guidance from their general. Should others have borne more responsibility?

If victory was to come at Hillsborough it would have been via Johnny Giles, not Law, the young Irishman frequently getting the better of Megson but too little avail. Even when allowed the opportunity to score, rather than create, he found Springett equal to his efforts.

As the game progressed there were two things that many of those packed onto the Hillsborough terraces were convinced would happen. One, was that they were not likely to see any goals that afternoon, and two, United were going to finish the game with only ten men, as left-half Nobby Lawton made five rather horrendous tackles on Wednesday players in quick succession, but somehow managing to escape with just a booking.

The crowd, however, were to be proved wrong on only one account – United finished the game intact. As they reflected on the ninety minutes, the Wednesday support would have settled for one out of two, as they did see a goal and it was scored by Tony Kay, ten minutes from time. A quick throw-in by Eustage to the Wednesday captain saw him turn on the spot and blast the ball past a helpless Gregg.

United attempted to fight back. Giles saw his shot deflected round the post by Swan, but the closest they came to scoring was three successive corners as the Wednesday defence stood firm.

Three wins in eleven was not Manchester United standard, far from it. Things had to improve, and fast as no-one wanted a prolonged stay at the foot of the First Division.

As a dismal September drew to a close, it was reported that the German's were considering re-opening an inquiry into the Munich disaster. Their investigation had originally ruled that the crash had been caused by a layer of ice on the wing, but research in Britain and America had revealed that slush on the runway was a much likely cause due to the greater drag effect on a plane's take-off run and that the slush spray could damage vital parts. If such findings were proven, then the sacking of pilot James Thain could well be over-turned, although a BEA spokesman was to add "The new report is irrelevant to the dismissal of captain Thain. It contains no reference to the reasons for which he was dismissed."

Thain, who had been dismissed by BEA on Christmas Day 1960, and was now a farmer, felt confident that at long last, his name would be cleared. "Since the accident there have been numerous reports on the effect of slush on runways and I feel that if the Germans are big enough to re-open the enquiry, I will be vindicated." Sadly, his hopes were to be dashed and it would be a further six years before his name was cleared, although the Germans continued to point the finger in his direction.

It was Blackpool next stop. The illuminations were shining bright along the Golden Mile and a couple of hundred yards or so from the promenade, United flickered briefly, but just didn't have enough power

212

Blackpool Football Club Limited

SATURDAY

6th OCTOBER, 1962

Manchester U.

Kick-off 3-0 p.m.

WEST STAND

Section **D**

Seat No. **K 13**

Price **8/-**

to dazzle their opponents and snatch a much sought-after victory.

Whether it was the fresh, seaside air or the tantalising smell of candy floss, hot dogs or fish and chips wafting up Bloomfield Road, United certainly looked reinvigorated from the first whistle.

Straight from the kick-off, Giles went dancing down the right, teeing up Herd, but the United number nine, back from injury, was to see his shot saved. Minutes later, having once again got the better of left back Martin, Giles moved along the by-line before cutting the ball back into the path of the ever-alert Herd, who hammered the ball into the bottom corner of the Blackpool net.

For the away support in the season best crowd at Bloomfield Road of 33,242, this was the United they knew, and craved for again, but they were also to see the present day United in the twenty-first minute when Ray Charnley, the Seasiders towering centre-forward not for the first time in the afternoon, got the better of Bill Foulkes, flicking the ball towards McPhee, allowing his forward partner to beat Gregg for the equaliser as his fellow defender dallied.

Five minutes before the interval United regained their lead and, again, it was thanks to the Giles/Herd partnership. A goal bound shot was cleared off the Blackpool line by Jimmy Armfield, but the ball went only as far as Johnny Giles who quickly returned into the goal-mouth where Herd calmly picked his spot.

The home side upped the tempo in the second half, taking the game to United, but only after the hero of the hour blotted his copybook. As Blackpool pushed forward, a clearance from the United defence was picked up by Herd and off he went for goal. Faced with just the advancing Waiters, the Blackpool 'keeper, the hat-trick was scorned as Herd's shot went wide of the post.

It was a golden opportunity, and a match winning one at that, but it served as an elbow in the ribs to Blackpool who laid siege on the United goal. High balls flew forward in the hope of reaching Charnley with the penalty area as packed as promenade down the road, but it wasn't until fifteen minutes from the end that Gregg was finally beaten.

Charnley shot, but the ball struck Gregg and rebounded out. Parry shot, but the ball struck another defender and again rebounded into the melee. Charnley, his long legs stretching out in front of a quartet of players, managed to prod the ball past Gregg for the equaliser.

As Blackpool were far from convincing, it was yet another point lost, their defence very suspectable of being caught on the rebound as their forwards attacked. Against anyone but United they would have been put to the sword. Looking at it from another angle, against a more capable side United would have lost their fourth consecutive match. At least their travelling support could forget the dropped point with a night on the town and a trip through the illuminations.

Seeing the name of Manchester United at the foot of the First Division was an unaccustomed sight, but it was certainly no misprint as the decline in fortunes continued and, for many, the only way out of the current situation that the club found itself in was to open the Old Trafford cheque book and bring in new recruits. Only established top-class individuals would fit the bill, and the majority of clubs would be reluctant to part with any of their star names, but money talked, and if First Division safety came at a price for United, then so be it.

It was estimated that it would cost an outlay of around a quarter of a million pounds to obtain suitable replacements for the current under-performing individuals on the Old Trafford pay-roll, with speculative guesses that four players were necessary if United were going to avoid relegation, never mind climb to a respectable position in the table.

There had certainly been no formal approaches made, but moves were certainly rumoured to be afoot, with three of Busby's fellow countrymen heading the list of possibilities. The canny Scot obviously declined to comment, but his list of wants was believed to include Pat Crerand, the Celtic playmaker, Dundee full-back Alex Hamilton and from the other half of the 'old-firm', Alex Scott, the Rangers outside right, who was currently out of favour at Ibrox. Also earmarked as a possible signed was promising Preston North End utility forward Peter Thompson, a player long admired by the United. Had it not been for Munich then he most certainly would have been wearing the red shirt, as whilst recovering from his injuries in hospital at that time, Busby received a letter from Thompson's mother saying that she wanted her son to play for United. Unfortunately, by the time the United manager was fit to deal with club matters, he had signed for Preston.

If United could sign only one of that previously mentioned quartet, then Crerand would without any doubt be the one, as the half-back line appeared to be the Achilles heel in the United set up, with Maurice Setters, Nobby Stiles, Jimmy Nicholson and Nobby Lawton all showing indifferent form. It was also considered that to get the best out of Denis Law, then a playmaker was required, rather than the more defensive styled half-back, a description that applied to the previously mentioned quartet.

Busby, however, was up-beat. "I must admit we set out with high hopes that this season we would really do something, and in terms of results I am afraid we have not obtained all we were hoping for.

"But don't write us off yet awhile. I think we may still show the soccer world a thing or two."

"We have had some bad results. But I am pretty confident about the immediate future as soon as we have the services of such experienced players as Herd, Pearson and Charlton." Charlton was due back in action within days rather than weeks, while Herd and Pearson had both been out with thigh and ankle injuries respectively.

Having Charlton back in the side was something that Busby considered akin to having a new player within the ranks, as he had missed those first dozen games of the season, but at long last the United manager could pencil the Ashington born forward onto his team sheet for United's home fixture against Blackburn Rovers on October 13th.

It had been widely reported that Charlton would make his long-awaited return in the United reserve side against Blackpool at Bloomfield Road, but with the performances of late, Busby had second thoughts on the matter and thrust him straight back into the first team. Rusty or not from lack of playing time, his presence was very much required.

It was certainly 'welcome back', but in no way was it 'many happy returns' for Charlton and for those United supporters whose daily read was the 'Guardian' they did not need the headline in the locally printed newspaper to tell them what they already knew only too well following the 3-0 defeat at Old Trafford - "Manchester United At Their Lowest Ebb".

"Charlton returned to United's forward line at inside-left after his operation and the fact that he was United's best forward says much for modern surgery, but little for his colleagues" wrote the 'Guardian's' Brian Crowther. The journalist was also to tell those who were not present, or remind those who were, that "Blackburn Rovers never found it necessary to raise their game above the ordinary in beating Manchester United 3-0 at Old Trafford.

"For twenty-seven minutes of the second half, Rovers were without Pickering, their centre-forward, and though in this period United had most of the game territorially, they lacked the wit to take advantage. Indeed, one has never seen United reach such depths, and one can but hope that the realisation of their present plight will prove remedial."

It took Blackburn twelve minutes to send the groans echoing around the ground. Harrison pushed the ball into the centre towards the unmarked McGrath, whose shot from just outside the penalty area flashed past Gregg. The United 'keeper looked to have been caught unawares.

United only managed one dangerous attack during the first forty-five minutes, which ended with Herd heading the ball downwards only to see it bounce off the diving Else. It was to prove a crucial save, as the ball was quickly despatched down field, catching the United defence in disarray. Harrison sprinted past Brennan as the defender struggles to get back in position, and with a view of goal, the Blackburn outside-left took the ball in his stride and hit it firmly past Gregg.

Thirteen minutes into the second half it was 3-0, Lawther taking a pass from Pickering to score with relative ease.

United were somewhat fortunate that it was only three, and could thank Gregg in one instance as the 'keeper saved a penalty kick from Douglas after the same player had been fouled by McMillan.

Herd tried hard and unselfishly, while the two wing men, Giles and McMillan saw little of the ball, while Law on the other hand appeared only half interested and was booked for taking a kick at a prostrate Douglas. "A bunch of individual misfits" was the opinion of one match reporter. Leslie Duxbury, a journalist with the 'Express' wrote: "As I have said before, no one man is going to pull this United outfit permanently off the floor, not Law, not Charlton. The defence was again so terribly slow and square. Nobody moved a muscle to stop McGrath blasting Blackburn's first goal. For the record – Charlton supplied one shot, Law a couple of headers, McMillan two misses and Herd perhaps a little more effort than his colleagues.

"It was another sad display by United. The slouched off the pitch to a chorus of slow hand claps and boos."

James Courage of the 'People' wrote: "What's gone wrong with Manchester United? Soccer fans all over the country were asking that question last night when they heard that Matt Busby's boys had crashed 3-0 at home to Blackburn Rovers.

"For even with the £115,000 Denis Law and fit-again Bobby Charlton, playing in his favourite position of inside-left, United took a larruping. All the hopes that Matt has built on buying big for the team he loves seem to be crumbling away ... to the Second Division.

"Is It the old story - you can't buy success! Matt Busby will admit he's paid big for more than one player before now and been wrong. But how long will Law, the man Busby reckons the greatest player in Europe, be content to hang around for relegation?"

The very much in-vogue friendlies continued at Old Trafford on October 17th, but there were no throngs of red and white bedecked supporters heading down Warwick Road, or over the swing bridge from the Trafford Park direction. Indeed, the red turnstile gates were firmly closed and silence enveloped the ground, with only the muffled sound of leather upon leather and the odd inaudible shout being heard by anyone passing.

Inside the ground, only a few witnessed the forty-minute kickabout as United played host to England, who were preparing to face Northern Ireland in Belfast three days later.

With the gates locked, and casual observers and members of the press banned, it was only word of mouth that reported England's 3-0 win, [Greaves, O'Grady and Halliwell were the scorers], with England manager, former United player Walter Winterbottom calling the shots by telling Matt Busby to have his United side put the England defence under as much pressure as possible for the first twenty minutes. Given United's recent performances, it was asking quite a lot!

Due to international call-ups, United had Saturday October 20th off, but the lack of action did not see a refreshed and invigorated United return to action in North London four days later as Tottenham Hotspur didn't simply defeat United, they demolished them, scoring six before United could register one of their own.

Looking at the United side – Gregg, Brennan, Cantwell, Stiles, Foulkes, Setters, Giles, Quixall, Herd, Law and Charlton, in particular the

No. 819

TOTTENHAM HOTSPUR
Football and Athletic Company Limited

BLOCK   **PARK LANE STAND**
W and X   (Unreserved Section)

v.

MANCHESTER UNITED

RE-ARRANGED LEAGUE FIXTURE 1962/63
(For date and time of kick-off see National Press)

PRICE

8/-   The Tottenham Hotspur Company do not Guarantee that the proposed match will be played.
R. S. JARVIS
Secretary

UNRESERVED SEAT

forward line, one wonders how on earth did such a line-up concede six? This eleven, worth an estimated £213,000, were arguably the team that Busby would have liked to have started the season with and, had he been able to do so, then perhaps results, in some instances, might have been different, but here they were at White Hart Lane, a side full of individual talent and experience, conceding six, before managing two in reply in the final ten minutes of the game as Spurs relaxed in the knowledge that the game was, and had been for some time, well and truly over.

Tottenham, League and F.A. Cup winners in 1960-61 and Cup winners again in 1961-62, were a formidable side and would go on to win the European Cup Winners Cup in the current season. They had class in the likes of Blanchflower, Mackay, White and Greaves, not to mention their co-stars, to outwit the best of opponents and they were rampant against a United side who tried and toiled throughout the ninety minutes.

Despite Noel Cantwell back in his more familiar full-back role, and Maurice Setters reclaiming his place after injury, Greaves should have given Spurs the lead in the 10th minute, but lobbed the ball wide as Gregg moved off his line. But he was to atone for his error five minutes later, tapping the ball home after Gregg could only parry a powerful shot from Mackay. Soon afterwards he rounded Foulkes before seeing his shot smack against the post.

Foulkes deflected a Medwin shot against the post, while another effort crashed against the cross bar before the Spurs winger made it 2-0. Five minutes prior to the interval it was 3-0, Medwin again following a Blanchflower free-kick. United were all over the place, unable to match the free flowing football of the North London side.

After the break, United had their moments. Quixall wormed his way through the defence only to be denied by Brown in the Tottenham goal, while Law sent a curving shot round the outside of the post. It was, however, only momentarily as within five minutes of the re-start it was 4-0, Baker splitting the United defence with a perfect pass to Greaves who didn't waste the opportunity.

The seemingly constant attacks always had United on the back foot, while they somehow managed to keep their frustration intact, which must have been difficult for those who were considered to have something of a short fuse. Perhaps more so when Jones made it 5-0 in the 70th minute and Greaves added the sixth eight minutes later.

Seven minutes from time, Herd pulled one back, a mere consola-tion, with Quixall scoring from the penalty spot three minutes from time after Charlton had been fouled.

In the form they were in, Tottenham would have beaten any side in the country, quite possibly any side in Europe for that matter and, if United looked for any consolation in the 6-2 defeat, it was in the fact that Tottenham had hit nine past Nottingham Forest the same after-noon that United lost 1-0 to Sheffield Wednesday.

The White Hart Lane humiliation left United on their own at the foot of the table with eight points from their fourteen fixtures, a point worse off than Fulham and Leyton Orient. Their goals against column of thirty-one was only five less than that of neighbours City. The Maine Road side cared little, as they had a four-point advantage over their cross-town rivals.

"It's a case of many good players doing badly at the same time" muttered Matt Busby, although behind closed doors he must have been wondering just what was going wrong with his team.

But even if there were a 'good players doing badly' there were countless eyes watching United's progress, or that should be lack of it, with much of the interest being focussed on individual performances rather than results, with representatives of other clubs being in regu-lar attendance at United's Central League fixtures, with others keep-ing a watchful eye on those who appeared to be unhappy and would perhaps relish a move away from United and also the foot of the table.

An approach from Queens Park Rangers for Albert Quixall had been rejected out of hand with the comment: "we cannot possibly afford to part with him", while across London neighbours Arsenal had received a similar rebuff in their enquiry as to eighteen-year-old Jimmy Nichol-son's availability. "Nicholson is not leaving. He is one of the players booked for my future plans" uttered Busby as a response.

Despite their precarious League position many were off the opinion that United were far from being relegation candidates, after all, they now had eleven full internationals on their books following Sammy McMillan's recent selection for Northern Ireland – surely no team with such a wealth of resources could find themselves heading for the Second Division. Or could they? Many would, however, be wrong in their assumption, as West Ham United found themselves relegated back in 1932 when they had ten internationals, six of whom had represented England, on their playing staff.

Since the dawn of the 1962-63 season each dropped point, each defeat, was considered the kick in the pants that Busby's team required to get themselves back on track and into winning ways, but that wake-up call simply fell on deaf ears. Until now.

Conceding half a dozen goals against Tottenham could well have knocked the stuffing out of many teams, resigned them to their fate even although it was only October. Every goal conceded would have been accompanied by the 'here we go again' feeling, knocking any confidence that was there to pieces. So, it was strange that the 6-2 White Hart Lane reversal, turned out to be the result, unwelcome as it was, that made United realise, for the time being at least, that they were perhaps doomed towards the Second Division before Christmas had been celebrated and the bells heralded in a new year.

United had been fortunate that their seven home First Division fixtures up until the last Saturday of October when West Ham United pulled up outside Old Trafford, had enjoyed favourable attendances. The Lancashire 'derby' figure of 63,437 against Everton had never been matched, while the other half dozen fixtures attracting between 37,721 and 51,685. It was surprising to many that those figures were not much lower with results, such as those that the Old Trafford faithful had endured of late, would have reduced the noise from the turnstiles on a match day to being barely audible.

But the neon 'Manchester United' sign high above the Scoreboard Paddock shone brightly and Old Trafford on a match-day was akin to the streets of the city, awash with red and white – one with the scarf bedecked followers of Matt Busby's team, the other with the livery of the corporation buses. The colours of the former carried with pride despite the recent fall from grace.

The United Supporters Association could boast of some 4,000 members, along with their own headquarters that could boast a bar and billiard room amongst its social facilities, which also included a Sunday League football team. Monday nights would also see interested parties being given a tour of the Old Trafford inner sanctums. It was certainly

a far cry from the four dozen or so members when the supporters club was founded in 1946. Transport to away games was arranged, where they would be entertained in the supporters' club of the opposition, the hospitality would be returned in Manchester.

"But we don't give them any money" said Chairman George Hornsby, "United don't need it, but if there is anything we can do for the club, we are happy to oblige." Although not officially recognised by the club, the two worked hand in hand whenever a big-match ticket allocation was necessary.

"We are fortunate to have such a fine bunch of supporters" a proud Matt Busby proclaimed. "They are very discerning, and I believe they know their football as well as any supporters anywhere."

With the current campaign being nothing short of a disaster, many of those supporters were of the opinion that things could certainly not get any worse following the humiliation in north London and a ray of sunshine had to appear over Trafford Park sooner, rather than later. However, for many of the casual supporters that United would attract on match-day, they had had enough. They could see no chink of sunshine through late October gloom and decided that their Saturday afternoon could be better spent elsewhere instead of standing on the cold concrete terraces of Old Trafford.

And so, it was on Saturday October 27th that the Old Trafford turnstile operators did not get their usual fortnightly exercise in clicking the foot pedals that allowed the paying customer through the gate, as only 29,204 decided to turn up to watch the bedraggled United face West Ham. Four thousand fewer than had witnessed the 3-0 defeat against Blackburn Rovers.

Perhaps strangely, Busby kept faith with the eleven who had toiled against Tottenham, paying no heed to those who were suggesting that he wielded the whip and the big stick and ring in the changes. To be honest, any changes that could have been made would certainly not have strengthened the side, as this was a Manchester United who were a far cry from having strength in depth in every position, with some of the Central League side being little more than adequate.

Busby's faith, along with that of those who decided to continue with their Saturday afternoon ritual at a wet and windswept Old Trafford, was rewarded as the bottom of the table side recorded a rare victory, defeating West Ham 3-1. It was a performance that showed encouragement rather than a transformation, an out-patient rather than a permanently discharged case.

The Upton Park side were no whipping boys, whilst United's performance was far from flawless, although had it not been for Leslie in the Londoners' goal then the score line could well have been further enhanced. Albert Quixall in particular, showed himself to still be a class act, capturing many of the newspaper headlines, such as – "Quixall Clears Those Clouds" – 'Daily Express' and "No Release For Quixall After Restoring Esteem" – 'Daily Telegraph'. Headlines not simply achieved via his two goals. His performance would once again have numerous interested parties making their interest in the restless individual known, but if he could simply set his mind at rest and continue along similar lines, then he, rather than Law, could well be the man to transform his beleaguered club's season.

Law, for once, decided that he was more beneficial to his team playing as a forward rather than a jack-of-all-trades, attempting to cover every blade of grass. Eric Todd of the 'Guardian' was of the opinion that if he showed more performances in this mode then "Manchester United would lose their anonymity."

As could be expected, West Ham began confidently, Gregg saving well from Musgrove, but their early promise took a dent in the seventeenth minute when right-back Birkett failed to clear his lines, Charlton headed the ball through to Stiles and, as the diminutive wing half moved in on goal, he was rather unceremoniously brought down by Leslie. Quixall made no mistake from the penalty spot.

It was a lead that United held until the half hour. Gregg had already denied Byrne with another fine save, but he was unable to prevent Musgrove rounding off a Bradbrook - Woosnam - Peters move. The groans were clearly audible and many were of the opinion, 'here we go again'. But five minutes from the interval, United regained the lead. Giles swung the ball into the West Ham penalty area, Leslie palmed it out, but not to safety, only to the foot of Quixall, who hammered the ball high into the roof of the net from ten yards.

Having the advantage was something new for United and, like kids having found the key to the sweetie shop, they continued to enjoy the best of the play as the second half progressed. Herd failed to make the most of a trio of opportunities, while Leslie denied the United front line on numerous occasions. West Ham did have their moments, Seeley missing a glorious chance to equalise from three yards out, with Gregg sitting on the ground.

Despite United having the upper hand, there was always the fear of that equalising goal outdoing all that went before, but with ten minutes remaining, the outcome was put beyond doubt when Herd headed a Leslie clearance back towards goal and in nipped Law to force the ball home off Lyall's legs.

The final whistle brought sighs of relief, with the result shifting United off the foot of the table, it was only up a couple of rungs, but it was hoped that it would bring much needed confidence and belief to a team that had quite clearly lost both.

As mentioned, a few lines back, Denis Law had enjoyed a more favourable ninety minutes by embracing the role of a forward and not trying to justify his transfer fee or prove his worth to the supporters and in his column in the 'Sunday Pictorial' respected journalist, Sam Leitch, gave his thoughts on Law, having watched him against Tottenham. He wrote: "Law looked a fidgety, frustrated fellow, lacking the sort of support Greaves has always had at White Hart Lane.

"Now Denis seems infected with the general lack of confidence that shackles half a million pounds worth of Red devils. Arrows mark their path to the Second Division... is Law getting the best out of United? Or are United getting the best out of Law?

"But United are not exploiting Law's remarkable talents.

"Some of his colleagues look as if they resent him swooping down on them from all over the place.

"If Matt can afford to have patience at the foot of the table, he must apply it in the case of Law. The team must be built round him and his spring-heeled energies."

Leitch went on to quote a former Scottish team mate of Law's who said: "On the field he's not an easy fellow to get on with. At first his style takes some getting used to, as does his habit of wanting to do your job as well as his own.

"I reckon a club has to have Denis at least six months before either he or the team benefits. By that time the boys have got over their 'give-it-to-Denis' complex."

So, was he a law unto himself and could United afford to wait six months for the special Denis Law blend to mature into the sparkling, sweet tasting success that Manchester United and their followers craved?

In answer to the second of the two questions, the answer was a most definite NO. Football is all about results, current ones at that, whilst supporters long for the silverware which goes hand in hand with continuous runs of positive outcomes. Only one team can win the League or the F.A. Cup and they want it to be their team. From a United perspective that Thursday afternoon in 1958 wiped out a side who were more than capable of winning cabinet loads of trophies, both at home and abroad, but that was in the past, an unfulfilled dream. The seasons since then have been like climbing a mountain, taking tentative steps, gaining a firm foothold and making sure you took the correct path back to the top. The team of today, having pro-gressed so far, have had to retrace those steps and set off again, but with players like Law, and perhaps the odd addition, they would surely once again reach the summit, which at present, remained hidden behind thick cloud.

The answer to question one regarding Denis Law being a law unto himself was YES, quiet possibly. He was a more than talented individ-ual, a player who possessed incredible skills. Skills that others could only stand and admire and if anyone in the United side could win a game on his own, then it was the Aberdonian. Every player with similar

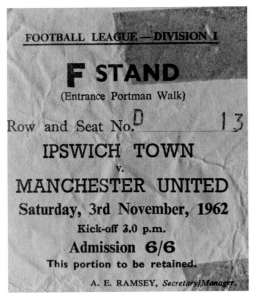

talents and capabilities also had that mean selfish streak. It was part of the make-up, a requirement even, if you were to be a success in your chosen profession.

This was proved on the afternoon of November 3rd when United travelled to East Anglia to face Ipswich Town, a team who, under the guidance of Alf Ramsey, lifted the Third Division South championship trophy, when United were doing likewise with that of the First Division at the end of the 1956-57 season. Season 1960-61 saw them lift the Second Division title, reaching the top flight for the first time in their history. What was even more of a surprise was their immediate success in the First Division, taking the title at that first time of asking, with a two-point margin over Burnley. All this whilst United re-built and struggled.

But Ipswich Town had never come face to face with an on-form Denis Law and on that November afternoon in 1962, he was to silence the doubters and prove to everyone that he could be relied upon to conjure up the goals when required and here was a player who could certainly help, if not lead, Manchester United to that ultimate peak.

There had been a possibility that the match would not go ahead due to the dreadful weather and, by tea time, Ipswich Town would have gladly have taken the postponement rather than the result, as there could not have been many occasions when they scored three at home and still managed to end up on the losing side.

The Ipswich crowd and the players were barely settled when Law struck in the second minute, picking up a Quixall pass before scoring. Crawford equalised, but it was nothing more than a minor hiccup to the visitors as Ipswich were soon on the back foot once again when Herd scored from thirty yards out, having taken a pass from Stiles.

Law claimed his second of the afternoon twelve minutes after his first. Charlton cut inside and slipped the ball back to Herd out on the left. The United number nine hit the ball low and hard into the Ipswich penalty area and there was Law in a flash to crash the ball home from

eighteen yards. He completed his hat trick in the 21st minute following a brilliant run down the centre by Giles. This was the Manchester United everyone knew best.

Thirty seconds into the second half Blackwood scored a second for Ipswich, adding another just short of the hour mark and at 4-3 many thought United would wobble and concede more. But it was not to be. Up popped that man Law again, five minutes from time to score United's fifth.

It had been an eventful afternoon for the four-goal hero or the "blond headed panther who prowled in search of that kill" as one journalist described him, as he was also to receive a couple of warnings from the referee, the second for almost coming to blows with an Ipswich defender.

Despite having won their last two fixtures, three if you take into account a 3-1 victory against the Austrian side First Vienna, a somewhat meaningless friendly thrown into the fixture list for some unknown reason, most probably just to keep that buzz of European football under the Old Trafford floodlights alive until it could return on a permanent basis, the defensive fragility of the team was still painfully obvious having conceded four in the last two fixtures, or if you like, ten in the last three.

Strangely, unlike the concern shown by the man on the terracing, it didn't appear to worry Matt Busby, not even when his team was to concede a further seven goals in their next three outings, as he continued to field the same rear guard. Of those three fixtures, two were drawn, the first, a Lancashire derby at Old Trafford against a Liverpool side that had not won away from home all season. A passionate affair that kept the packed ground on their toes right until the final blast of the referee's whistle. For those who left early, their weekend was well and truly spoilt.

United gained the initial advantage six minutes before the interval. An exquisite pass from the on-form Quixall split open the Liverpool defence, Herd, for once, managing to evade the close attention of

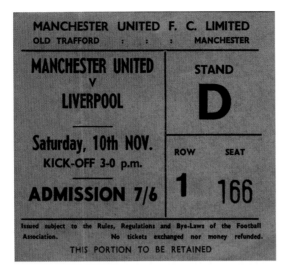

MANCHESTER UNITED F. C. LIMITED
OLD TRAFFORD : : : MANCHESTER

MANCHESTER UNITED
v
LIVERPOOL

STAND
D

Saturday, 10th NOV.
KICK-OFF 3-0 p.m.

ROW   SEAT

ADMISSION 7/6   1   166

Issued subject to the Rules, Regulations and Bye-Laws of the Football
Association.   No tickets exchanged nor money refunded.
THIS PORTION TO BE RETAINED

Yeats and beat Lawrence with relative ease. Six minutes after the interval, it was all-square. A powerful left foot shot from Callaghan was palmed out by Gregg, but only to the feet of St John who wasted little time in sliding the ball home for the equaliser.

Eighteen minutes later, it was 2-1 to United amid some considerable controversy. Giles, moving into the Liverpool penalty area, was caught by Melia and tumbled to the ground, the referee pointing to the penalty spot. The visitors were of the opinion that the United winger had lost control of the ball prior to the point of contact, but there was little doubt that Melia had caught Giles from behind and the baying United supporters were unanimous in their approval of the referee's decision.

Liverpool, despite their poor record on the road, mounted attack after attack as they sought the equaliser. Hunt missed two glorious chances, but with five minutes remaining and the score still 2-1 in United's favour, it looked as though the two points were in the bag. Many headed for the exits confident that victory was United's.

They would have barely set foot outside the ground when Liverpool forced a corner. Yeats out-jumped the United defence and headed A'Court's flag kick towards goal. Gregg dived and got his hand to the ball, but just as it looked as if it would go out of play, up popped Melia to prod the ball home to the jubilation of the vast travelling support.

Three minutes later, and not content with a point, Liverpool once again surged towards the United goal and were a mere step away from being awarded a penalty when Hunt was unceremoniously upended in a double tackle from Setters and Foulkes. From the resulting free-kick on the edge of the United eighteen-yard line, Moran ignored the defensive wall and hammered the ball past Gregg to give Liverpool a 3-2 lead.

From having the game practically sewn up at 2-1 with five minutes remaining, United looked to have dropped both points in a remarkable finale. But it was not all over yet. From the re-start, Cantwell hoisted a clearance, more in hope than anything else, towards the Liverpool goal. The ball was flicked on and Giles managed to get on the end of it, hold off challenges from Yeats and Moran, he hit a left-footed shot into the corner of the net for a last gasp equaliser. There was barely time to re-start the game before the final whistle echoed around the ground.

In the course of the last few fixtures, with United looking like a team that should hold a more respectable position in the First Division table, one player had stood above all others, with the upturn in fortune arguably down to his performances. Many would have been more than happy to have seen Albert Quixall removed from the Manchester United pay roll and banished to some nondescript lower league side, while Quixall himself had shown his unhappiness on the banks of the ship canal, by suggesting that his footballing career would perhaps be better continued in pastures new.

But it had been the former Sheffield Wednesday man who had almost single handed earned both points against West Ham United and against Liverpool, with all eyes fixed on his blond headed counterpart Law, he showed that the dark shadows that had followed him around in the early days of the season had disappeared, the axe that hovered above his neck had also gone as he coaxed, cajoled and conducted the rhythm of the United attack.

Quixall, however, was to be upstaged a week later when United again scored three and although he did have his hand in one of the goals, the plaudits went to Denis Law for his double in the 3-2 win against Wolves and to Maurice Setters who, like Quixall, had not enjoyed those early weeks of the campaign.

As in the previous Saturday, the match evolved around a small percentage of the ninety minutes, thirteen minutes to be more exact, in a fixture that was considered as one of the greatest between the two clubs.

Wolves took the lead in the 12th minute through Stobart, with the same player doubling that advantage four minutes prior to half time. "They ran off at half-time with their dismal record of six games without victory proudly forgotten" wrote Clement Freud in the 'Observer'. He was to continue: "Two cups of tea and three cakes [on my part] later, Wolves returned and gave an exhibition of such lethargic futility in front, such blatant misunderstanding behind, that the Mancunians first took heart, then took a goal." United were perhaps fortunate it was only 2-0.

The outcome was to change on the hour. Giles went past Thompson, cut inside and his centre found Herd who guided the ball home. Six minutes later Setters slid the ball to Quixall and as the Wolves

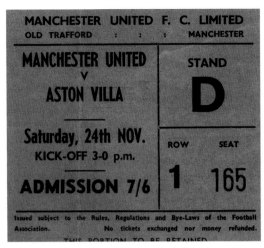

MANCHESTER UNITED F. C. LIMITED

OLD TRAFFORD : : : MANCHESTER

MANCHESTER UNITED
V
ASTON VILLA

STAND

D

Saturday, 24th NOV.
KICK-OFF 3-0 p.m.

ROW   SEAT

1   165

ADMISSION 7/6

Issued subject to the Rules, Regulations and Bye-Laws of the Football
Association.   No tickets exchanged nor money refunded.

THIS PORTION TO BE RETAINED

defence stepped forward in anticipation of an off-side decision, the ball was quickly returned to Setters who saw his powerful drive parried by Davies in the Wolves goal, allowing Law to jink in and tap the ball home.

It was Law who was to stun Wolves with the winner in the 73rd minute, dispossessing Stobart before running past three defenders before side footing the ball home.

"Law is an endearing character: unshirking industry on the part of a high-priced footballer is always good to watch and no-one begrudged him the winning goal which he achieved with a dazzling solo one-step" wrote Freud. "That was it from a goal scoring point of view. Hundreds of boys ran on to the field, and why on earth shouldn't they if they feel like it? The nasty suspicion that the crowd had only come because they hadn't read newspapers for three years, and still thought that Wolves versus Manchester united was the match of the year, faded as it was generally agreed that this had become a wonderful match."

So, Law had his ninety minutes of glory in the Midlands, but Quixall was not going to give up his recent ascent to the 'United Man of the Moment' crown so easily, and it was reclaimed against another Midland side, Aston Villa a week later when his two goals gave United a point in the 2-2 draw.

It was a point that was to come at some expense as Villa played the ninety minutes with "exuberance, though not malevolence", according to the 'Birmingham Daily Post', although it would be safe to say that United, and Denis Law in particular, would disagree as he limped off the pitch as early as the thirty-fourth minute, never to return, following a challenge from Crowe.

At this stage of the proceedings, the scores were level. Noel Cantwell had put through his own goal, having given away the corner that his unfortunate mistake originated from. The equaliser came soon after, when Law lured Sidebottom out of position before laying the ball back to Charlton, whose shot was handled on the goal-line by Fraser. From the penalty spot, Quixall was never going to miss.

With Law gone, Quixall revelled in the role of the main attacking force coupled with that of the mid-field schemer, but reduced to ten men, United were always going to find themselves up against it from a forceful Villa side.

Dougan restored the Midland side's lead with a neatly headed goal from a Burrows cross, but within three minutes, Quixall once again equalised, this time rising like a bird to head a Giles cross into the corner of the net.

Had those drawn games been converted into victories then United's continuing improvement would have taken on an even better look than their fourth bottom position. Their sixteen points saw them sit three clear of third bottom Fulham, while above them, six clubs sat on seventeen, with ninth place Blackburn Rovers only three points better off. Positive, or negative, results could bring about a dramatic change in fortune either way.

Whilst Albert Quixall had witnessed a resurgence in his United career, others, such as David Gaskell, had seen theirs take a downward spiral. Having sprung into prominence with his impromptu appearance in the 1956 F.A. Charity Shield fixture against Manchester United as a sixteen-year-old, he had always been something over an understudy to Harry Gregg, stepping in whenever the Irishman suffered an injury, never really been able to call the goalkeeper's position as his own.

He had played in twenty-one of the forty-two league fixtures of the 1961-62 season and kept his place in the side for the opening ten of the 1962-63 campaign, but following the 5-2 defeat at the hands of Burnley and Gregg's return yet again from injury, he found himself amongst the others kicking their heels in the Central League side.

Gaskell was content to wait upon his recall to the United first team, whenever that might be, but one Central League performance, a 2-1 victory against Sheffield United at Bramall Lane on November 24th, saw the United 'keeper in the headlines, but not in the manner as to which he had been accustomed.

Following the fixture, a senior Sheffield police officer revealed that they received a complaint from a woman spectator regarding the conduct of a United player during the match. When asked by a reporter if he knew anything about the matter, Gaskell replied: "I had my name taken by the referee.

"There was a penalty awarded to Sheffield and a bit of arguing.

"Something was thrown and hit our centre-half Frank Haydock in the face.

"I haven't a clue about any police investigations. They have not spoken to me."

What Gaskell had not revealed was that when being cautioned by the referee, he gave him a false name for which he was severely censured and fined five guineas. The referee had also reported the Sheffield club for misconduct by spectators and ordered to post warning notices on their ground for one month.

Gaskell had waited over a month before his appearance in front of the F.A. Committee, whilst having to wait a further month before an appearance in court which had resulted from that same Central League fixture.

'The Bare Truth About A Goalie' proclaimed the 'Daily Mirror' second page on February 26th, with the article going on to tell that Gaskell had pleaded not guilty at the court hearing in Sheffield of using insulting language and making an insulting gesture.

It was alleged that with United leading 2-0, Sheffield United had been awarded a penalty, which Gaskell saved before turning to the crowd and held two fingers up "in a derogatory manner". The penalty kick was, for some reason, ordered to be re-taken and a goal was scored, after which Gaskell was said to have lowered his shorts and wiggled his bare behind at the crowd. A nurse who supposedly witnessed this claimed that "the crowd was absolutely furious" and added that Gaskell [and his team mates] used obscene language. One man in the crowd had apparently tried to get onto the pitch to confront the United 'keeper'.

In his defence, Gaskell denied pulling down his shorts, saying that when he dived to try and save the penalty kick, they had come down a little and he had immediately pulled them up and added that he had never used obscene language. In regards to the two fingered gesture, he said he had made this to the players not the crowd.

Although, when asked by reporters following the match as to what had happened in regards to be spoken to by the police, Gaskell had said that no conversation had taken place, but in court he mentioned that when interviewed by police officers he had told them "I am always pulling my shorts up. I wear blue swimming trunks underneath."

Following the two-day hearing, Gaskell was cleared on both accounts – using insulting language and using an insulting gesture likely to cause a breach of the peace.

The headlines quickly swung from one United goalkeeper to another, following Harry Gregg's performance against Sheffield United, ironically at Bramall Lane where Gaskell had found himself in hot water, as the Northern Ireland goalkeeper saved a penalty in the 1-1 draw.

Matt Busby was forced into making his first change to his line-up in seven games, as Denis Law had not recovered from the twisted knee picked up against Aston Villa the previous week. Although the presence of the fiery Scot might have made the difference between one and two points, United extended their unbeaten run to six games.

Having scored sixteen goals in their previous five games, many might have been disappointed that United only managed the one solitary strike against the Yorkshire side, particularly after Bobby Charlton gave them the lead in the 18th minute. But while it had been the United front line who had been grabbing the headlines and the plaudits, it was the defence who stood out at Bramall Lane.

Charlton's goal was his first since his return following his hernia operation and, throughout the ninety minutes, he showed flashes of his old England form. His goal, conjured up by his audacity and skill, saw him get the better of Coldwell and Richardson on the left, before cutting inside and blasting the ball past Hodgkinson from a narrow angle.

A mere handful of minutes had elapsed before Sheffield United were level, Brennan tripping Hodgson in the penalty area, leaving the referee in little doubt in awarding the kick. Simpson's spot-kick going in off the post with Gregg well beaten.

The goal did little to inspire the home side, who lacked much in the way of inspiration, while United were little better and the game lapsed into a dogged battle that may well have got out of hand had referee J. R. Lonynton not kept a firm grip of the proceedings. Some officials might have allowed a few of the tackles to go unchecked, but with the risk that, as the game progressed, things could have got out of hand. No such risks were taken and four names went into the book, two from each side, Stiles and Setters of United.

United's tackling and approach was robust, tough rather than reckless, but it was to see them concede two penalties, the second of which, ten minutes from the end, had it not been saved by Gregg could well have given Sheffield United, who had dominated the second half, both points. Hodgson weaved his way into the United area, but was brought down by Noel Cantwell. Gregg on this occasion was equal to Simpson's kick, guessing that the Sheffield player would opt for the same side as before. He was proved correct and pulled off a fine save.

A point was better than none, more so when you found yourself at the wrong end of the table.

For one of those United players who fell foul of the referee, it was on par for the course, as he was something of a marked man when it came to match officials and he had also just been given a fortnight suspension by the Football Association Disciplinary Committee.

"I just cannot go on like this" said an upset Maurice Setters, following his latest brush with authority. "I feel I've only got to tackle a player to be in trouble.

"If everyone had been booked for doing what I did, almost all the twenty-two players would have had their names taken.

"I have never in my life gone out on the pitch with the intention of deliberately fouling a player. It is his living as well as mine."

The suspension of Setters, considered by some to be the 'bad boy' of English football, came on the back of a referee's report from United's away match against Wolves at Molyneux on November 17th, when he was booked for showing dissent following the award of a free-kick against him. He had been warned on September 18th as regards to his previous misconduct.

Matt Busby found himself not only without the services of Setters, but also his other wing-half, the tigerish Nobby Stiles, for the visit of Nottingham Forest to Old Trafford. Into the side came Jimmy Nicholson for his first start in two months. Thankfully Denis Law was fit to return, allowing Lawton to step back into the half-back line and handing back the number ten shirt to the Scot.

United's star continued to soar upwards, defeating Forest 5-1, a result that gave them much respectability in the First Division table – 14th, seven and six points respectively above the bottom two clubs, Leyton Orient and Fulham, although they were ten off second place Burnley and a further two off leaders Everton.

Forest were in a much better position, some eight points better off, and had they defeated United would have found themselves sitting fourth. But it was not to be, as United maintained their fine form of late and their average of three goals per game, with the haunting form of three months ago now nothing but a distant memory. "On the crest of a revival" wrote one correspondent who had observed the defeat of Forest.

The opening twenty minutes gave little indication as to the eventual outcome. With nine minutes gone, a Giles corner was headed high into the air by Quixall and looked to be going out of play, that was until Herd decided otherwise, appearing at the back post to head home.

With Quixall pulling the strings, as always was the case in these effervescent days, United looked forward to a rewarding afternoon, but ten minutes later Forest struck back through Addison thanks to an inch perfect pass from Quigley. Perhaps things would not, after all, turn out as expected thought the majority of the surprisingly sparsely filled Old Trafford ground.

At this time, although an imposing arena, it was far from being the largest, although it had been one of those selected to host group stage fixtures in the World Cup when the competition was due to come to England in 1966. With a capacity of 65,000, similar in size to that of Sunderland and Sheffield Wednesday, it was still, however, smaller than the other selected stadia of Sheffield Wednesday [65,000], Arsenal [68,000], Aston Villa [70,000] and Everton [75,000].

The attendance for the visit of Forest - 27,946, was only 641 more than had watched the thrilling 3-3 draw with Liverpool a matter of weeks previously, but those who had bothered to seek their afternoon entertainment down beside the ship canal, they were once again treated to six goals, but on this occasion, there was no sharing of the spoils and, having been given a rude awakening by Forest's equaliser, United got down to the business at hand.

Within a couple of minutes of Forest drawing level, United regained the lead. Giles rounded Gray with comparative ease, before picking out Quixall. The ball was quickly despatched towards Herd who took the ball on the turn, sending a low hard drive past Armstrong.

That lead was increased in the 26th minute when Law cleared from the edge of his own penalty area towards Giles, who in turn lobbed the ball forward to Charlton. Taking the pass on the centre line, he set off down the right before sending the ball soaring past a helpless Armstrong with a vintage drive.

After the interval it continued to be more or less one-way traffic, although at times, the Forest creative pairing of Palmer and White were given too much freedom, but their defensive team mates were equally lax when it came to marking the United front line.

It wasn't, however, until the 73rd minute that United increased their lead, Giles taking up a pass from Law, left Wilson mesmerised before lashing the ball past Armstrong.

With a minute remaining, Charlton was carried off following a wild lunging tackle from Wilson, and as he disappeared down the tunnel, Law brought the proceedings to a close with United's fifth. Faced with two Forest defenders, plus the goalkeeper, he still managed to steer the ball past the trio and into the net. But all good things must come to an end, and so United's unbeaten run of seven games, with their barrowload of goals, ground to a halt on Saturday December 15th at the Hawthorns where West Bromwich Albion scored three without reply.

"A ramshackle Manchester United defence was the decisive factor of a match all too easily won" was the opinion of John Arlott in the 'Observer' the following morning, adding: "Without even playing, or needing to play, more than in an orthodox manner and at fair pace, the West Bromwich Albion forwards could make their way through the middle or along the wings to goal at almost every moment.

"Not only was the Manchester United defence completely beaten three times, and fortunate to escape a dozen times more, but it was incapable of supporting or supplying its potentially brilliant inside-forwards in any real counter-attack."

Setters was still relegated to the naughty boy step, whilst Charlton had to sit this one out through injury, his place taken by Moir, seeing first team action for the first time since the end of September. Law, described by Real Madrid's Di Stefano only days before as 'the greatest footballer in the world' could well have been the man to undo the Albion defence, but he found himself at the edge of the United penalty area as often he did at the opposite end.

It was a scruffy United performance compared to some that had gone before. Free-kicks and corners were given away like charity donations and with such frequency that a goal never seemed to be far away, and it was something of a surprise that it took West Bromwich until a few minutes before half-time to register their first goal. Cram beating Gregg with a low, hard drive from the edge of the penalty area into the corner of the net.

Control was resumed following the break with a second goal only minutes after the re-start. Smith meandered down the right, outfoxed Foulkes, before floating the ball casually over the head of Gregg as he advanced from his goal. United attacks were, at best, scarce. Quixall subdued and Herd wandering aimlessly. The absence of Setters against his former club, both in strength and leadership, being well and truly missed.

With twenty minutes remaining, Jackson added a third with a right footed volley and that was it, as Albion took their foot of the pedal and coasted through the remainder of the game. Had they not been inclined to do so, then United would have surely suffered their biggest defeat of the season. "No First Division match should be as easy to win as this" was John Arnott's final comment.

United avoided being placed under the microscope by the media, their performance examined in much closer detail and their slovenly ninety minutes pushed to the side, when it was revealed that they were considering reporting the match referee, Gilbert Pullin of Bristol, to the Football Association for making 'belittling comments' to Denis Law during the match at the Hawthorns.

It was not the first time this season that the G.P.O. technician had found himself in hot water, as he had been exonerated by an F.A. enquiry back in October when he had been accused of threatening an Oxford United player during a match at Torquay.

At the Hawthorns, it had been Albert Quixall who had heard the comments and said to the official that he would report him, which he did at the interval to Matt Busby. "I told the referee I would report him and I did" said Quixall. "I've never heard anything like it from a referee before. But at the moment I cannot reveal what comments I did hear. The matter is in the club's hands. At first, I thought he must be joking. It was so unusual. It all seemed so laughable. You just wouldn't believe it if I told you some of the things I heard."

That something had occurred out on the pitch other than the actual football, was something that the men of the press were not long in picking up. When asked about the incident, Law was cautious in his reply. "I'd like to tell you the lot, but I can't at the moment.

"All I can say is – I don't mind being cautioned or even sent off if I deserve it. But this sort of thing is different.

He was later to add: "I would rather leave the matter in the hands of the club. I have seen the boss about what happened and all I can say is that it was a most unusual experience and one I have never had before in my football career."

Goalkeeper Harry Gregg added: "I wasn't involved in anything, but at half-time I could see Denis was upset.

"He isn't the kind of player who gets annoyed easily about anything, but he was really disturbed about things which happened before the interval. "In fact, I've never seen him so upset before."

Rounding on Matt Busby as he left the Hawthorns, the United manager was put on the spot regarding the matter and confirmed that a number of his players had approached him and made serious allegations towards the match official. "Denis and the other players have been in to see me, but I do not think it would be wise to take the matter further at this stage beyond saying that the allegations will be discussed by the board tomorrow evening. Then we will decide what action, if any, we should take in this unfortunate matter."

Few knew anything about what had been said, or alleged to have been said, but Steve Richards of the 'Daily Herald' wrote: "I understand that some of the alleged remarks came at the start of the game, when Law had not been involved in any incident, and later when he made ordinary mistakes – like inaccurate distribution – which occur during any match."

As for the referee. "I am amazed to hear of the charges" said Pullin. "Frankly I can't recall any such incident. At no time did I threaten Law with disciplinary action. Beyond that I cannot comment. I've heard nothing officially of any complaint."

Following the Old Trafford board meeting, the club announced that they would be reporting the official to the Football Association, and no sooner had this news leaked than an army of black clad officials stood up in support of their threatened comrade, with Bill Rogers, secretary of the 12,000 strong Referees' Association saying: "We are watching this situation closely. I think it is wrong that a club should make it known publicly they have protested about a referee.

"I am surprised it should be a club with a great reputation like Manchester United.

"As I see it, Mr Pullin is in a terrible position. Every time he puts a foot on a Soccer pitch he could be pilloried and every one could be gunning for him.

"He is one of our members. We will protect him."

And if there are any signs that he is suffering because of the publicity over this protest then we will protest to the F. A. about Manchester United's handling of the affair."

"As a club they are perfectly entitled to say what they think about any referee, but It should be done privately to the F.A. and Football League.

"It is all wrong that referees should have to face this sort of publicity."

When asked if he had read the referee's version of what had said to have taken place Bill Rogers rather surprisingly replied: "No - but my impression is that professional footballers are getting altogether too touchy these days. It seems a referee can't make any remark without risking action of this kind.

"After all. It is not referees who pull shirts, take up petulant attitudes and carry on petty gamesmanship. We are merely carrying out instructions.

"I think players have got the wrong idea since these unlimited wages came in.

"Once the message gets through to them that referees are merely doing their job as instructed, then this spate of warnings, cautions and sending off will cease. The public doesn't come to see this sort of thing."

Pullin had to wait until mid-February for the case to be heard, a hearing that was completely alien to anything that had gone before, leaving press and supporters alike able to do nothing more than speculate as to what the eventual outcome would be.

Bill Rogers, the Referees Association secretary, who had previously been quite voracious in his support of Pullin commented: "I can't see an F.A. Commission censuring a referee without due cause. Obviously, he has left himself wide open somewhere.

"Referees can't be put in a glass case. Players have to face this type of commission, so there is no reason why referees should not have to.

"But if Mr. Pullin contacts me we will obviously look into it." Had a clearer picture to that afternoon's events come to the fore?

Many were of the opinion that the stiff collar, unsmiling men of the Football Association, men who were often far removed from the actual game itself, would simply dismiss United's complaint before those in attendance had made themselves comfortable. For once, they were wrong.

The three-man commission of Mr. Noel Watson, Mr. Len Shipman and Mr. K. A. Milner met for nearly two hours and questioned Pullin, Law, West Bromwich Albion winger Alex Jackson and Manchester United's Albert Quixall. Also called into the hearing were Players' Union secretary Cliff Lloyd, United manager Matt Busby, West Bromwich Albion manager Archie Macaulay and his chairman, Major Wilson Keys.

Following the inquest, the commission released the following statement: "From the evidence adduced, the commission is satisfied that Mr Pullin made certain unnecessary remarks to player Denis Law during the match and that the player was justified reporting the matter his club.

"The commission has decided that Mr Pulllin be severely censured, warned to his future conduct and informed that must not in future make unnecessary remarks and observations to player during the match.

"The Manchester United club officials and players are informed that their action in making Press statements before the complaint was considered by the Disciplinary Committee is deprecated and their attention is drawn to the letter on this subject sent to all English clubs in 1957. No order is made as to payment of costs of the commission."

No player had ever won a case against a match official before, but the three-man commission, having read about and listened to United's complaint, came to the decision that Gilbert Pullin had made "unnecessary remarks" to Law and he was severely censured and warned about his future conduct.

Following the hearing, Pullin refused to comment and also refused to pose for a photograph shaking hands with Law, even although Denis stood with his hand outstretched. Law was unphased, and said they had already shaken hands privately. He added that he was very happy about the way things had gone at the hearing.

As for Pullin, it was only a matter of days before he announced that he was hanging up his whistle, tendering his resignation as "the findings of the Commission will be with me wherever I go."

Saturday December 22nd saw Arsenal make the pre-Christmas trip to Old Trafford, but for those who decided that an afternoon's football was a more appealing attraction than the packed shops and streets of the city centre, their decision was only partly rewarded and their admission money wasted as they were to see only limited action in more ways than one.

As kick-off approached a thin film of mist hung over the ground, but with the referee's pre-match inspection allowing him to see both goals and both linesmen, he felt himself under no pressure to consider the conditions worthy of a postponement.

In the opening stages of the game, play swung from end to end. A Barnwell - Strong - Sneddon move saw the latter fire over, while at the opposite end Charlton's centre brushed over the blond head of Law. The Scot came close again, having dispossessed Barnwell, but Magill was on hand to avert disaster. An acrobatic save by Gregg denied Eastham, the ball saved on the goal line, while Charlton, picking up a pass from Setters, cut inside and unleashed a shot from twenty-five yards which skimmed the cross bar before disappearing into the crowd. McClelland in the Arsenal goal was also to deny Herd twice, Charlton and Law.

Gregg saved from MacLeod as the second half got underway, while United had appeals for a penalty turned down, but four minutes after the interval Arsenal took the lead through Barnwell, who beat Gregg from twenty-five yards.

By now, if you were sitting in the main stand, the Stretford End had disappeared from view and, with fifty-six minutes played, the referee decided to call play to what was initially a temporary halt in the hope that the now thickening fog would rather miraculously lift. Not surprisingly it didn't and the match was brought to a premature end.

Boxing Day found United on the banks of the Thames at Craven Cottage, where they were given a warning as what was to come, not in regards as to the actual outcome of the ninety minutes, but to the adverse weather and the conditions underfoot. They were perhaps fortunate that their journey south had not been in vain as nineteen other League fixtures were postponed, with a further three abandoned. Only three of the eleven First Division fixtures were completed.

The fog of the previous week had lifted, but was replaced by ice and snow, making the fixture far from memorable, not that they were going to be that in the first place as Fulham sat in second bottom place, while United could be as indifferent as they cared to be. But at the end of the often farcical ninety minutes, the general opinion was that had bone hard pitch augmented by a constant fall of snow, United

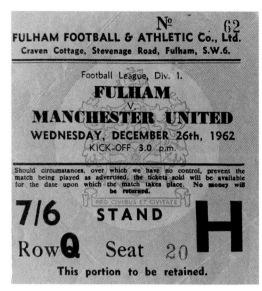

would have undoubtedly have run riot.

Although United won by the only goal of the game, both sides were defeated by the conditions. The usually effervescent Law rarely ran, often trotting, sometimes walking, but still managed to be at the forefront of everything United. There was little, however, to warm the paying public, many of whom would have decided that they would have better off at home long before the end.

In a nutshell, the outcome of the game hinged on one minute of action. Fulham danger man Keetch, who despite the conditions, had managed to torment the United defence for the best part of the first half, but with five minutes remaining he was shown a distinct lack of festive spirit when he was unceremoniously grounded by a strong tackle. A ball rolled towards Charlton and from the edge of the penalty area he hit a swerving shot past Macedo as the Fulham 'keeper groped helplessly for the ball. Keetch, although able to play on, was little more than a passenger limping around up-front, before drifting back into mid-field.

United should have already enjoyed having the advantage, but the usual dependable Quixall had missed a penalty in the thirteenth minute following a foul on Law. But following Charlton's goal and the injury to Keetch, there was only ever going to be one winner.

The tracksuit bottomed Macedo kept Fulham in the game with notable stops from Charlton and Stiles, while the United defence were troubled more by the conditions than the Fulham forwards.

Given the poor underfoot conditions, it could have been considered a well won two points as a mere slip could have resulted in an opposition goal. They were, however, to be the last two points United would win until April 9th, and it wasn't all down to poor performances.

Fulham were due in Manchester on December 29th for what was the usual Christmas home and away fixtures against the same club, and there was every likelihood that two points would again have been claimed. But it was the weather that gained the upper hand in the First Division that afternoon, with all but two fixtures taking place. The United – Fulham return was not one of them.

Snow and ice-bound pitches, equally dangerous terraces and approaches to grounds all played their parts in disrupting the Saturday afternoon rituals of countless supporters up and down the country. Their weekend was made even more dismal with the dreams of winning a small fortune on the football pools also being scuppered as they were declared void, the systems, guess work or whatever in trying to forecast draws or away wins not being needed due to the number of games called off. Only ten were to be played in the whole of the Football League.

At the same time last year, football had suffered at the hands of the weather with thirty-two postponements, but the thirty-five of December 29th was the most ever recorded by the Football League, and although it was early days there was talk of extending the season until May. It was perhaps a sensible precaution as fifteen years previously, more than one hundred League and F.A. Cup fixtures had been postponed or abandoned between February and March, with the season extended into June. Some were to comment that snow in June was something that had also been previously recorded!

In his programme notes for the postponed match against Fulham, Matt Busby wrote: "In a matter of 48 hours time, we will enter upon another new year and I need hardly say that I believe 1963 will prove to be a prosperous one for Manchester United.

"In a week, of course, we will see the start of the annual trek to Wembley for First and Second Division clubs and we have been fortunate in the draw for the Third Round in that we have a home tie.

"But by far the most impressive feature of the first half of the season has been the form of the Central League side, who have struck top form in the last dozen matches.

"This is a great sign for our football future and there are also indications that in the F.A. Youth Cup we will also make considerable impact in the next four months."

'Manchester Evening News' correspondent David Meek also sang the praises of the Central League side, which in itself was worth applauding, but as one year comes to an end, it is as much about reflecting on the recent past as the future, but perhaps those late summer, early autumn performances were regarded as forgettable, and some certainly were, and it was much better to look forward rather than back.

As Matt Busby mentioned, January saw the F.A. Cup come to the fore, with United having been given a home tie against Huddersfield Town on the 5th of the month. It, like all but five in the competition, was to fall foul of the weather.

United had been optimistic on the Thursday night about the game taking place forty-eight hours later, but a rapid deterioration in conditions saw the hope of any football being played a nigh impossible and, sure enough, the already printed match programmes was confined to the waste paper bin. The tickets, however, were of course valid for the re-arranged date and but it would be two months before they would be put to use.

From the cold, [there was an average temperature of -2.1ºF], slush and snow of Manchester thoughts were once again transported back to Munich and that afternoon of February 6th 1958. In that first January week of 1963 it was announced that United's £250,000 claim against British European Airways had been settled out of court and the action withdrawn. A B.E.A. official said that an application would be made to the High Court on January 11th.

At that time, no figure as regards to the actual settlement was disclosed, but following the High Court hearing, it was announced that the club would receive £35,000. Announcing the terms of the settlement, a B.E.A. spokesman said: "All allegations of negligence and wilful misconduct made against B.E.A. have been unreservedly withdrawn and B.E.A., denying all liability, will pay the club £35,000 and costs in settlement of the club's claim, which totalled £273,000." The action, which was due to be heard at the High Court on January 21st was subsequently withdrawn by United.

The third round F.A. Cup tie against Huddersfield Town due to have been played on January 5th, was re-scheduled for Monday 21st, but was again to lose out to the weather, losing out a second time on January 30th. By this time, United should also have fulfilled First Division fixtures against Birmingham City away and Leyton Orient at home, as well as a fourth round Cup-tie if they had been successful against the Yorkshire side.

Clubs were obviously losing money through those continual postponements. Some sought ways for beating the weather, like Leicester City, who tested a new 11 foot wide and 70 yards long polythene tent, which was heated by hot air blown through a tube. When put to use, it saw the temperature rise from 26ºF to 36ºF within seventeen minutes. Littlewoods Pools were another who were losing money and they were much bettered place to combat this loss without the need of venturing out into the cold.

On January 20th, the Pools Promoters' Association announced that due to the number of games that were being postponed each week they were going to appoint a panel of 'experts' to decide what they thought the actual result of the individual games would be. The panel, just to make it a little realistic would meet at 3.00pm on the Saturday afternoon and announce their results at 5.00pm. No doubt after countless cups of tea, pints of beer, or glasses of whisky!

Not all fixtures were postponed, despite sometimes bone-hard pitches or played amid swirling snow or a near blizzard, although actual training was at times a struggle. The Isle of Man government offered clubs training facilities on the island, with around twenty pitches available. Bolton stayed nearer to home, making the journey to Southport to train on the beach.

United, having seen all their January fixtures being called off, needed action and it came as something of a relief when as scheduled they met City as arranged on February 2nd. It was, however, not Manchester City at Maine Road, but Third Division Coventry City at Glenmalure Park, Dublin.

Coventry manager Jimmy Hill, whose fixture against Shrewsbury had been postponed, used his Irish contacts to discuss the possibility of arranging a game in Ireland and when United's fixture against neighbours City was confirmed as a no-go, he contacted Matt Busby who eagerly agreed to cross the water for ninety minutes of action.

In Dublin, the conditions were far from perfect, the match almost not taking place at all, as there was an overnight change in the weather, leaving the conditions under-foot icy, whereas before it had simply been heavy. They were, however, considered good enough to endure ninety minutes football and the Irish public were treated to a four goal encounter, with the honours shared. The outcome mattered little, it was nothing more than a kickabout, a training exercise, but the Third Division side would draw much more from the match than their loftier opponents.

It was United who took the lead in the 26th minute, Albert Quxall taking a neat pass from Law before scoring, but ten minutes before the break, Coventry equalised. Sillett lobbed a long ball forward and somehow the United defence failed to pick up the run from Farmer, who quickly latched onto the ball before coolly hooking the ball over the advancing Gregg.

Six minutes later, Coventry were in front. A three-man move between Hale, Farmer and Humphries stretched the United defence and a pass from the latter of the aforementioned trio allowed Whitehouse to beat Gregg.

Law was his usual effervescent self, turning up here there and everywhere, while Quixall found the conditions not exactly to his liking, leaving it down to Charlton to round off the scoring ten minutes from time, with his powerful shot almost dismantling the cross bar from the uprights. The goal was also to flick something of a switch as it immediately saw hundreds of youngster's swarming onto the pitch.

The ninety minutes, whilst not being considered a money-making venture, the fixture simply hoping to see all the relevant costs met, turned out to be profitable from the purpose of both teams enjoying the practise and also receiving an equal split of the £600 gate money.

Whilst eager to put his players through their paces in Dublin, or anywhere for that matter, Matt Busby had other things on his mind, with the subject matter in his daily briefings with his assistant Jimmy Murphy predominated by one thing – the possibility of luring Pat Crerand, the Celtic and Scotland half-back, south to Manchester.

Gorbals born Crerand had found himself left out of the Celtic side to face Falkirk in the Scottish Cup, the second time he had found himself on the side lines in recent weeks, something that was certainly not to his liking. So much so, that he asked the Parkhead directors to put him on the transfer list. Such news alerted numerous suitors, with Newcastle United and Tottenham Hotspur amongst the early clubs to register an interest should he definitely become available.

Available he certainly became and any hopes of Newcastle United, Tottenham Hotspur or anyone else for that matter hoping to sign him seemingly bit the dust when it was revealed that Matt Busby, having returned from Dublin was off again, this time heading up the only too familiar road to Glasgow for talks with the Celtic management.

Busby, however, had been involved with talks in Manchester prior to this in regards to the Celtic half-back, but these had been totally unofficial and behind closed doors, conducted across his office desk with Denis Law.

The United manager was keen to add a play-maker to his side, someone to pull the strings and make things happen. He had the destroyer type individual in Maurice Setters and Nobby Stiles, coupled by the imposing figures of Noel Cantwell and Bill Foulkes behind them, but he felt his team lacked that little bit of finesse and he had two players in mind who could come in and provide his team that missing link. One was Pat Crerand, the other was Jim Baxter of Rangers.

Denis Law had obviously played with both, knew them both on and off the park, so Busby called him into the confines of his office and put the question to his fellow Scot – "Crerand or Baxter?"

The reply was immediate – "Crerand". And so, off to Glasgow went Busby to conclude the deal.

Crerand at this point was not involved, and was completely unaware of United's interest, never mind their agreed deal with Celtic. He arrived for training as usual on the Monday morning [February 4th], but when asked about a move by waiting journalists he simply replied: "I still don't know the full terms. I cannot say what I will be doing." Neither was there a meeting with Matt Busby, as the United manager had returned south in anticipation of the often postponed Huddersfield Town Cup-tie being on that night.

Many were of the opinion that Crerand and his fiancée were more in favour of a move to the bright lights of London and Tottenham Hotspur, but things quickly swung in United's favour as Celtic manager Jimmy McCrory announced; "We are not going to auction Crerand. We have agreed a transfer fee with Manchester United manager Matt Busby and there is no snag on that account". There was perhaps no 'snag' as regards the transfer fee, but there was apparently one in regards to Crerand's accrued share of benefit, as under Scottish League rules, a player may receive from the transferring club £150 for each year of service up to five years. All that, however, was seemingly overcome as the couple headed south to Manchester the following day for talks with Busby and a look round the city itself.

Having flown south on the Tuesday night, it didn't take Crerand long to decide that the manager, the club and the city were for him, a mere twenty minutes to be exact, and he duly put pen to paper on a £50,000 deal at 10.30am the following morning. Once he was told that the terms on offer were £55 per week, coupled with results and crowd bonuses, he simply asked for the pen.

"There were no snags, Pat has signed for United and we are both happy. I am delighted to have him at Old Trafford. I have been watching him for two years and have always been impressed by his play" declared Busby. The player himself was equally happy with the move. "I am sure I am going to like it here. Mr Busby and everyone has helped to make Noreen and myself feel right at home. Now I am only waiting to get into one of the famous red jerseys.

"Manchester United is the only English club I have ever thought of joining and when I heard the terms they were offering I just gasped – and signed."

With Celtic, Crerand [pictured] was on £26 per week, plus £10 appearance money!

With the weather still being much more than just a little bit temperamental, when Crerand's United debut would be was something of a guessing game. It was pencilled in for the forthcoming away fixture against Burnley three days later despite the Turf Moor pitch being covered with 21cm of snow. Also under doubt was the new signings availability for the F.A. Cup, as the competition rules required a player to be registered for fourteen days in order to qualify. With postponements throwing the competition into disarray, United sought confirmation from the Football Association.

As it turned out, there was no debut for Pat Crerand at Burnley, neither was there to be any concern over when he could appear in the F.A. Cup, as the third-round tie against Huddersfield Town remained as 'pending', nothing more. The fourth-round had been scheduled for January 26th, with the fifth round having been down for February 16th. Looking back, on that Saturday of the third-round ties, only three were played, one of them ending in a draw, then on the scheduled fourth round date saw one tie played plus three third round and so it continued.

Crerand's United debut eventually came on February 13th, against Bolton Wanderers, not a few miles up the road from his new stomping ground, but in Cork, yet another friendly.

Again, the conditions were far from ideal, but this time they could be regarded as considerably worse than those in Dublin, and had it been a league or Cup-tie then there was every possibility that it would never have gone ahead, or at least have been abandoned at half time. "Farcical" was how they were described in the 'Express'. Speaking after the final whistle, Bolton goalkeeper Hopkinson was to say: "I almost couldn't get off for the interval. I had virtually become cemented into the deep mud."

But if it was bad for the players, it was little better for the crowd of around 6,000, a far cry from the expected 20,000, but with no cover, only a stand without seats, the majority of those who left their homes were drenched in the downpour that accompanied the proceedings.

The conditions did little to hamper Crerand on his debut, as he gave a forceful and constructive display that was enough to defeat a defiant Bolton side, who took the lead through Francis Lee in the 15th minute following a free-kick which saw the ball sticking in the inches deep mud, preventing Gregg from preventing the eventual outcome.

With Bolton continuing to threaten, it was Crerand who claimed the equaliser, driving home from twenty yards out, igniting the blue touch paper which saw United score a further three. A Quixall penalty after Edwards handled. Law – beating three opponents and walking round right-back Hartle, before firing home from eighteen yards, and finally Giles, with a lob over the head of the advancing Hopkinson. Bolton claimed a second from the penalty spot through Lee after Crerand fouled Hill.

Despite giving away the penalty, Crerand was more than happy with his debut. "It was a great day for me and I was delighted we won. But I have never seen mud like that before and I never expect to have to play in anything like it again.

"And on that penalty, I do not think I gave it away at all, but it was really wonderful that I managed to score a goal on my first game with the team."

Crerand got a second run out in the Emerald Isle on February 20th when United faced a Dublin XI at Dalymount Park, as once again Old Trafford was unable to host the Huddersfield Town Cup-tie. Again, he was to show that here was a player of quality in United's comfortable 4-0 victory, but the overall performance from United didn't exactly meet with the approval of those in attendance.

Due to Crerand's arrival at Old Trafford, there was immediate speculation amongst clubs as to who might be surplus to demand. Joe Harvey, manager of Newcastle United, who had shown an interest in signing Crerand, was still on the search for a half-back and the rumour mill had him linked with Maurice Setters and Jimmy Nicholson. Mark Pearson was another Old Trafford player reportedly on the Newcastle radar. Harvey was quick to shoot down the rumours, although many were of the opinion that there was no smoke without fire. None of the trio, however, found their way to Tyneside, although the rumours regarding Setters leaving Old Trafford gathered momentum when Matt Busby announced that he had taken the captaincy away from the former West Bromwich Albion man and given it to Noel Cantwell.

MANCHESTER UNITED F. C. LIMITED
OLD TRAFFORD : : : MANCHESTER

MANCHESTER UNITED
v
BLACKPOOL

STAND
D

Saturday, 23rd FEB.
KICK-OFF 3-0 p.m.

ROW   SEAT

ADMISSION 7/6   1   166

Issued subject to the Rules, Regulations and Bye-Laws of the Football
Association.   No tickets exchanged nor money refunded.
THIS PORTION TO BE RETAINED

Cantwell, like Setters, was a tough tackling, no nonsense defender, but one who perhaps did not attract the same amount of attention from referee's and whose did not feature somewhat regularly in their little black book. Following the announcement, the always turning rumour mill went into over-drive, with the general opinion being that Busby and Setters had fallen out. "Maurice is part of the structure here" retorted the United manager. "There is no question of his being for sale." He was, however, reluctant to discuss the reason behind the change in captaincy, although it was generally believed that the all too frequent brushes with authority would not be too far from the top of any list. It was also something that Busby muttered "might have something to do with it".

Having lost the captaincy, it would have eased some of the 'pressure' surrounding Setters, as more often than not, his booking came from his overreaction to a match official's decision. All Setters was to say was: "I am disappointed. But this will not make me a different kind of player."

The trio of Manchester United players did not find their way to St James Park, but the enthusiastic, action starved United support did find their way to the now unfamiliar Old Trafford on Saturday February 23rd. At long last football returned to this Mancunian oasis. It wasn't the frequently postponed F.A. Cup third round tie against Huddersfield Town though, but a league fixture against Blackpool which had actually been scheduled in the original fixture list for that same afternoon.

Rusty both sides certainly were, something that was reflected in the often mundane ninety minutes on the overly sanded Old Trafford pitch, but this could well be expected with competitive action being little more than a mere memory. It was, however, football and it allowed those Old Trafford regulars their first glimpse of Pat Crerand in a red shirt.

Law was missing with a recurrence of a knee injury, so the unification of the Scottish duo had to wait, leaving Phil Chisnall to attempt to find some capitalise on the often-perfect ability of the former Celtic player to pick out a team mate with a carefully floated pass. Chisnall, no matter how hard he tried, could never be a mirror image of Law and Crerand's choreography was often wasted.

Throughout the ninety-minutes, which saw numerous mis-kicks, United had the majority of the scoring opportunities with Tony Waiters in the Blackpool goal saving well from Giles [twice], Charlton and a twenty-five-yard drive from Crerand. At the opposite end Blackpool did come close when their debutant Napier hit the join of the cross bar and post.

Ten minutes before the interval, Quixall picked out Herd with a perfect pass, but the United centre-forwards effort went over the bar. But to the surprise of many, the referee did not award the goal-kick, but instead pointed to the penalty spot, having noticed a handball by Gratrix. Not for the first time this season, the usual dependable Quixall saw his spot kick saved, this time by the excellent Waiters.

Charlton, again, came close to scoring on a couple of occasions in the second half before United eventually took the lead in the 68th minute. Gratrix failed to clear a Qiuxall pass into the Blackpool penalty area and Herd accepted the gift to score with ease. But within five minutes Blackpool were level. Setters grappled with Quinn inside the United penalty area, leaving the referee with no option than to award a penalty. Unlike his opposite number, Gregg could not prevent Charnley from scoring, the ball going in off the post.

As the minutes ticked away, United continued to press forward, but to little avail and there was no further scoring. The point saw United remain in the somewhat comfortable position of just below mid-table, twenty-two points from their twenty-four games. Seven more than bottom club Leyton Orient, who had played two games more and four more than second bottom Fulham, who had played one more. Had United taken both points, then they would have been a further couple of places higher. No matter what, they were still a far cry from putting pressure on the leading pack.

Yet another point was dropped as February moved into March and football finally resumed on a regular basis with United travelling to Ewood Park to face Blackburn Rovers on the 2nd of the month where they were held to a 2-2 draw.

Considerable numbers of United supporters made the short journey across Lancashire in the hope that the tartan partnership of Crerand and Law would click into gear and United could continue on a path to First Division safety, while the home support were simply grateful to be back in their usual spots on the terracing for the first time since December 15th. Conditions were still rather firm underfoot, but the visitors, having taken the lead in the fifth minute, appeared to master such treachery best.

The opening goal was something of a gift to United, as Else in the Blackburn goal, apparently dazzled by a glaring sun, dropped a Giles corner and Law wasted little time in prodding the ball home.

Returning after injury, Law was back to his usual self – dribbles, flicks, back-heels, the complete repertoire, leaving the Blackburn defence often mesmerised. He could well have added a second just after the interval, turning the ball against the post after Else had parried a Setters shot.

On the hour mark, Blackburn drew level through Byrom and six minutes later they were in front. Quixall attempted a long pass back to Gregg, but it was far from accurate, going instead to the feet of Pickering. The Blackburn forward, pushing all thoughts of his wedding a few hours earlier to the back of his mind, accepted the present and crashed the ball past Gregg as Quixall held his head in shame.

Redemption, however, was at hand for Quixall as seconds later, kick-starting the move that was to produce the equaliser. Pushing the ball wide to Herd, the United centre-forward sent a high looping cross into the Blackburn penalty area where it was met by Charlton whose shot flew into the net off the back of Bray, the Rovers right-back.

One point was better than none, although once again United failed to hammer home their superiority in mid-field, while Law could have done much better with a couple of ideal scoring opportunities. The likes of Blackpool, Manchester City and Fulham, three clubs who could be found below them, all won. There was still a diary full of fixtures, seventeen to be exact, to be completed, but the danger zone wasn't exactly an arm's length away. Fixture congestion could well be a bigger, more threatening opponent, more so if there was by chance something of an extended F.A. Cup run.

Interest in the F.A. Cup finally got underway on March 4th, two months later than scheduled. There had been heading towards a dozen postponements, but finally Huddersfield Town crossed the Yorkshire/Lancashire border and an hour and a half after the first blast of the referee's whistle, they were wishing that high winds, fog, sleet, snow or whatever had placed Old Trafford once again as being unplayable.

The night belonged to two men, distant individuals, but connected by the thread woven between the two clubs. On one side there was

MANCHESTER UNITED F. C. LIMITED

STAND	ROW	SEAT
D	**10**	155

F.A. Challenge Cup—3rd Round

Manchester Utd. v. Huddersfield T.

AT OLD TRAFFORD   KICK OFF 3-0 p.m

SATURDAY, 5th JANUARY, 1963

Admission 7/6   *L. Olive*
Secretary

Issued subject to the Rules, Regulations and Bye Laws of the Football Association.

KEEP THIS PORTION

Denis Law, facing his former club, but showing little in the way of compassion to his former paymasters. On the other was a man who had served United well, suffered on that fateful Thursday in 1958, while being unfortunate not to already own an F.A. Cup winners' medal, robbed of the honour through the jinx that was all too common up Wembley Way on Cup Final day over the past couple of decades. Despite conceding five on the night, Ray Wood was blameless and saved his team from an even heavier defeat.

It took United two minutes to claim the advantage. Forty yards from goal Law trapped the ball, rotated a full circle, beating the mesmerised Bettany, before sending a through ball to Quixall who ran clear and shot past Wood. Five minutes later, Herd, in mid-field passed to Setters, who in turn sent Law scurrying away, shrugging off two tackles before blasting the ball high into the net.

The third goal in the nineteenth minute had more than an element of luck about it. Giles, wide on the right, sent the ball low into the Huddersfield goalmouth, with the unsighted Wood moving too late to prevent the ball going in off the post. The general opinion was that it was a cross more than a shot.

Law struck again nine minutes later, latching onto Herd's back heel, feinted to one side, mis-kicked, lost his balance, but still managed to divert the ball past Wood. 4-0 and Huddersfield had still to have a shot on target. Twenty-eight minutes gone and they were also longing for the full-time whistle.

In the second half Huddersfield managed a couple of goal bound headers from Stokes and McHale, but they simply fell invitingly into Gregg's arms. Two of only three saves he had to make. His former team mate Ray Wood was obviously the busiest of the two 'keepers, pulling off numerous notable saves, one in particular even producing

100

a round of applause from Albert Quixall after Wood had palmed his volley over the bar.

Shots flew high and wide, but there was no second half goal rush. Wood was relieved, while the crowd was disappointed, only having a solitary Law effort three minutes from time when many were long since gone, to cheer.

"What a terrible match to pick for a return to my old happy hunting ground of Old Trafford" commented Huddersfield goalkeeper Ray Wood. "United were two goals up before I had even touched the ball – bar picking it out of the net! But they were great goals."

Despite the often-mundane performances from United, ordinary alongside poor, the Manchester United directors were never of the opinion that they needed a change in manager. A fresh face, with fresh ideas, as football embraced a new era. Matt Busby, despite eighteen years at the helm, still had all the requirements the club sought, whilst retaining the ambition to guide his team to what was considered unfinished business. Those personal targets, on what could be considered, current form, looked a long way off, but the opportunity to achieve, and better, the success of the past was presented to the United manager in the form of a new five-year contract.

Due to the countless postponements, fixtures moved from league to Cup with much regularity, as they did from mid-week to weekend. Supporters often found those mid-week encounters a problem, unable to get time off work, or dashing from office or factory and making the kick-off with minutes to spare. Over 47,000 had watched the defeat of Huddersfield, while Old Trafford welcomed its biggest crowd of the season – 53,416 for the visit of Tottenham Hotspur on March 9th.

Many might well have been present, thinking that they were going to witness United put a dent in Tottenham's championship aspirations, if those thoughts had entered their head then they were in for a huge disappointment. For those unable to be present, relying on the men of the press to narrate the story of the afternoon, they were left in little doubt that they had been spared, fortunate not to have been present, not simply in having to watch Tottenham score twice without reply, but to squirm in embarrassment as the red shirts squandered chance after chance.

"All the enthusiastic but undisciplined energy of a fairground attached itself to Manchester United's marksmanship at Old Trafford on Saturday, and Tottenham Hotspur, like the proprietors of a coco-

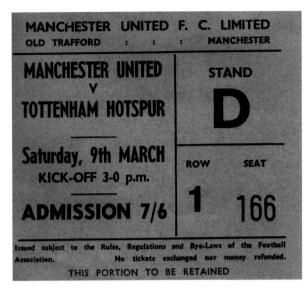

nut shy, learnt what rich profits can lie in an ebullient but ill directed aim." – the 'Times'. No matter what newspaper you read, the story was the same. The game was lost by United, rather than won by Tottenham, although whilst those scoring opportunities were cast to the wind, Bill Brown in the visitor's goal had an inspired afternoon. For every missed United opportunity, he pulled off an equally important save. Even when 2-0 down the opportunities arose, at least four or five in the last twenty minutes. It was perhaps fortunate that six of the eight clubs below United also lost that afternoon. Anything otherwise would have seen a drop of at least a couple of places.

Crerand constantly split the Tottenham defence open with characteristic twenty- or thirty-yard passes, but his accuracy was not match by the likes of Law and Herd on the receiving end. Charlton was perhaps a more guilty culprit than the two Scots.

Tottenham took the lead in the thirty-third minute, Brennan misjudged the flight of the ball from a Smith cross and it hit Jones on the head rather than the Spurs man heading past Gregg. Law spun on a sixpence to wriggle past three bemused defenders, only to see his shot bulge the side netting. Crerand brought Greaves crashing to the floor inside the penalty area, but the referee turned blind eye. And so, it continued.

After the interval a thirty-five-yard run by Greaves failed to bear fruition as Gregg dived full length to save. Brown pushed a pile-driver from Giles onto the bar, but then, in the sixty-fifth minute Spurs grabbed the goal that would decide the outcome. Mackay got the better of Crerand. Jones centred; Greaves, his path to goal blocked by two defenders passed the ball squarely to Saul who took his time in side-footing the ball past Gregg.

From then on, it was more or less all United, flowing forward time after time, but achieving nothing. They had four or five excellent scoring opportunities following that second Tottenham goal, but all that they produced were muttered comments from the disappointed supporters as they trudged homeward.

The long lay-off from competitive football was proving far from beneficial. Before the enforced break, there had been only one defeat in nine games, but since returning to action United had failed to win in their three league outings. Taking the Cup-tie against Huddersfield out of the equation, United were in danger of drifting back to their early season form.

If the league form was a worry, and there was no sign that the relegation zone was opening its arms to embrace Manchester United, then the F.A. Cup might just prove to be a welcome distraction. Like the First Division, its fixtures were running haywire.

Replays for one round were being played on the same day as ninety minutes from the next were contested, while two different rounds could well appear on the same days list of fixtures. From a United perspective, they were to find themselves facing Aston Villa at Old Trafford on March 11th in the fourth round and, if they were successful, they would face Chelsea, again at Old Trafford, on Saturday the 16th in what would be the fifth round.

A solitary day off from a strenuous ninety-minutes is not much time to re-charge the old batteries at the best of times, but it was made considerably harder when playing conditions were far from perfect. Those same conditions also affected overall performances, making the prediction of results much more difficult than normal. In any case, few would have been foolish enough to bet on Matt Busby's unpredictable eleven during the current season.

In the Old Trafford fourth round tie Aston Villa were something of a mirror image of what United had been in their game against Tottenham Hotspur. The scoring opportunities were not as numerous, but they were to prove ineffective when going forward, while their inefficiency in defence cost them the tie, or at the very least, the possibility of a replay at Villa Park.

Without Sleeuwenhoek, and to a greater extent centre-forward Dougan, Villa were immediately hampered, while having to adapt to the bounce of the ball on the bone hard pitch, also saw valuable time lost in coming to grips with their opponents. They were also, like United, well aware as regards the importance of the ninety minutes, something that was not lost on certain individuals as contests within the contest soon developed.

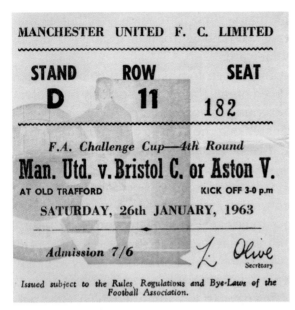

MANCHESTER UNITED F. C. LIMITED

STAND **ROW** **SEAT**

D **11** **182**

F.A. Challenge Cup—4th Round

Man. Utd. v. Bristol C. or Aston V.

AT OLD TRAFFORD   KICK OFF 3-0 p.m

SATURDAY, 26th JANUARY, 1963

Admission 7/6   *L. Olive*
Secretary

Issued subject to the Rules, Regulations and Bye-Laws of the Football Association.

Charlton and Herd both went close, but it was Crowe who almost gave United an early lead, putting a pass back inches past his own post in the fifteenth minute.

Law was spoken to by referee Sparling following a tackle on Tindall, while a clash with Thompson saw the United man requiring treatment from the trainer. Wylie and Setters were also spoken to following a midfield clash.

Eight minutes before the break, the jeers turned to cheers when United took the lead through Quixall, the former Sheffield Wednesday man now just as an important cog in the United machine as any other individual.

Charlton wandered out to the right and combined with Giles and Law to allow Quixall to beat Sidebottom with a low ground shot that in all honesty, the goalkeeper should have saved. "I was quite embarrassed about the goal" said Quixall afterwards. "I think it was its slowness rather than its speed that beat Geoff Sidebottom."

Villa took it on the chin and came close to equalising near to half-time when Gregg pulled off an exceptional save, pushing a powerful drive from Woosnam upwards onto the crossbar. They were equally effective as the second half got underway, enjoying a fair share of the play. But for once, the United defence looked impregnable.

United themselves were far from dangerous in their finishing with their best efforts in the second half coming from Herd, who produced a fine save from Sidebottom following a twenty-yard run and from Stiles who shot narrowly wide from twenty yards.

With the game drawing to a close, Villa, not having abandoned hope, threw everything at United, seeking that elusive equaliser that would have produced a replay. It was not to be. Those who had remained until the final whistle let out a sigh of relief, while those who had left early were equally relieved when they opened their morning newspaper to read that the solitary goal had been enough and they were once again Old Trafford bound on Saturday.

But let's look further forward for a moment, to next season, and imagine if those same supporters turned up at Old Trafford to watch United take on one of their First Division stablemates, that is if they managed to avoid relegation, and one or even more of their opponents were not members of the Players Union. The United players would be well within their right to refuse to play. Farcical? Not if the 'closed-shop' ultimatum by the Players Union was not given the red light.

A meeting was arranged in Manchester with the one hundred or so 'rebels' within the First Division, clubs who were not already members being told to pay their half-crown membership or there would be a threat of strike action when their clubs were faced. Fortunately, it was something that failed to materialise.

The only strike action that was to be seen at Old Trafford five days after the solitary goal victory over Villa, were in the respective goal mouths of United and Chelsea as the next step on the Wembley journey was taken.

The Londoners, under Tommy Docherty, were, like United, something of a work in progress. They had been relegated from the First Division last season, but were back on track for promotion in the current campaign, sitting atop the Second Division table.

But despite having talented individuals such as Eddie McCreadie, Terry Venables and Bobby Tambling within their ranks, they had struggled against Tranmere Rovers in round three, requiring a replay to get through, then finding Charlton Athletic an easier nut to crack in order to earn the right to face United in that fifth-round tie.

Matt Busby's belief that this was United's year to make the journey to the national stadium took on something of a more positive look rather than being considered little more than a throw away comment that he hoped his players would pick up on and generate some often-needed self-confidence, more so when faced with something considerably more than just an ordinary ninety-minutes football.

A victory against Chelsea would find them two steps from Wembley, one hundred and eighty minutes, barring any replays, from what many players regarded as the pinnacle of any career, an appearance in the F.A. Cup Final.

But they were to take their supporters through an often-stressful afternoon, going from being powerful, promising and assertive to faltering, fussy and failing in the game's simple things.

MANCHESTER UNITED F. C. LIMITED

STAND   ROW   - SEAT
D   2   199

F.A. Challenge Cup—5th Round

Manchester United v. Chelsea

AT OLD TRAFFORD

Admission 7/6   L. Olive
                                 Secretary

Issued subject to the Rules, Regulations and Bye-Laws of the
Football Association.

KEEP THIS PORTION

Against Chelsea, the first forty-five minutes were ordinary to say the least. United were still without the cup-tied Pat Crerand. The man who had in his few outings in the red shirt shown that here was the player that United and their supporters had long looked for. A ring-master, someone to run the show, pull the strings and get the best out of those around him. Without him, they often lacked inspiration.

Had it not been for two mistakes from Chelsea and England under-23 goalkeeper Peter Bonetti, then it may well have been the Londoners whose name went into the draw for the sixth round. With sixteen minutes gone, and neither side having shown anything of promise, Quixall, showing no signs of missing his side-kick in Crerand, chased a Setters pass to the goal line. His cross into the Chelsea penalty box should have been dealt with at ease by Bonetti, but it was fumbled and fell to the feet of Law who had little more to do than prod it into the empty net.

A minute into the second half, Setters, once again, sent Quixall off down the right, but on this occasion the United inside-forward took it upon himself to shoot from twenty-five yards out. It should have proved an easy save for the usually competent goalkeeper, but once again the ball slipped from the 'keeper's grasp, hit a post and trickled, as if in slow motion, over the line.

Chelsea had opened rather defensively, with Sorrell man marking Law, but they had now to open their game up and in doing so, enjoyed the better of the mid-field head-to-heads. This good work, however, was wasted by indifferent and indecisive finishing. Something that could also be said of United and the good work that Quixall put in.

With twenty minutes remaining, Chelsea pulled a goal back. Sorrell, having for once departed from the shadow of Law, scoring from close range. On another day, it would have been backs to the wall stuff for United, but the Chelsea wingers – Murray and Blunstone were more often than not neglected. Throw in the fact that Shellito had to clear off the line from Law, then on points, United deserved their victory. If, however, they did indeed have Wembley in their sights, they would need more drive and determination, along with a greater sense of teamwork than was shown against the Second Division leaders. Having said that, Pat Crerand would be back for round six.

The United laundry ladies were on overtime, either that or a new set of playing kit had to be invested in, as two days later the kit hamper was again filled as United headed to London to face West Ham on league business at Upton Park and what was their sixth game in sixteen days.

West Ham's fixture list had been equally crowded, as they too had a continuing interest in the F.A. Cup, but they possessed something that United often lacked – teamwork. Individually, with the likes of Law, Crerand, Quixall, Herd and Charlton on board, they were superior when it came to individual talent, but with nine of the West Ham eleven having come through the Upton Park youth system, they had more of a comrade in arms feel, they were like a brotherhood. If a United player got the better of one claret and blue shirt, another would immediately pop up, as if from nowhere, to take his place.

During the first half-hour, West Ham produced only two shots of note, from Brabrook and Bovington, but they were to take the lead in the thirty-eighth minute when a Sealey free-kick soared over the United defence, centre-half Brown raced in behind Maurice Setters and bundled the ball past Gregg.

Despite their lead, West Ham rarely looked in command, United on the other hand always seemed to be edging towards a goal. Herd headed against the bar and both he and Law created space for a shot, but on each occasion, their efforts went wide. Of the two sides, the visitors looked the more likely winners.

The outcome, however, was decided within a sixty-second time span. Hurst, Sealey, Scott and Boyce had all watched their shots cannon of United defenders, while Rhodes in the Hammers goal had tipped a Giles effort over the bar. With thirteen minutes remaining United claimed the equaliser when a Charlton corner was met by the head of Herd, who moved in front of Rhodes to nod home.

Many saw this as the turning point in the course of the game, and they were soon proved correct, but not in the way they had expected. Within a minute of Herd's goal, the home side were back in front.

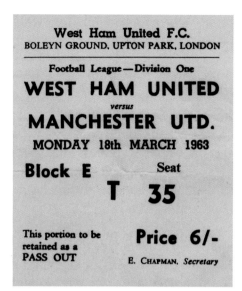

West Ham United F.C.
BOLEYN GROUND, UPTON PARK, LONDON

Football League — Division One

WEST HAM UNITED

versus

MANCHESTER UTD.

MONDAY 18th MARCH 1963

Block E   Seat

T   35

This portion to be
retained as a   **Price 6/-**
PASS OUT   E. CHAPMAN, *Secretary*

From the re-start, Bovington sent a long ball down the middle, with Hurst and Brennan in hot pursuit. The West Ham forward lunged at the ball, Brennan stretched and stuck out a foot, but turned away in despair as he watched the ball flashed past Gregg.

One minute from time, United were well and truly beaten. A Bobby Moore throw-in was quickly switched to Sealey and from the edge of the penalty box he chipped the ball over the head of Gregg to give the Hammers a convincing 3-1 victory.

The defeat was something of a shock to the system, it wasn't disastrous by any means, but it was a setback, another two points lost in the quest for First Division safety. There was still some thirty points to play for, but it was virtually the same for the seven others – Blackburn Rovers, Manchester City, Blackpool, Bolton Wanderers, Birmingham City, Ipswich Town and Leyton Orient, who found themselves below United in the lower regions of the First Division.

Of that seven, United had still to play only three – Birmingham, Orient and Ipswich. From the division front runners, they had to lock horns with fourth place Liverpool and second place Leicester City [twice] in consecutive fixtures. There was much to play for, and much to lose. Then again, win those fifteen remaining games and the teams above United lost all theirs, then United would be champions!!

Ipswich Town were next up. Having lifted the First Division championship the previous season, their fall from grace had been swift and dramatic, little more than free-fall. They were second bottom, a mere point better off than bottom club Leyton Orient. It was perhaps more of a 'must win' for Ipswich than United, but with the home support behind them, few, if any, considered it anything other than a home win. If that had been their choice when filling in their weekly Football Pools, then they were not going to be celebrating come five o'clock on Saturday March 23rd.

For whatever the reason, United turned in what was described in one newspaper as being a "pathetic performance", by "a ragged collection

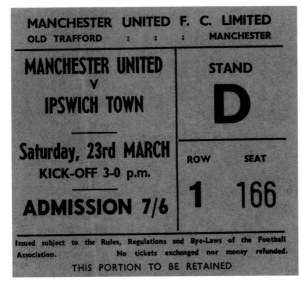

MANCHESTER UNITED F. C. LIMITED
OLD TRAFFORD : : : MANCHESTER

MANCHESTER UNITED
v
IPSWICH TOWN

STAND

D

Saturday, 23rd MARCH
KICK-OFF 3-0 p.m.

ROW   SEAT

ADMISSION 7/6

1   166

Issued subject to the Rules, Regulations and Bye-Laws of the Football
Association.   No tickets exchanged nor money refunded.
THIS PORTION TO BE RETAINED

of individuals", ninety minutes when they touched rock bottom. Another correspondent who had a seat in the Old Trafford press box penned: "Warm sun, thin applause, now and again cheers – and time for the occasional yawn. It might have been a cricket match.

"For ninety-minutes, a team which has groaned into the sixth round of the Cup, and Ipswich, the dying past-masters of the League, shillied and shallied their way to boredom."

For those supporters who decided that this was a game to miss [the attendance was 21,000 less than the last league fixture against Tottenham and 16,000 less than the Chelsea cup-tie] they were certainly proven correct. Matt Busby had seen little need to change the line-up in recent weeks, so it wasn't as if there was any unfamiliarity within the ranks. It was simply a very poor performance.

Even so, United had more than enough opportunities to win the game, but they severely tested the patience of the crowd with their lacklustre performance. Their apathy was unbelievable, their lack of understanding even the basics of the game was incredible.

That only one goal was to separate the two teams shows the lack of opportunities that arose even with the quality of the United front line and that goal was not produced by some flash of genius, or some creative brilliance. It was down to nothing more than a defensive error.

With half an hour played Carberry strolled down the wing and floated over a right footed cross. Up went Gregg and Brennan, along with Crawford the Ipswich centre-forward, all missing the ball which dropped invitingly to the feet of Leadbetter, who even with his eyes closed couldn't fail to miss.

It was a goal that should have awoken United from their slumbers, given them a kick up the backside, never mind an elbow in the ribs and invigorated the £300,000 outfit into action, seeking the equaliser with perhaps the winner thrown in for good measure.

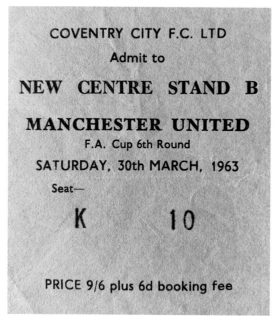

COVENTRY CITY F.C. LTD

Admit to

NEW CENTRE STAND B

MANCHESTER UNITED

F.A. Cup 6th Round

SATURDAY, 30th MARCH, 1963

Seat—

K   10

PRICE 9/6 plus 6d booking fee

Alas, it was not to be. The forward line continued to be completely out of sorts, with the best scoring opportunities falling to Cantwell and Setters, a pair not exactly noted for their scoring abilities. It was little wonder that many made their way home well before the final whistle as slow hand claps, boos and jeers echoed around the ground.

The finger was pointed at Matt Busby in a letter to the 'Manchester Evening News and Chronicle' which said "United need a shake up; Busby must crack the whip and lash some fight and team spirit into the side. The players are not fighting for the ball."

A victory against a relegation haunted Ipswich would have been ideal preparation for the F.A. Cup quarter-final tie against Coventry City the following Saturday, a fixture ideal for a giant killing and one that the Midland side would have been looking forward to more than their illustrious opponents.

Third Division Coventry City, 66-1 outsiders and undefeated in twenty-three games, had already pulled off one Cup shock in defeating Sunderland 2-1, scoring twice in the final eight minutes, in front of over 40,000 ecstatic supporters, Highfield Road's biggest crowd for twenty-five years. There was every possibility that they could offer a repeat performance, so unpredictable were United. It had also to be remembered that Coventry had recently drawn 2-2 with United in Dublin, with victory having been only seconds away, before Bobby Charlton scored with that last gasp equaliser. "There are 20,000 Irishmen who won't agree with the present odds for the Cup – Coventry 66-1 and Manchester United at 9-2" said Coventry manager Jimmy Hill.

But no matter how indifferent the current Manchester United side could be, they were still a major attraction with their all-star cast, so much so that a crowd limit of 44,000 was put in place, with the Coventry allocation of 33,000 selling out in a matter of hours, when an estimated 45,000 flocked to Highfield Road. Although ticket sales were not planned to commence until 5.30pm, there were people outside the ground at 5.45am and by twelve noon there was a queue estimated at around 15,000. Heavy rain began to fall in mid-afternoon, so it was decided to start selling at 3.30pm, with the first 1,000 being offered one stand and one terrace ticket. After that it was two terrace tickets per person. Some of those disappointed supporters would be fortunate to get their hands on a ticket a few days later, as United returned 2,500 of their 11,00 allocation.

The 'sold-out' signs on the windows of the Coventry ticket office mattered little, as those disappointed supporters were soon besieged by ticket-touts, offering the four-shilling terrace tickets at £1.

While Jimmy Hill took his Coventry side to Worthing to escape the clamour surrounding the tie, Matt Busby was handed a selection problem when Noel Cantwell failed a fitness test. Not only did he have to decide who would fill the left-back role, he had to give equal consideration to who would lead the team on the day. His options for the latter were possibly greater than those for the former, with Maurice Setters and Bill Foulkes both having had the captaincy in the past, but he by-passed both and handed the leadership to Denis Law. Tony Dunne was to come in at left-back in place of the injured Cantwell.

The doubt over the eventual outcome of the Cup-tie was overshadowed by the possibility that the game might not go ahead. As the United supporters began arriving in Coventry, match official Mr. E. Crawford took one look at the pitch when he arrived at Highfield Road at 12.15 and told club officials that he was far from satisfied with its overall condition, in particular a section of water in front of the stand and a waterlogged goal area. The thirty-six hours of heavy rain having taken its toll. Taken aback by his complaint, the ground staff and volunteers immediately set to work, forking and sanding the surface.

It had been planned to open the gates at noon due to the heavy rain, but those plans were scuppered by the referee's decision and the rain-soaked fans began a chorus of 'Why Are We Waiting?' completely unaware of the drama taking place on the other side of the gates. Eventually, almost an hour later than intended, they were allowed in, while the ground staff continued to spread barrow loads of sand and sawdust on the worst affected areas of the pitch.

A huge contingent of red and white clad United supporters arrived in four special trains at Coventry Station waving flags and banners, ringing bells and twirling rattles. Others arrived by coach and car.

The tickets that been so eagerly sought after suddenly became plentiful with kick-off half an hour away. Several shops close to the ground spoke of people coming in and leaving tickets for anyone who wanted them. Many of those tickets coming from United supporters.

Busby was well aware of what his team faced. "We know we've got something on today. But we are confident we can get through" he was to say. It was an opinion shared by Peter Lorenzo of the 'Daily Herald', but the journalist was to add: "Manchester United are possibly the most disjointed, certainly the most disappointing team left in the Cup. And that's why I take them to end the long unbeaten run of Coventry this afternoon... and march to Wembley.

"So much expense, so much experienced talent *must* come good at some time.

"Class, ability, tremendous potential is stockpiled in United's boots. And that, so far, is where it's stayed. Rhythm, blend and character is worryingly absent from the Matt Busby all-stars – at the moment.

"But I refuse to believe that such a formidable force on paper will not eventually prove its capabilities on the field.

"And, if United are to show it at all this season – now is the hour, this is the crucial test."

United were also to hope that the five-minute, pre-match act, by Ken Dodd that followed the half-hour community singing, was to be the only comedy performance of the afternoon.

Due to the overall condition of the playing surface, there was no accompanying glitter and sparkle from the First Division side, United more than content to simply play it by ear.

Coventry set the pace early in the game and the United defence, like the sawdust and sand had done for the rain, soaked up the pressure of the Sky Blue front line. Playing directly into the face of Tony Dunne, who had not seen first team action since mid-October, Coventry had their avenue of attack marked out, and by the fifth minute, they were in front. Humphries evaded Dunne, not for the first time, and from the bye-line sent a low, curved cross into the middle of the goalmouth. Foulkes and Bly challenged for the ball and it ended in the net. Few cared how it got there, or who put it there.

An explosive start, but one that Coventry neither built on nor matched, and it wasn't until mid-way through the second half that they once again threatened the United goal.

United equalised in the twenty-seventh minute. Setters took a throw in to Quixall, who in turn passed to Law, the ball quickly moving on to Charlton, his low, right-footed shot beating Wesson with ease. It remained at 1-1 until five minutes into the second half when Charlton claimed a second. Again, it came via a throw in as he gathered the ball on the left before firing a twenty-yard drive past Wesson. It was a goal that gave United confidence, although back came Coventry.

Humphries had the ball in the net, but the referee had already blown for hands against Bly, although he was later to deny this and say that the ball hit him in the face. Bly himself came close to scoring when only an acrobatic save by Gregg pushed the ball against the underside of the bar before it bounced to safety.

So near yet so far, and if it wasn't at that moment that Coventry City and their supporters realised that their Cup dream was over, it was hammered home when Albert Quixall maintained his record of having scored in every round when he claimed United's third. Giles lobbed the ball into the goalmouth, Wesson dived for it at the same time as Bruck attempted to kick it clear, neither attempt was achieved and the ball simply rolled to the feet of Quixall who tapped it home.

No-one could deny United their victory, but even with those recent irregular performances there should never have been any doubt that it would be the first division side who would make the last four of the competition. "Luck Was With The Busby Men In Tingling Tie" was the headline in the 'Coventry Evening Telegraph' following the game, but with a few lines it was admitted that "Manchester United deserved their win because they were just the better side on the day, but it took two pieces of individual brilliance by gifted Bobby Charlton to haul them through a sticky patch and if luck had been kinder to Curtis and Co. we might once again have been hailing the Sky Blues as giant-killers."

'Nemo', the Telegraph's man at the match considered United to be "a ragged ill-organised and ill-disciplined bunch" in the opening minutes of the game when it was all Coventry. It was a description that could have been levelled at United in many of their previous fixtures and it was the truth, not some sour grapes from a defeated foe.

Having reached the semi-final of the F.A. Cup changed nothing. This was a season like none other since that of 1936-37 when relegation to the Second Division was last tasted, but there were still sufficient points to be won to eradicate all thoughts of dropping into a lower tier of the English game.

Going back to the Coventry Cup-tie, amongst the travelling United support that day was a, then, ten-year-old Keith Ennion. "I had been at all the previous Cup-ties" recalled Keith "and following the sixth round draw United had been paired with Second Division Sunderland or Coventry City of the Third Division. Sunderland were riding high in their league, so we obviously wanted it to be Coventry.

"Due to the weather around that time, the fixtures were all over the place and the same day as the Sunderland-Coventry game, United reserves were playing City reserves at Old Trafford in the Central League. At half time, it was noted on the old scoreboard at Old Trafford that Sunderland were leading 1-0, but when we arrived home, we discovered that Coventry had come back to beat Sunderland, so five days later we were to travel to Coventry.

"I'm sure the match was all ticket, so tickets must have been on sale the day after that Central League match. I travelled with my dad and elder brother in the car. I was only ten at the time.

"I can't remember the journey there but I do remember the rest of the day. It was an awful day weather wise – it rained non-stop before the game. At about 12.30 the gates opened and the ground, apart from the main stand, started to fill immediately. It was always like that in those days so that the fans could find their place on the terraces with all their mates together, unlike today where you have to sit apart, wherever your seat is, so you don't need to get in early. The atmosphere was building up by 1pm as the terraces were full. Again, these days it is impossible for an atmosphere to build up before a game because the music is played so loud to drown out any singing from the fans.

"The ticket allocation at Old Trafford must have covered all areas of the ground as there was a good contingent of United fans at the covered end where I was located at the wall on the front, with both United and Coventry fans around me and there was also a healthy support for United at the open end on the other side of the ground.

"Nearly sixty years ago, and yet I can remember certain instances from matches that long ago and yet struggle to remember scores from only a few weeks ago! As I said, it rained incessantly and I remember over the Tannoy system they were playing 'Rhythm of the Rain' by the Cascades (a hit from that time). I think they were trying to have a laugh at our expense! I always remember talking to the lad on my right who was telling me how their star player Willie Humphries was going to run rings around us. I told him they would never cope with Albert Quixall.

"At about 2pm the most ridiculous event happened. They had a big stage on the centre circle where Community Singing was to happen with Ken Dodd, of all people, leading the singing. I thought Community Singing only happened before the Cup Final at Wembley. There was always a lot of chanting in those days and nobody used to sing, but they had their 'Sky Blue' song to the tune of 'The Eton Boating' song. A song they still sing today. It was pretty impressive too. The game started and unbelievably Coventry scored in the first minute from memory with Willie Humphries scoring for them. This sent the kid standing next to me into raptures. I had the last laugh though as United went on to win the match 3-1."

Peter Lorenzo, the respected 'Daily Herald' journalist, perhaps a closet Red, wrote in his paper the Monday following that six round F.A. Cup victory that "The Old Trafford mail-bag should be considerably lighter this week – minus the shoals of poison-pen letters that have been lashing Matt Busby and Manchester United these last few weeks.

"For at Highfield Road on Saturday United did more than end the 23-game unbeaten run of courageous Coventry. They started on the road back to the top.

"His face tinged with excitement and relief, Matt Busby told me afterwards: "If we'd lost to this very fine side today, the after-effects might so easily have affected our plans and hopes for next season.

"I've always insisted we will be a very good side, and we will benefit enormously - psychologically and otherwise - from today's fine win.

"But if we had lost, everything would have gone the other way."

"For longer than he, his players or United's supporters care to remember. Busby has always been looking for the rainbow, insisting that the good days would be rolling back for a club whose name remains one of the most respected wherever football is played.

"On Saturday, for the first time in an age, those promises were translated into tangible and thrilling fact."

Lorenzo would be proved wrong, for the time being at least.

Any bumps and bruises picked up at Highfield Road had little time to soften or disappear completely as Fulham travelled to Old Trafford two days later looking to make it a Manchester double, having beaten City at Maine Road the previous Friday. They succeeded in their mission, extending their points total to fifteen out of sixteen, making it was difficult to believe that when United defeated Fulham 1-0 at Craven Cottage back on Boxing Day, a result that left the Londoners second bottom of the First Division, that there would be such a dramatic turnaround in fortunes. Fulham sat just above mid-table, comfortable with their thirty-two points, while United floundered four from the bottom, nine points worse off. They were only two points above second bottom Man-

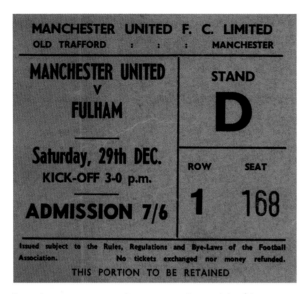

MANCHESTER UNITED F. C. LIMITED
OLD TRAFFORD : : : MANCHESTER

MANCHESTER UNITED
v
FULHAM

STAND

D

Saturday, 29th DEC.
KICK-OFF 3-0 p.m.

ROW SEAT

ADMISSION 7/6

1 168

Issued subject to the Rules, Regulations and Bye-Laws of the Football
Association. No tickets exchanged nor money refunded.
THIS PORTION TO BE RETAINED

chester City, although they did have a game in hand.

But that game in hand mattered little as Fulham's 2-0 victory brought United crashing back down to earth, inserting 'relegation' into the vocabulary of the Old Trafford support. It had been used fleetingly in the recent past and in more of a jocular manner when mentioned in the same breath as neighbours City, but now, it was no laughing matter, it was deadly serious, leaving many of the opinion that it was more than a distinct possibility come the end of the season.

"Busby Boys Are Back To Zero" shouted the headlines of the 'Daily Herald' the following morning, with Steve Richards writing: "For 90 minutes at Old Trafford last night Manchester United hurried to convince those who did not go to Coventry that they were a top side once again. They failed miserably." A couple of seats along the Old Trafford press box, Derek Hodgson of the 'Daily Express' scribbled: "United were so bad in the first half that the dreaded name Ipswich was whispered. Recollections of that Black Saturday turned Mancunians pale, yet so sloppy was United's football the comparison was being drawn."

United started slowly, allowing Fulham to dictate the play, and those alarm bells were ringing loud and clear in the eighth minute when Brennan gave O'Connell the space to have a shot at goal from ten yards, but the Fulham outside-left shot wide of the goal. He was to make amends four minutes later when a Leggat shot was blocked and the ball fell to O'Connell, who drove the ball firmly into the bottom left-hand corner of the net.

A Mullery shot from all of thirty-five yards skimmed the cross bar and had it not been for Tony Dunne then Fulham's account would have been more than doubled. The full-back repelling attack after attack.

Plodding away, United saw one effort headed away for a corner by Robson, then Chisnall, on the brink of passing to Giles, was intercepted by Keetch. But in general, their finishing was undistinguished. Two Charlton efforts were all they had to show for their forty-five-minute endeavour.

Within six minutes of the re-start, United thought they had managed to draw level, Setters heading past Macedo, but to the disapproval of the rather meagre crowd of barely over 28,000, it was disallowed for offside. That it was the United half-back who found himself in such a forward position said much about the attack in general and it was Setters who once again came close to scoring, denied on this occasion by the post. He was also to set up Charlton, whose rising drive struck the cross bar.

Fulham had weathered the storm, and with eleven minutes remaining, Brown sent Leggat pounding towards the United goal and his left footed shot from twenty-five yards left Gregg helpless.

United's Sixth Round F.A. Cup victory had placed them alongside Liverpool, Leicester City, Nottingham Forest and Southampton in the draw for the semi-final, the latter two clubs in need of a replay, and it was in that order that the balls came out of the maroon velvet bag, with United out last to face the winners of that sixth-round replay.

The cellar area of the First Division was a cold, dark place. Any small crumb could provide succulence, with a chink of light giving hope for the days ahead. Manchester United needed both and the visit to Villa Park on April 9th was to bring, albeit only momentarily, sustenance in the form of a 2-1 win.

Noel Cantwell returned at left-back to bring some stability to the defence, Quixall switched inside-forward positions due to a Law injury, with his number eight shirt given to Nobby Stiles. It was the diminutive Collyhurst boy who was to be the unlikely match winner.

For once, it was the opposition that was considered 'pitiful' by the national press, with the two points gained being the easiest obtained for some time. The United defence stood firm when put under pressure, but as a team, they were not great by any manner of means.

Villa lacked the effort and determination of their opponents, but more importantly lacked a player in the class of Bobby Charlton. Having missed the early months of the season, he was now fundamental in United's quest for both cup glory and First Division survival.

It was Charlton who created United's first goal in the sixth minute. Finding himself unmarked on the edge of the Villa penalty area, he quickly passed to Stiles who side footed the ball home. But by that time, United could well have found themselves at least a goal down. Cantwell having cleared from Dougan, but having also almost gifted Villa a goal when his pass back to Gregg was intercepted by Baker, and with the united 'keeper on the ground, the Villa man somehow managed to shoot wide of the United goal.

Pass-backs to Gregg were more or less all that the United 'keeper had to contend with during the first forty-five minutes and even they disappeared in the second half after Stiles returned the compliment to his United team-mate almost on the hour mark, which saw Charlton score with his now trade-mark long range drive.

Villa managed to pull a goal back through a Thomson header from a Baker cross, but while other, more capable, sides might have gone on to secure an equaliser, or even victory, the Midlands side could only sit back and soak up the pressure from the United front line.

It was a victory only notable in the sense of the actual score-line, as Villa were too poor to judge if indeed United had turned a corner and the prospect of a semi-final appearance was going to coincide with a run of positive league results that would lift the name of Manchester United away from the First Division relegation zone.

Easter was usually a telling time on the football calendar, two or three fixtures played over the course of the weekend, often deciding championships, promotions and relegations, with only a few games being left to play. But Easter 1963 was different, and although the results mattered to many, there were still more than enough fixtures remaining for clubs to clinch titles, promotions, or to avoid the dreaded drop into a lower division. It also to be a testing time for Manchester United, not simply because it meant playing three games over the course of three days, it was more to do with what the fixture list had thrown their way – sixth placed Liverpool on the 13th followed by home and away fixtures against their semi-final opponents and league leaders Leicester City home and away on the 15th and 16th. Failure to take anything points wise from that trio of fixtures could well see United in serious trouble at the foot of the table, as prior to the trip to Anfield, they were only four points better off than second bottom Manchester City, with Ipswich Town and Birmingham City sandwiched in between.

The 'Liverpool Echo', on the morning of United's journey along the East Lancs Road, was of the opinion that the fixture, whilst always an attraction, was made even more compelling by the fact that it could well be an F.A. Cup Final rehearsal. Their journalist, Leslie Edwards, pulled no punches in his article that appeared alongside a United team group photograph on the front-page writing: "Manchester United have never been the force they were before the Munich crash. They did miraculously well to maintain their First Division status despite the loss of so many of their talented players. Any other club, less well-off for up-and-coming reserves, might have dropped not only into the Second Division, but the Third.

"While Mr Busby was convalescing after his long battle for life, United took on their staff a great number of strong, young players of promise. Many of them have not developed as they should – in more ways than one.

"Even the signings, at tremendous cost, of Quixall and Law have not enabled the club to regain their place, held for seasons after the War, as the greatest footballing machine in Britain.

"The repute of United as a side standing or falling by their ability to play football has occasionally been tarnished. Tottenham, Burnley and Leicester City have taken on the United reputation for giving entertainment free of rough play and petulance."

Quite an assessment, but none the less true and to the point, and the plight of the current Manchester United was highlighted even more strongly following the defeat by a solitary goal at Anfield. It was a defeat that threw an assortment of questions into the mixing pot regarding United's all-round ability and their chances of remaining in the First Division, but they were relatively minor in comparison to the one asked in regards to the form of talisman Denis Law.

"What has happened to Denis Law, Britain's most expensive footballer?" asked Leslie Duxbury in the 'Sunday Express'. "Last year's hero of sunny Italy has been out of form so long I have almost forgotten why he ever qualified for a six-figure price tag.

"Against Liverpool yesterday he was again so pale and fitful that one had consciously to recall that he was in the team."

Duxbury was not alone in his thoughts; others were of a similar opinion. Ray Raymond, another member of the press corps penned: "Manchester United are in trouble up to their eyes. If they continue to fritter away chances as they did in this substandard game, they'll not escape relegation.

"Unless Denis Law can produce his real form their troubles will increase. Law, after promising much, failed to make any impact on this game until the closing minutes, and then he and St John were spoken to by the referee." Terence Elliot was another scribe who told the tale of woe concerning United, but added an encouraging postscript. "It was sad to see Matt Busby's team slipping nearer the deep freeze of relegation but their fans must surely have noted that if Liverpool can do no better than this, the Cup could be well within the Old Trafford reach."

So, defeat at Anfield. Despite Law being out of sorts, United should, in reality, have been at least two goals in front at the interval. Stiles, the stand-in inside-forward missed two glorious opportunities within the space of two minutes when it appeared much easier to score than miss. The first saw Charlton send an inviting cross into the goalmouth, but Stiles, standing in front of goal, headed wide. Seconds later, the ball rolled through to Stiles, who had only Lawrence to beat, but he hesitated, perhaps thinking himself offside, allowing the Liverpool 'keeper to snatch the ball off his toes.

Charlton was always a threat, but with his fellow forwards lacking in inspiration, it placed a heavy burden on the United defence and it was to Crerand, Foulkes and Dunne to keep Liverpool at bay and limited them to just the one goal. The crowd, however, had to wait until the seventy-second minute for that goal and, by then, they were flustered by the lack of goalmouth action, the often inconsistency of the referee and the actions of one or two of the United players.

Stiles upended Liverpool centre-half Yeats despite being a good six inches shorter and responded to the baying crowd with a two-finger gesture. Gregg was spoken to for apparently throwing the ball at a linesman who had awarded a corner kick, while Foulkes, having charged Hunt off the ball, was relieved that the referee did not award a penalty.

The goal, when it came, was created by Stevenson who, having intercepted the ball strode forward before passing to Hunt. The ball was then slipped to St John who brought it under control before sending it high into the roof of the United net from ten yards.

There was almost an equaliser when the ball bounced awkwardly in front of Yeats, but Charlton's shot bounced off the centre-half's body and went out for a corner. Law came close with a rare effort, but it was inaccurate, like most of the United shooting, and flew harmlessly over the cross bar.

Leyton Orient appeared doomed, with sixteen points from their thirty-four games but United's defeat on Merseyside changed the look at the bottom of the First Division, a sight that was far from being pleasing to the eye.

Birmingham City had played thirty-one games and had twenty-four points. Above them sat Manchester City with twenty-five points

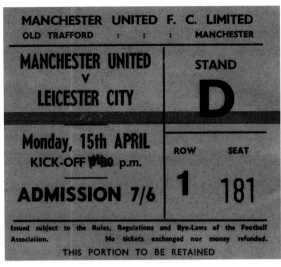

MANCHESTER UNITED F. C. LIMITED
OLD TRAFFORD : : : MANCHESTER

MANCHESTER UNITED
v
LEICESTER CITY

STAND

D

Monday, 15th APRIL
KICK-OFF 7.30 p.m.

ROW   SEAT

1   **181**

ADMISSION 7/6

Issued subject to the Rules, Regulations and Bye-Laws of the Football
Association.   No tickets exchanged nor money refunded.
THIS PORTION TO BE RETAINED

from thirty-two games. United were also on twenty-five points, but had played a game less. A rung above were Ipswich Town on twenty-seven points, but they had fulfilled thirty-five of their fixtures. It remained nail-biting times. More so as Leicester City, who were now level on points with Tottenham Hotspur at the top of the table and chasing the championship, were next up in a double-header.

Leicester City had dropped two points in their championship challenge when they lost at West Ham at the same time as United failed to achieve success at Anfield, so they were eager to get their title hopes back on track at Old Trafford. United, having struggled against the lesser lights of the First Division, and also in recent weeks, would need to step up a gear or two if they were to take points off Leicester and dent their title aspirations further.

For a while, Leicester must have indeed thought that their championship dreams were turning into a nightmare, as they were outplayed by a United team who looked transformed from that of recent weeks and, in all honesty, it was a game that they should and would have lost had it not been for their grit and determination.

Following heavy rain, the game began in sunshine, but the soft underfoot conditions almost saw the 2,000 travelling Leicester supporters celebrate a goal early on when Gregg slithered to collect a back-pass that he only just managed to keep in play.

With eleven minutes gone those travelling supporters were to breathe a sigh of relief when a Setters shot struck Sjoberg who was standing on the goal line and bounced to McLintock who managed to clear. Law and Crerand both fired shots over the bar, while Banks saved a low drive from Herd. It therefore came as no surprise when United took the lead in the sixteenth minute, Herd's shot glancing off King and ending up in the opposite corner as to where it was intended. Banks in the Leicester goal being totally wrong-footed.

Having gained the advantage, United continued to press and should, in all honesty, been four up by half-time. In another attack, Stiles headed the ball towards the Leicester goal with Banks way off his line, but it Sjoberg once again who was ideally placed to head clear. Herd headed over from three yards out, while other United efforts were charged down. Leicester were unable to use their noted counter-attack to their advantage.

But eight minutes into the second half they eventually managed to gain a foothold on the game. Riley crossed into the middle and although Cross initially stumbled over the ball, he managed to regain his footing and beat Gregg from close range.

United were reduced to ten men soon afterwards when Stiles went off injured, but they continued to press forward and were rewarded with a second goal in the sixty-second minute. As Charlton moved towards goal, he was tripped by Norman just outside the penalty area and from the resulting free kick, Quixall tapped the ball sideways to Charlton who unleashed a powerful drive past Banks that the goal-keeper had no chance of saving.

Within a minute, it was all-square once again. A scramble on the right of the United penalty area resulted in the ball running lose to Norman who drove home from twenty-five yards.

Stiles returned to the fray after a quarter of an hour and although limping, managed to make himself more awkward than threatening, while Law was having yet another of his inconspicuous afternoons.

Despite dropping a much-needed point, the men of the press were of the opinion that Manchester United were, albeit slowly, getting near to the form that was expected of them. "Matt Busby's team of wayward talents had one of their great occasions yesterday" wrote Derek Hodgson in the 'Sunday Express'. "Before a 50,000 Old Trafford crowd, against the most consistently successful side in England, all Busby's expensive jewels glittered in one riotous colourful match." Hodgson rounded up his match report by saying: "If these two teams do meet at Wembley my shirt will be on Manchester United."

The 'Daily Telegraph' correspondent fancied both United and Leicester to win their respective semi-finals and added: "those lucky enough to obtain tickets are in for a thriller if the teams contest the issue with the same speed, enthusiasm and polish as they did in this encounter."

Derek Wallis, in the 'Daily Mirror' was of the opinion that "United played the sort of football that made nonsense of their League position", but with those first half opportunities, they should have achieved a victory. Rather ironically, the two teams below them, Manchester City and Birmingham City also drew, the former 1-1 at Nottingham Forest, the latter 2-2 at Everton, another club who had an eye on the First Division title.

Twenty-four hours later, the action moved to Filbert Street. Would United be able to conjure up as many goal scoring opportunities as they had done on home soil, or would Leicester have realised that, as Derek Wallis suggested, United were not as bad as to what people made them out to be?

For the return fixture, Leicester City, attempting to re-gain the leadership of the First Division, made four changes, three positional to the team that snatched a point in Manchester. Out went Cheesebrough and in came Heath, Cross moved into the half-back line, while McLintock went to inside forward and Gibson took the outside-left spot. United were un-changed, with Stiles recovering from the knock that saw him off the field for a quarter of an hour the previous day.

Two hours prior to kick-off, the streets around Filbert Street were busy, with many already queuing to make sure they gained admission. Fifty minutes prior to kick-off, the gates at one end were closed, the double-decker terracing full. Soon afterwards the gates at the Filbert Street end were also slammed shut.

There was much at stake for both sides, so as could be expected, the action was fast and furious. United produced three threatening attacks in the first ten minutes, one producing an excellent save from Banks after Law's shot was deflected. Heath hit the post in the fifteenth minute and fifteen minutes further on, there was a suspicion that Crerand had handled in the penalty area, but play went on. Leicester cursed, while United once again breathed a sigh of relief. But it was only a matter of time, minutes in fact. Cross picked out nineteen-year-old Heath, and his shot from ten yards out bounced off Gregg's body, but the Leicester reserve continued his run and the ball bounced off his chest and into the net.

It was a lead that was not to last any length of time, as within two minutes United were level. Law heading home a Stiles cross. With luck, United could have had a second, but as had occurred the previous afternoon, they were denied by a header off the goal line. On this occasion it was King denying Charlton. All-square at half-time, but the second period was to explode into a flurry of activity and goals.

Five minutes into that second period Leicester again took the lead. Riley crossed and Keyworth headed home. Two minutes later it was

2-2. Law controlled a Setters cross on his thigh, bounced it up in the air and, with his back to goal, flicked it over his head and past Banks into the net.

For those on the terraces and the others locked outside, it was a nervous time, as the game threatened to go either way, but they were somewhat calmed in a three-minute spell when Leicester scored twice. Keyworth notching them both in the fifty-third and fifty-sixth minute, from Riley passes. It was a one-two that hit United badly and with their noses in front Leicester were in no mood to relinquish their advantage.

Fourteen minutes after Keyworth's second, Law pulled a goal back from a Stiles pass, forcing Leicester onto the defensive for the majority of the remaining twenty minutes. Law had a header saved by Banks and Herd, not once, but thrice shot when many considered a pass would have been more productive.

The 4-3 victory took Leicester back to the pinnacle of the First Division on fifty-one points, equalling their 1928-29 record, but it still left United in a hapless 19th place. They only had Birmingham City's defeat for comfort. And whenever did Denis Law notch a hat-trick and not finish on the winning side?

There was just over a week before United were due to face Southampton in the F.A. Cup semi-final, the south coast club having hammered Nottingham Forest 5-0 in their sixth-round replay, following their 3-3 draw, and already tickets were at a premium for the Villa Park head-to-head, with ticket touts asking £4 for thirty-shilling seats. A small amount compared to the £5 that Shay Brennan had to fork out when faced with the judge at Salford courthouse.

The United full-back had been arrested following a 60 m.p.h. police chase and was only caught when he stopped at traffic lights. Charged with driving while unfit through drink, he was fined £35, banned for twelve months and had his licence endorsed.

Fortunately, he didn't lose his place in the United starting line-up, as there was now strong competition amongst the first team squad for selection, more so with the possibility of a Wembley final on the horizon.

Any thoughts about walking out under the twin towers had to be extinguished for the time being as not only did Southampton need to be defeated in the semi-final, but there was also the more pressing manner of securing their First Division status.

Having scored three against Leicester City in a vintage, effervescent display, Law, at last, looked to have brushed aside his recent indifferent spell and it was down to the United number ten to rescue his

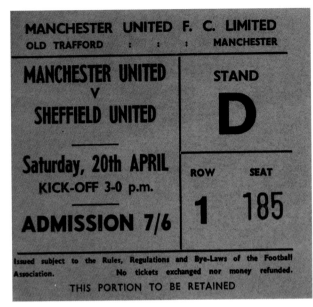

MANCHESTER UNITED F. C. LIMITED
OLD TRAFFORD : : : MANCHESTER

MANCHESTER UNITED
V
SHEFFIELD UNITED

STAND

D

Saturday, 20th APRIL
KICK-OFF 3-0 p.m.

ROW   SEAT

1   185

ADMISSION 7/6

Issued subject to the Rules, Regulations and Bye-Laws of the Football
Association.   No tickets exchanged nor money refunded.
THIS PORTION TO BE RETAINED

team once again in the 1-1 draw with Sheffield United at Old Trafford on April 20th.

Sheffield United had a debutant in Jones up front, but it often looked as though the United front line were newcomers, such was their indifference. Crerand, Charlton and Law all came close in the opening ten minutes, but it was following the latter's miss that the ball was quickly despatched up-field. Allchurch crossed from the goal-line and Hartle ran round Brennan to shoot past Gregg.

The United 'keeper didn't look his usual self, fumbling a couple of shots that he initially looked to have covered, while Brennan sent a pass back towards him in something of a forceful manner whilst harassed by Hartle. United were fortunate it was only one!

It should have been back to level pegging in the sixty-third minute when Quixall got the better of Graham Shaw, but as he moved into the penalty area the full-back stuck out a foot and sent the inside-forward crashing to the floor. Such was the force of the tackle, Quixall required treatment and turned down the opportunity to take the resulting penalty. Strangely, no-one seemed to want the responsibility, many turning the backs to the ball and it was only after Law spoke to Bobby Charlton that the dilemma was solved. From the spot, Charlton's kick was only half-hearted and Hodgkinson saved with ease.

As the game moved towards the final ten minutes it began to look as though United had dropped yet another two points in an inept performance, but it was thanks to Law that a point was salvaged, heading past Hodgkinson. A goal that was acknowledged with only a minimum of cheers. Only one man left Old Trafford with a smile on his face and that was Norman Kirkman, Southampton's northern scout, sent on a spying mission by his manager Ted Bates and there was little doubt that he would be reporting back that the Manchester United that he had witnessed over the ninety minutes were once again far from being any-where near like playing to form, turning in yet another sluggish perfor-mance and could quite easily be defeated in that forthcoming semi-final.

The point gained hardly improved the chances of staying in the top flight as both Ipswich Town and Manchester City both won away from home. Ipswich 3-0 at Sheffield Wednesday, City 3-2 at Arsenal. City's vic-tory allowed them to leapfrog their neighbours, leaving them equal on twenty-eight points with Bolton Wanderers. United had twenty-seven points, Birmingham City were on twenty-five. All had played thirty-four games. Leyton Orient continued to be out of the picture, bottom with nineteen points from thirty-six games. Grim it certainly was.

Two days after that totally indifferent performance against Shef-field United, the Old Trafford gates were again open and, somewhat surprisingly the turnstiles made a few more revolutions than they had for the Yorkshire sides visit as 5,000 more turned up for the visit of Wolves. Perhaps some were there in the hope of picking up a spare ticket for the F.A. Cup semi-final three days later, others through force of habit, while some might even have turned up to see if United were really as bad as those unflattering newspaper reports.

Matt Busby had been reluctant, as was often the case, to make changes to his team other than through injury, so it was something of a surprise to find Harry Gregg omitted from the eleven to face Wolves. Admittedly, he hadn't enjoyed the best of games against Sheffield United, but with that F.A. Cup semi-final on the horizon, his experi-ence would be invaluable. His replacement, David Gaskell, had not featured in the first team since the 5-2 defeat at Burnley on Septem-ber 22nd. A long time without a first team game.

Strength in depth was not exactly something of a strong point in the current Manchester United squad. If any of the main players were missing, their replacements were not exactly like-for-like, with only Noel Cantwell and Johnny Giles, who currently found themselves on the side-lines, worthy substitutes. It could be argued that the only real plus point was the flexibility and versatility of certain players. But due to the current perilous predicament at the foot of the table, there was no possibility of fielding anything but the strongest side against Wolves and it could only be hoped that the selected eleven could all stay well clear of injuries.

United stunned their doubters with a goal in the fifth minute. There was an opportunity sixty seconds earlier when Setters passed to Charl-ton, whose centre floated tantalisingly into the Wolves penalty area, but

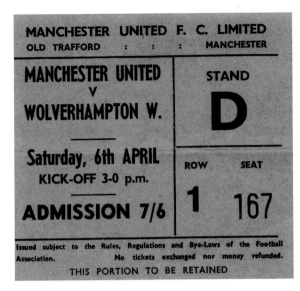

before it reached a red shirted head, Davies in the Wolves goal jumped and plucked it out of the air. Then Law picked out Quixall with an inch perfect pass and he, in turn, centred towards Herd, whose header went far beyond the reach of Davies.

In bygone days, such a start would have meant only one thing, a constant tidal wave of red shirts and a hatful of goals, but this was now and although Charlton was only inches too high from twenty yards and Law headed over when considerably closer to goal, United, known for their generosity as hosts, allowed Wolves considerable room and presented them with the equaliser in the twenty-fifth minute.

A Goodwin free-kick from twenty-five yards appeared to be of little danger and Foulkes decided to allow the ball to pass over his head, in the knowledge that both Dunne and Gaskell were behind him. Goalkeeper and defender both went for the ball, but it was Dunne who got there first and his attempted header towards Gaskell was far from accurate as it drifted past the 'keepers outstretched arm and into the net.

Wolves, on another day, could have found themselves 3-1 in front at the interval as Stobart missed from three yards out and Crowe, having tormented the luckless Dunne, shot wide.

United were their usual ragged and dysfunctional selves, with only Charlton looking anywhere near to his best, and the pessimists in the crowd made themselves heard loud and clear. But instead of the unwelcome sounds drifting down from the terraces doing little to help the bungling red shirts, it had the opposite effect and from seemingly out of nowhere, with five minutes of the first half remaining, United scored. Dunne passed to Charlton, Charlton to Herd and from there it went to Law who darted past Showell before sending the ball low past Davies.

The goal failed to produce anything in the way of confidence as United continued to show a lack of urgency as the second half progressed, again allowing Wolves too much time on the ball. They were fortunate that the Midland's title challenge had disappeared and numerous chances were missed. Broadbent had a shot saved, Stobart had a goal disallowed for an infringement, with another, by Wharton, chalked off for offside. United were also grateful to Gaskell for one or two rather unorthodox saves as the game moved towards a close.

But it wasn't all Wolves as United did have their chances. Quixall and Stiles combined to set up Law in the seventy-ninth minute, but the ball was hooked off his toe. Two minutes later it was Crerand to Charlton and from the wing his centre found Herd, but with Davies off his line, his shot went narrowly wide.

A more than welcome two points. They were now a point in front of Manchester City, but had played a game more. The four-point gap over second bottom Birmingham City was far more encouraging.

And so, it was off to Villa Park and the F.A. Cup semi-final against Southampton. Many were of the opinion that Leicester City, who faced Liverpool in the other semi-final at Hillsborough, like United, had their thoughts more focused on the First Division. Leicester in their championship challenge, United riddled by fears of relegation, leaving Liverpool and Southampton a clear path to Wembley.

"Only an outright fanatic would suggest that Manchester United are certain to beat Southampton. The difference in league status counts for no more than it does the fact that United have the costlier equipment", wrote Eric Todd in the 'Guardian'. In the 'Daily Herald' Peter Lorenzo stuck by his early season tip that United would win the cup and gave his main reason for going for Matt Busby's off-form team "experience".

As mentioned earlier, United were not blessed with an overly strong squad, but were fortunate to have Noel Cantwell and Johnny Giles waiting in the wings if required and twenty-four hours prior to the semi-final tie Busby was dealt a blow in his match preparations as both Albert Quixall and Shay Brennan were ruled out through injury, so it was to Cantwell and Giles that he looked as their ready-made replacements.

Semi-finals can be dour affairs, devoid of class and entertainment no matter how much quality can be found within the supporting cast. Grey, empty, miserable and desolate was how the correspondent covering the game for the 'Times' saw the ninety minutes, adding: "A dream, which is some sort of chemical madness, evaporated and we were left with a game that deserved little better than a goalless draw." It was a sentiment echoed by Alan Hoby of the 'Sunday Express' who wrote: "As a football entertainment drawing 68,312 customers with a record gate of £28,499 7s. 6d., this wildly-awaited semi-final was a big bore. As a parade of skills, a pageant of excitement and drama, it was not only the most depressing of anti-climaxes, but a parody of all that is best in English football." And it was repeated by Maurice Smith in the 'People' – "From Blunderland to Wonderland … from Villa Park to Wembley. Such is the Manchester United 1963 Cup story. In 40-odd years of watching I have never seen a more halting, more unpromising semi-final victory.

"Villa Park authorities proudly told me this was the biggest-ever-pay-day. To me – no fault of Villa's of course – it looked like a £28,000 highway robbery as far as the standard of football was concerned."

Surely, they couldn't all be wrong!

And they weren't, as every match report related much of the same. However, when Matt Busby was asked by 'Daily Express' journalist Terence Elliot as regards to the loads of criticism on the game and if he was still happy, the United manager simply sat back and smiled, answering: "I'm delighted, simply delighted, we are back at Wembley again." But Busby was not blind to the fact that it was a far from perfect ninety-minutes, "what semi-final ever is" he added. "You get very few. There is so much at stake, so much anxiety. Such a build-up that we often get an anti-climax."

Perhaps much of the disappointment arose from the fact that only one goal was scored and that it came mid-way through the first half, leaving the remainder of the game as an uninteresting spectacle. The stretcher bearers, who ran here there and everywhere to attend to a seemingly constant stream of fainting cases, were considered as showing more urgency than the two teams.

United were destructive rather than creative, seldom inspired to attack, but they almost broke the deadlock in the eleventh minute when Herd, collecting Cantwell's long clearance, sent a long pass out to Giles on the right and, taking the ball on the run, shot and hit the post. A prostrate Reynolds in the Southampton goal managed to flick the ball away from danger as it rebounded off the woodwork. Two minutes earlier Crerand had sent Stiles off on a run, but he lost control on the edge of the penalty area.

There was little of note until eleven minutes later whence came the game's only ray of sunshine. Herd moved wide and sent the ball curling over the head of Knapp. Reynolds appeared undecided as to whether come or remain on his line. The ball fell invitingly towards Law and it looked as though he missed with his header, but he was allowed a second opportunity and managed to scramble the ball home despite a desperate dive from Reynolds.

Law had the ball in the net again just before half-time, but the referee disallowed it for an infringement that few had seen.

Southampton fought to the end and almost forced a replay with two late efforts, on both occasions they were denied by Gaskell. The first of the two saw him dive acrobatically to save from the ever-threatening Paine and then, five minutes from time, he ran from his goal to stop O'Brien with his finger-tips.

With stronger support, Southampton centre-forward Kirkby might have won the game for the south coast club as he had the beating of Foulkes all afternoon, but cutting a somewhat lone figure, the Setters inspired United defence seldom had cause for alarm.

Noel Cantwell maintained that it was "Better to win in a negative fashion than to lose playing entertaining football", a statement that many would go along with, more so when a season of such negativity could, in the end, bring success in the form of silverware. For the purists, and of course those with no interest in either side, just in football as a whole, it was, as Ken Jones of the 'Mirror' said: "As entertainment this game wouldn't have been booked for a seaside show in the Orkneys."

Denis Law scores in the semi-final clash with Southampton at Villa Park

Although the press corps, along with many in the packed Villa Park, considered the game a rather mundane ninety-minutes it was never-the-less an afternoon to remember for the young Keith Ennion. Having been at all the games in the previous rounds, this was one he didn't want to miss. "I used to go to all the reserve matches at Old Trafford if we didn't travel to the away matches and my brother went to a few as well. My dad didn't watch the reserves much, but would go to the Youth Cup matches. This meant that I had a full token sheet. My brother was six short and my dad about twelve short. Because of this we only qualified for two tickets for the semi-final and my dad decided to let my elder brother take me on Lingley's coaches. My brother was only fourteen. This probably wouldn't be allowed these days.

"The M6 hadn't been built in those days and it took the coaches three hours to get to Villa Park with a short stop at Newcastle-under-Lyme bus station. Southampton were allocated the Holte End and a few seats in the main stand, but I think from memory, United had most of the rest of the ground.

"We entered the ground at about 1pm and my brother and I were on the wall at the front of the Witton Lane end just to the left of the goals as we were looking at the pitch. The atmosphere was brilliant again, with all their supporters decked out in yellow and black, which were their colours for the game, as both clubs had to change colours for the day. They sang 'When The Saints Go Marching In' regularly. The United fans were still in the chanting stage at that point but started singing following that game.

"United's mascot, Jack Irons, was walking round the pitch decked out in red and white as always, along with the other mascot whose name I have forgotten. Southampton also had a mascot decked out in their colours. They were walking round the perimeter of the pitch trying to get the fans whipped into a frenzy, and other supporters were climbing over the wall at the front and walking round with them and no police or stewards tried to stop them.

"When United entered the field of play it was met with about five hundred toilet rolls thrown from behind the goal at the United end.

"The best memory of the game was Law scoring the only goal of the day right in front of us. The coach on the way home stopped at a pub somewhere near Stoke and I remember a United fan from the coach bringing me and my brother a lemonade to us outside the pub as we were not allowed in."

In the other semi-final, Leicester City overcame a resilient Liverpool with a 1-0 victory, whilst suffering none of the backlash suffered by their Wembley opponents. Many felt that Liverpool were unfortunate not to win, but as Cyril Chapman of the 'Birmingham Daily Post' wrote: "City are through to Wembley, which after all was the main topic of the exercise." The same could certainly be said of United's victory.

CHAPTER FIVE
NO TEARS FOR CITY

That Cup Final date with Leicester City was still a month away, pushed back to May 25th due to the mid-season postponements, the snow and ice proving more than formidable opponents, whilst causing United untold problems in the build up to that big day in North London. Looking at the First Division fixture list at the star of the season, April 27th would have seen the curtain come down on the league campaign with an away match at Nottingham Forest, the Cup Final was due to be played seven days later. Enough time for any aches and pains to clear up along with a couple of days relaxation thrown in for good measure.

But 1962-63 was no ordinary season. Not only were Manchester United in something of an unfamiliar position in the First Division relegation zone, but they had also to fulfil seven league fixtures in twenty days, with the last of those coming a mere five days prior to the Cup Final. Twenty days to salvage a season and avoid the embarrassment of the Second Division.

First up was the visit of Sheffield Wednesday to Old Trafford and following what was one of their worst performances of the season, there was every possibility that United would indeed be a Second Division side by the time the team bus drove up Wembley Way.

"I did not think a team with so much talent could sink so low" wrote Derek Wallis in the 'Daily Mirror'. He added: "Manchester United's most deplorable failures this season must have looked positively brilliant compared with their appalling performances at Old Trafford last night."

Mayday it certainly was, but no distress call could save United against Sheffield Wednesday, leaking three goals in thirteen first half minutes. They had survived the opening twenty-five minutes, when Wednesday looked far from threatening, but then Shay Brennan was out-thought by Dobson, who found Finney completely unmarked and headed home comfortably.

Five minutes later Quinn was given more than enough space to run through and deflect a Dobson corner past Gaskell. The third

MANCHESTER UNITED F. C. LIMITED

OLD TRAFFORD : : : MANCHESTER

MANCHESTER UNITED

SHEFFIELD WEDNESDAY

Saturday, 16th FEB.

KICK-OFF 3-0 p.m.

ADMISSION 7/6

STAND

D

ROW   SEAT

1   167

Issued subject to the Rules, Regulations and Bye-Laws of the Football Association.   No tickets exchanged nor money refunded.

THIS PORTION TO BE RETAINED

goal followed in the thirty-eighth minutes when Setters headed clear another Dobson corner, but only as far as Megson who headed the ball down and crashed the ball home.

United appeared to wake up after the interval, forcing six corners in the opening fifteen minutes, but the Sheffield defence stood firm and it was not until seven minutes from time that United finally broke them down when Setters pulled a goal back, heading home a Crerand free kick. But it was too little too late.

Had Ron Springett not pulled off two excellent saves in the fifth and sixth minutes, then it might have been altogether different, but then again, this was Manchester United. One down, six to go.

Next stop was a few miles up the road from Old Trafford at Turf Moor Burnley, not exactly a happy hunting ground for Matt Busby's team in recent seasons as December 28th 1959 had seen the only success in the past five seasons. The others were all defeats – 4-1 in November 1962, 5-3 in October 1961, 4-2 in March 1959 and 3-0 in March 1958. Not all were instantly forgettable, as the last of the quartet, in the wake of the Munich air disaster, was a bruising affair that would live long in the memories of those who were present and would be seen as something of a red rag whenever the two sides went head-to-head at later dates.

It was a heated, tempestuous affair that exploded just over mid-way through the first half amid unnecessary fouls, raised fists and lost tempers, coming to a head when nineteen-year-old Mark Pearson was sent off for a tackle on Burnley right-half Les Shannon.

But it was in the aftermath of the game that the blue touch paper was well and truly lit when Bob Lord, the Burnley chairman, said of the United players: "Some of them were running around out there like a lot of teddy boys. If this lot is allowed to ride roughshod it could upset the whole of organised football." He fuelled the fire even further by adding: "Manchester people are still swayed by what happened at Munich. It isn't a good thing for the game.

"There is too much sentiment about Manchester United... in Manchester. All the talk since Munich seems to have gone to the heads of some United players. We weren't playing rough. We didn't start it.

"All they have had to withstand in recent weeks seems to have been a bit too much for some of these young men."

If Bob Lord had any thoughts of Manchester United's current predicament, he wisely kept them to himself, but there was still an undercurrent to the fixture, as no sooner had the first blast of the referee's whistle been heard when police were called to the terracing behind David Gaskell's goal to seek out the troublemakers. They were called upon again in the second half, but on the field of play it was relatively peaceful with only Foulkes and Lochhead being spoken to by the referee following some pushing and shoving.

But despite their recent failures at Turf Moor, not to mention their current erratic form, United gained a rare success, a valuable two points, although had Burnley struck early on when United looked nervous, apprehensive even, frightened to attempt anything that might lead to a goal for their opponents. As would Simpsons twenty-five-yard drive, had it been a mere six inches lower. Gradually, however, confidence grew, their defensive play took on an air of solidity and assurance, while the attack only lacked the goals to match the overall effort shown.

Scoring opportunities at either end were few and far between, as rare as the glimpse of actual class from any of the twenty-two players and it was one of those games when you had the feeling that it was destined to end goalless. A thought that lingered in the mind until the seventieth minute.

Giles was lying injured, almost on the half-way line, as the ball rolled loose to Quixall and, for a matter of seconds, as the referee waved play on, the United number nine considered booting the ball out of play to enable his team mate to receive attention from the trainer. His hesitancy was matched by that of the Burnley players who were caught out when Quixall noted a lack of urgency from the claret and blue shirts and decided to forget about his team mate momentarily, sending a forty-yard pass into the penalty area where Law rose majestically to head past Blacklaw.

Although there were still twenty minutes remaining, United manned the barricades and repelled whatever came their way. Previous defeats and backbiting were forgotten, this victory was of more importance. The short journey back to Manchester was a happy one, more so as neighbours City had lost 3-0 at home to Blackpool and Bolton had lost 1-0 at Everton. Birmingham City had managed to pick up a point in a 3-3 draw at Fulham.

Birmingham City's share of the spoils in London was enough to give them a one-point advantage over second bottom Manchester City. Bolton Wanderers, Manchester United and Aston Villa all held a two-point edge over the Midlands side, with United and Villa having a slight advantage with a game in hand. Two down, five to go.

It had been the end of October, beginning of November when United last managed to win two successive league fixtures. They had drawn, won and drawn again, but putting two consecutive victories together had proved beyond them, but if ever there was a need for such a statistic then it was now. Arsenal's visit to Old Trafford would tick off that game in hand and two points would see United jump a couple of places higher, moving closer to safety.

The paying public continued to eye United as something of a reluctant source with whom to give some of their hard-earned cash. Something like a street corner busker whose singing you thought wasn't bad, but you didn't feel like donating some of the loose change in your pocket to him.

Arsenal's visit was also a Monday night, with any spare money having been spent in the local shops or across the bar of the local pub over the course of the weekend. Watching United was not so much as a priority these days and there was of course, also a trip to Wembley to budget for.

Two victories on the bounce continued to elude United as Arsenal inflicted a 3-2 defeat on the Cup finalists, but from that defeat came praise – "United Show Top Form – In Defeat" and "United Take The Glory In Defeat" were the headlines above the match reports in the 'Daily Mirror' and 'Daily Mail' respectively, but it was points, not plaudits that were required to save United from relegation.

"Three brilliant breakaways by Arsenal, three moments of hesitation by United's defence.

"Three superbly taken goals – and the defeat they definitely didn't deserve keeps Matt Busby's team still uncertain of First Division safety in a year of Cup triumph.

"But on this form, they might still make it. They have the fight again. They have the finishing power" wrote Frank McGhee in the 'Mirror'.

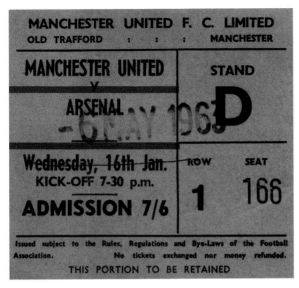

MANCHESTER UNITED F. C. LIMITED
OLD TRAFFORD : : : MANCHESTER

MANCHESTER UNITED   STAND

v

ARSENAL   D

-6 MAY 1963

Wednesday, 16th Jan.   ROW   SEAT
KICK-OFF 7-30 p.m.
                          1   166
ADMISSION 7/6

Issued subject to the Rules, Regulations and Bye-Laws of the Football
Association.   No tickets exchanged nor money refunded.
THIS PORTION TO BE RETAINED

But it was still a defeat, two points dropped, no advantage gained over their rivals at the foot of the table. It was also a concern within the ranks and on the terracing, as five minutes from time Maurice Setters was carried off the pitch five minutes from the end, following a clash with Arsenal's Billy McCullough and was taken to hospital for an x-ray on his ankle.

It was McCullough and Laurie Brown who stood solidly in the heart of the Arsenal defence, repelling United attacks, that on another day, would have seen them won the game in the opening forty-five minutes. Law hit the bar, had another blocked by Clarke, who had already kicked a goal bound Charlton effort off the line, while other efforts were scrambled away with much relief.

Arsenal took the lead in the thirty-first minute with their first on-target shot. John McLeod picked out Joe Baker who out-stepped Bill Foulkes and beat Gaskell with a low, well-hit shot. Eight minutes into the second-half, McLeod was the provider once again, having only minutes later seen a powerful drive blocked by Gaskell, on this occasion he passed to Strong, whose initial effort was only partly stopped by Gaskell, allowing the Arsenal inside-right to nip in and snatch a goal from the rebound. The ten minutes that followed saw enough action to satisfy any appetite, leaving the 35,000 breathless.

Baker and Stiles were both booked following a flare-up, then with fifty-six minutes on the clock McClelland could only parry a thirty-yard Charlton shot, the ball running free to present Law the opportunity to snatch the rebound and reduce arrears. McClelland saved brilliantly from Quixall then, five minutes later, Baker and Strong surged down the right, Sammels mis-kicked but Skirton made no mistake with the chance that was to restore Arsenal's two goal advantage.

One minutes later it was 3-2. Giles centred and Law launched himself horizontally and somehow managed to hook the ball over his head and into the net. A linesman's flag was to deny Law his hat-trick, the disappointed Scot gesturing wildly at the official's decision.

In the dying seconds, Charlton twice beat McClelland, first with a header and then with a right-footed lob, but on both occasions the ball was cleared from underneath the bar by centre-half Brown.

United gained an early victory, of sorts, over Leicester City in the Cup Final build up when, over a three-way telephone call, Matt Busby called correctly when a coin was spun to decide upon the colours either side would wear in the Wembley showpiece. The clubs had requested the change in order to avoid a clash of colours for those watching on black and white television, so having lost the toss, it was announced that Leicester City would play in white shirts with blue rings round the cuffs and collar, white shorts with blue stripes and white stockings. United would be in their usual red shirts, white shorts and red stockings. Three down, four to go.

With Birmingham City keeping United company in the First Division basement department, the ninety minutes at St Andrews on May 10th took on a completely different outlook compared to what was usually nothing more than just another date on the humdrum fixture list.

The defeat by Arsenal made little difference to the league table, as Bolton Wanders had also lost 4-0 at home to Sheffield Wednesday that same evening, although they had now played a game more than United, Birmingham and Manchester City. Aston Villa were perhaps in the most comfortable position of all, as although level on points, they now had two games in hand.

United couldn't allow the approaching cup final to prey on their minds. Victory at Wembley would be a superb achievement, particularly after such a dismal season league wise, coupled with the fact that it was still only five years since the horrors of Munich, the Second Division, however, was no place for Manchester United. Glory at Wembley or First Division safety? It was a difficult call to make.

Matt Busby also had additional worries as despite the domestic season rolling towards a finale, there were still international fixtures taking place. Denis Law and Bobby Charlton had faced each other at Wembley at the beginning of April, while Law was in action at Hampden against Austria and Charlton against Brazil, in between the fixtures against Arsenal and Birmingham City. Busby would spend a nail biting ninety minutes beside the telephone, hoping that it would not ring with news of an injury. Thankfully Law came through the match against the Austrians unscathed, whilst not having to endure the complete ninety minutes. None of the players did, as referee Jim Finney called the proceedings to a halt with eleven minutes remaining and Scotland leading 4-1 following a series of ugly fouls. The 94,596 Hampden crowd stood rooted to the spot as Finney blew his whistle, waved his arms in the air and ran off the pitch. It wasn't until a police announcement ten minutes later that the crowd realised that they would see no further action.

By the time the referee decided that enough was enough, two Austrian players had been sent off and the incident that made up Jim Finney's mind that this excuse for a football match had progressed far too long was an incident between Linhart and Denis Law. The two players clashed, the Austrian fell to the ground, seemingly in agony and off went Finney. "There was no saying how it was going to end. Things were getting completely out of hand" said Finney. "Someone might have been seriously injured." Uninjured and unperturbed by the eighty-odd minutes in Glasgow, Law lined up against Birmingham City, but perhaps he would have preferred to have sat out what was to be yet another inglorious ninety minutes in a season that many wished would hurry up and come to a close.

"Finalists Flop" was the headline in the 'Daily Mirror' the following morning. "Manchester United, tattered and tired after an ugly ill-tempered fracas – with both sides equally guilty – find themselves two weeks from Wembley with their survival in the first Division still in doubt", penned Frank McGhee their correspondent covering the match.

The 2-1 defeat, amid rain and driving wind on a quagmire of a pitch, was hard to take in a robust encounter that saw both goalmouths take a pounding as both sets of players, knowing what was at stake, went at it hammer and tongs from the offset.

With six minutes played, the first real goal scoring opportunity fell to Giles. Charlton carved out the opening, but with the goal more or less at his mercy, Giles shot wide. Another effort from Herd banged into the side netting. For twenty minutes they looked the better of the two teams, but the necessary, and much needed goals simply failed to materialise.

Harris was just wide with a shot at the opposite end and then Auld tested Gaskell with a powerful shot from the edge of the penalty area. But, although it was United who looked the most impressive of the two sides, it was the home side who drew first blood in the twenty-sixth minute. Leek pushed the ball through to Bloomfield and the City inside-right beat Gaskell with a low drive.

The goal stirred both sides, Birmingham gained confidence, while Law took it out on Auld and was spoken to by the referee. The enthusiasm of both sets of players was beginning to stretch just a little too far and carried over into the second half when Stiles, Leek and Smith were all booked, will several others managed to escape with only a lecture.

It was not until the seventy-fourth minute that a second goal materialised and, again, it fell to Birmingham City. Bloomfield was again involved, drawing Stiles and Cantwell away from goal before swinging the ball into the United penalty area and Leek headed home.

Desperation stations on the United bench. Busby shouted for Giles to move onto the right from his inside position, with Quixall coming inside – and within a minute they had pulled a goal back. Crerand and Quixall combined, the latter picking out Law who headed home. It was, however, too little too late and although a further two or three opportunities came their way, none produced a goal.

Those two points put Birmingham City level on points with United and Bolton Wanderers, but they had played one game more. Manchester City were now three points adrift. If it was any consolation, the two City's had conceded considerably more goals than Busby's team.

Four down. Three to go.

Ten days of the 1962-63 season remained. Ten May days that would define not just Manchester United's season, but their future. Three league fixtures against fellow strugglers Manchester City, the already doomed Leyton Orient, a couldn't care less Nottingham Forest followed by that seemingly long-standing engagement in North London.

In Leicester, the local 'Evening Mail' filled countless column inches with articles relating to the forthcoming Cup Final, both on the local side and on United. Potted history, player profiles, anything that might sell a few more copies than normal. A special issue was rolled off the printing presses, as there would be in Manchester, but the Wembley Final was to take second billing in Manchester, it was the support to the headline act, with the ninety minutes in Moss Side arguably the most important head-to-head between the two old rivals since the 1926 F.A. Cup semi-final, a game that City won 3-0.

Maine Road had witnessed countless memorable fixtures over the years, United, as house guests, engraving their name into the ground's history, not just in those 'derby day' encounters, but in those magical European nights of the recent past. Nights that Old Trafford couldn't host as it had yet to be blessed with floodlights. But never would the ground have hosted such a 'needle' fixture than this May 10th meeting.

Twenty-four hours before the meeting of the Mancunian duo, Birmingham City had seen all their good work against United thrown to the wind as they lost 3-1 at Burnley. Neither United or City could afford to lose. Victory for United would ensure safety as it would give them thirty-three points, whilst still having two games left to play. City, would have one game remaining, but would be three points behind, so unable to overtake their cross-town rivals.

If City were to be victorious, they would be a point above United with one game to play, compared to United's two. They would also be one point above Birmingham City. A draw would keep everyone guessing as to the eventual outcome, but in reality, it would be of little use to City. It was all ifs and buts. In reality though, everything lay in United's hands.

United were again without Maurice Setters, fielding the same eleven that faced, and lost to Birmingham City, in a game that was neither for the football purists nor the faint hearted. Something that was summed up in the 'Daily Mail' headline – "Soccer Gets KO In Relegation Rough House". What more did they expect? It was a blue versus red local derby. But there was much more than local pride at stake. It was win... or be relegated.

The local police were on high alert and had fifty men on duty inside the ground with a similar number outside, along with a mounted section. The latter were required as with the gates locked and the game having kicked-off, there were still an estimated 3,000 to 4,000 outside, a section of whom forced a gate, with some gaining admission, before the arrival of the horses. Many then decided to leave, although a few die-hards stayed on, judging the flow of the game by the noise of the crowd.

City opened briskly. Dobing tested Gaskell and Hayes was roundly applauded for tackles on Charlton. The home crowd were equally vocal when Charlton mis-kicked from ten yards out. But these were little more than a testing of the tonsils as the volume rose a few decibels in the eighth minute when City went in front. Dobing put an excellent pass through to Harley, who ran onto the ball and turned it past Gaskell, who appeared slightly caught out by the swiftness of the move.

With their tails up and confidence high, the light blue shirts continued to press. Gaskell could only parry a shot from Young, but Foulkes kicked clear with Harley ready to pounce. In the home defence Leivers, ably assisted by Gray and Sear, stood firm, not giving United an inch and it wasn't until the half hour mark that they came more into the game, Foulkes going close on one occasion with a header that went just over.

Before the interval, City again had the ball in the net, but to the annoyance and disappointment of the majority, a raised linesman's flag was enough to see it disallowed. On the first half showing alone, a City victory was certainly on the cards.

It wasn't a game for the faint hearted, either off or on the pitch. 'Back alley tactics' was how Don Hardisty of the 'Daily Mail' reported it. But overall, only three players were booked – Wagstaffe, Harley and Crerand, although there could well have been more. Harley was perhaps fortunate to remain on the pitch, his tackle on Herd leaving the United man with a ripped stocking down to his ankle and a blooded shin.

The tension and overall bad feeling continued to bubble away as the players made their way off at half-time. There was a scuffle in the tunnel, unseen by the majority of the crowd, but apparently, amid the pushing and shoving, Pat Crerand knocked out David Wagstaffe!

A buzz went around the ground as the players came out for the second half as United took the field with only ten men, those situated beside the tunnel being of the opinion that Crerand, the missing red shirt, had been sent off during the interval, but they were disappointed to see the United right-half run onto the pitch pulling on his number four jersey as the second half got underway.

City began that second half as they finished the first and Giles did well to clear from Hayes with Gaskell nowhere to be seen. United continued to be subdued and only attacked in fits and starts, although Law had the opportunity to equalise when put through by Giles, but his shot was only half hit and Dowd saved with ease.

If anyone was going to score, it was City and at no time did they look as if they would relinquish their advantage. Harley again came close to scoring, but on this occasion, Gaskell was equal to his header from a Young free-kick. Stiles was also to head a Hayes effort off the goal line. United were dependant on long range efforts, mainly from Herd and Charlton, but none were to cause Dowd or his defenders any problems. Law, on his old stomping ground, was a mere shadow of the player everyone knew.

But it was Law upon whom the outcome rested.

Six minutes from time, with both sets of supporters biting their nails and checking their watches, Wagstaffe, for some inexplicable reason, attempted to pass the ball back to Harry Dowd from all of thirty yards. Law caught the scent of an opportunity and he was off on the hunt. Reaching the ball at the same time as the City 'keeper, they tussled for possession and, as the goalkeeper's arms went round Law's legs, down went the United man.

The ball was trickling out of play, nowhere near the City goal. The referee had little hesitation in pointing to the penalty spot and after Dowd had received treatment for what many thought to be a kick on the head from Law, Quixall kept his cool and placed the ball beyond Dowd and into the bottom left hand corner of the net. Law couldn't watch his team mates spot kick, he stood facing his own goal, Noel Cantwell provided the running commentary.

It was more than an equaliser. It was a crushing blow to City. It was relegation.

United were level and managed to hang on for the final few rough, tougher and ruthless minutes. No player could hold onto the ball without being flattened.

It was a game that City should have won. Any non-Red considered them to be unlucky and outside the game after the final whistle, tempers were high. The referee was the 'villain' of the match. 'These Yorkshire referees are all the same' commented one blue and white scarved supporter. Others crowded outside the Maine Road office and voiced their disappointment, but they, like their counterparts ninety minutes earlier were soon dispersed by the mounted police.

Having earned a point from that bruising encounter, United required only one more from their final two games against Leyton Orient and Nottingham Forest to be completely safe, but in reality, they would still be safe even if Manchester City and Birmingham City won their final match, as they had a better goal average. If that was indeed the case, then it would be Manchester City who would be relegated to the Second Division.

There was a golden glow over Old Trafford. An ever-increasing buzz about the place, smiles all round and everyone had a spring in their step. 'Relegation' was finally banished from the vocabulary. 'Wembley' was now the word on everyone's lips. Yes, there were still two league fixtures to fulfil, but obtaining that one point was not something that was beyond the capabilities of this often-disjointed Manchester United side.

Neither was there any pressure on the opposition, who would be simply happy to play out the ninety minutes and see the end of this long and drawn-out season.

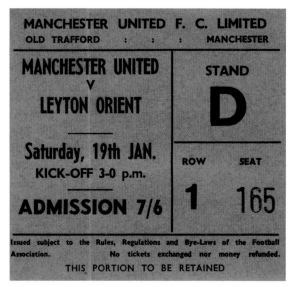

MANCHESTER UNITED F. C. LIMITED
OLD TRAFFORD : : : MANCHESTER

MANCHESTER UNITED
v
LEYTON ORIENT

STAND

D

Saturday, 19th JAN.
KICK-OFF 3-0 p.m.

ROW   SEAT

ADMISSION 7/6   1   165

Issued subject to the Rules, Regulations and Bye-Laws of the Football
Association.   No tickets exchanged nor money refunded.
THIS PORTION TO BE RETAINED

On what was the final Saturday of the 1962-63 campaign, United played host to Leyton Orient – Birmingham City did likewise to Leicester City, while Manchester City travelled to West Ham United. Although there was a hint of uncertainty, of the three, United had the easiest task on paper and so it was to prove, eventually.

Busby made only one change to the side that had drawn at Maine Road, bringing Maurice Setters back into the fold, following his recent ankle injury, which surprised many as it was suspected that Setters would not be seen in action again this season. Stiles was to miss out.

To any casual observer who was completely unaware of league positions or whatever, they would undoubtedly have taken United as the team heading towards the Second Division, as Leyton Orient were relaxed, playing some beautiful football, while United huffed and puffed, often showing signs of desperation.

The Old Trafford crowd were silenced in the ninth minute when Dave Dunmore back-headed the ball past Gaskell and by half-time slow hand claps and the barracking of certain players, including Bobby Charlton, echoed around the ground. Passing was careless, while there was little in the way of continuality in the play.

Seven minutes into the second half, it was Charlton and Charlton who combined to give United the equaliser. Stan, the Orient player, heading a cross from Bobby into his own net. United had the point that they might require come the end of the afternoon.

In reality it was never really the case of needing that point as no sooner had United drawn level, than the Old Trafford scoreboard was showing that City were losing 4-0 at West Ham. The loudest cheer of the afternoon echoed around Old Trafford.

Somehow, United managed to stutter along, keeping Orient at bay, whilst not exactly putting the visitor's goal under any real threat, then with nine minutes remaining came the deciding factor. George in the

Orient goal failed to hold a cross as he jumped with Bobby Charlton and the ball fell invitingly to Law to prod home off the post. Four minutes later, Bobby Charlton rounded George for the third.

Elsewhere, those four West Ham United goals increased to six, Manchester City clawing one back in meek response, while Birmingham City scored twice in a minute to beat Leicester City 3-2.

United still had one fixture to fulfil, but were now fifth bottom, level on thirty-four points with Ipswich Town, but with a better goal average. Below them were Birmingham City on thirty-three and City on thirty-one. Orient had managed only twenty-one.

It was now Cup Final week and tickets were, as always, like gold dust, but there was always that 'certain few' who, with no intentions of going to the game, or indeed little interest in it, managed to get their hands on considerable numbers of the sought after pieces of card.

Former Leicester City player Ted Jelly, who had in fact played in the 1949 Final, and who now owned two radio and television shops, placed notices in his windows proclaiming "free Cup Final tickets if you spend £50 or more".

There had already been an uproar in Leicester when the club chairman offered two tickets to film stars Elizabeth Taylor and Richard Burton and local scrap dealer Doug Cory had announced that he had fifty tickets and would exchange one for a hundredweight of scrap. In no time, those fifty tickets were gone, but by some magical means, he managed to secure a further fifty.

With no sense of urgency, or more to the point, need to secure a draw or a victory to ensure safety, Matt Busby could at last look towards Wembley's twin towers and rest key individuals in that final league encounter at Nottingham Forest. At least those who were left out knew their place in the Wembley line-up was guaranteed, for others, it was a case of wait and see.

Out went Bill Foulkes, Maurice Setters, Denis Law and Bobby Charlton and in came reserves Frank Haydock and Dennis Walker, along with Shay Brennan and Nobby Stiles. For the latter two individuals, they, as were one or two others, under the microscope. Brennan had not seen first team action since May 1st, but had played in every round of the Cup except the semi-final. Stiles had only missed the Coventry tie and had featured in eleven of the last twelve league fixtures.

At Forest, United had, perhaps surprisingly, held the advantage twice, taking the lead as early as the second minute when Giles picked up a pass from Herd and scored with a low shot that sneaked in beside the post. Addison levelled the scoring in the fortieth minute, having seen a penalty, after Haydock pulled down Julians, hit the post. Three minutes into the second half United were again in front, Herd scoring with a fierce drive, but Forest full-back Mochan put his side back on level terms in the sixty-seventh minute before Gaskell gifted the home side the winner ten minutes from time when he attempted, perhaps over confidently, to fist out a rather innocuous header from Julians and the ball simply skimmed his fist and flew into the net.

Losing such a goal would have given the United goalkeeper, and manager Matt Busby, much to think about on the journey home, with the highly experienced Harry Gregg waiting in the wings. Another player who would not have enjoyed the journey back to Manchester was Nobby Stiles, who suffered a recurrence of an old leg muscle injury. Another Wembley place was under consideration.

Tickets for the Final were, as always, at a premium and the Leicester scrap man and the television dealer had their Mancunian counterpart in tailor Alec Goodall of Salford. But Goodall was not cashing in on being able to lay his hands on the sought-after briefs as he simply sent letters to 800 customers enquiring if they were interested in a free trip to the Wembley showpiece. Response was obviously great, but there were only forty-two places up for grabs, enough to fill a coach, and the names of the lucky few were drawn out of the hat and off they went to Wembley on the eve of the game.

There was nothing under-hand in regards to Mr Goodall's generosity, his tickets being sourced from here, there and everywhere and it began to look as though the ticket touts hanging around Manchester Central station the night before the game were going to be equally generous, as their requests for £5.10/- for 45-shilling seats or £3 seats at £6, were being ignored.

United made Weybridge their Wembley headquarters and it was here that Matt Busby had to decide upon his starting eleven. It was a far from easy decision. The majority of the eleven picked themselves, but the United manager had to decide between Harry Gregg and David Gaskell, Nobby Stiles and Maurice Setters and Shay Brennan and Tony Dunne. In the end, it was Gregg, Brennan and Stiles who missed out, the latter perhaps not as disappointed as his two team mates, as the injury he had received against Nottingham Forest was always going to be too much of a risk.

"We have been trying to find our best form, but injuries have impeded us" said Matt Busby on the eve of the Final. "We have not played as badly

NORTH STAND

ENTER AT **E** TURNSTILES

(See plan and conditions on back)

ENTRANCE **82**
(LEFT)

Row   Seat

19   44

EMPIRE STADIUM, WEMBLEY
The Football Association
Cup Competition

FINAL TIE

SATURDAY, MAY 4th, 1963
KICK-OFF 3 p.m.

Price 63/-   *Chairman,*
Wembley Stadium Limited

THIS PORTION TO BE RETAINED
This Ticket is issued on the condition that
it is not re-sold for more than its face value.

as some people say, and I feel confident we will recapture our blend... I have been driving the team a bit during the last few days, and there are signs of returning to our best."

"Yes, this is my sixth Cup Final, two as a player and four as a manager, and the preliminary spell has been the least enjoyable because of the tension and the anxiety over the League position... I recall the 1948 team had a bad patch before they won at Wembley."

Winning the F.A. Cup was now more than simply prestige, a gleaming silver trophy in the boardroom and a new line on the list of honours. It was now a money-spinning exercise, with the victorious side at the new-look Wembley finding themselves with a passport to Europe and a place in next season's European Cup Winners Cup. "We want it to be a good final. But we are very conscious of the fact that a win will put us into a European competition next season" admitted Busby. "It will give us back something we want very badly. And quite apart from anything else, there is big money in it."

Having dropped from the dizzy heights of League Champions and European Cup contenders to being amongst the also-rans of the First Division, or to be blunter, relegation candidates, certainly hurt, but this was who the Manchester United of the early 1960's were.

The F.A. Cup Final was much, much more than the opportunity to win a trophy, it was an offer to reclaim some prestige, a chance to prove that this Manchester United side were much better than performances and league positions showed. No, they didn't lie, but this was a side capable of so much more and a victory could well be the first step on the road back to the summit where the club and its supporters belonged.

Somewhat strangely, considering their indifferent form, the majority of the national press had United down as favourites. Perhaps the 'Liverpool Echo' explains best. Their correspondent, Michael Charters, told the readers that if Leicester City, who had done nothing since their semi-final victory over Liverpool, couldn't pick up the threads

147

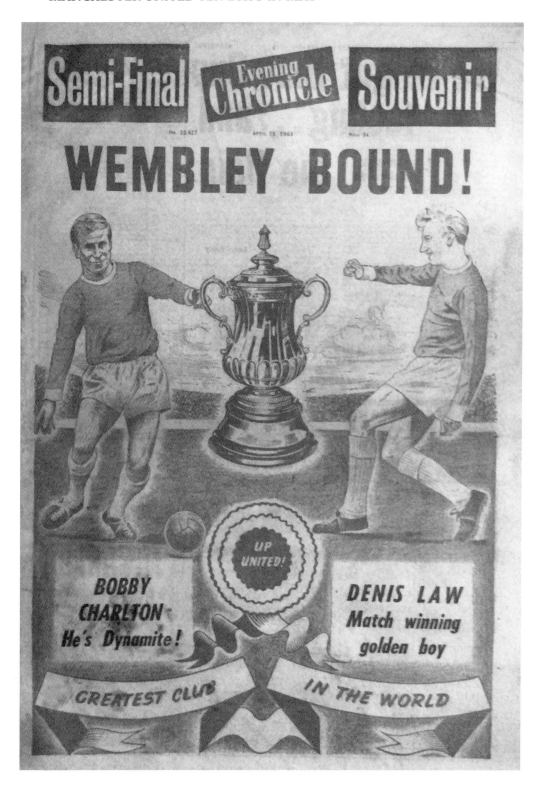

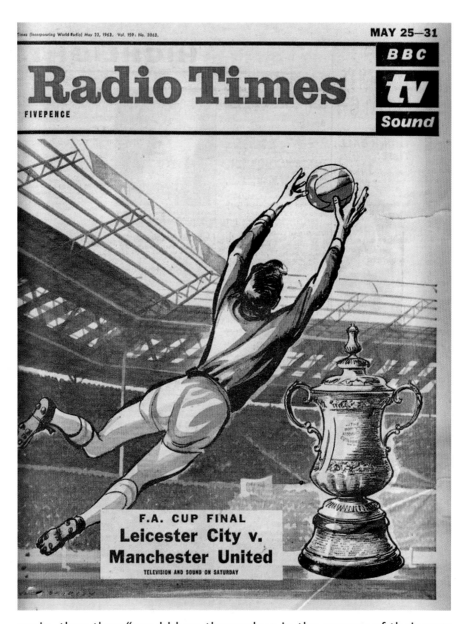

Times (Incorporating World-Radio) May 23, 1963. Vol. 159: No. 2062.

MAY 25—31

BBC

Radio Times

tv

Sound

FIVEPENCE

F.A. CUP FINAL
Leicester City v.
Manchester United
TELEVISION AND SOUND ON SATURDAY

again, then they "would lose themselves in the morass of their own defence-minded techniques. Even Manchester United, the team with so many talented players who cannot play talented football together, should be able to beat them."

Of United he wrote: "United are an enigma to themselves, their supporters and the rest of the football world. Many knowledgeable folk in the game have thought they would make Wembley from the third round onwards, because it seemed as though they were favoured

Matt Busby proudly leads his United side out at Wembley

with that intangible called "Cup luck." Certainly, they have had a far easier run to the Final than their opponents, and they are there without playing impressively in any game.

The fact that they have only just escaped relegation proves how they have been struggling. It is in their favour that their best display for several months was at Leicester when they lost 4-3, with Law getting a hat-trick. That, so I hear, was a flash of the United which everyone thought they would show all season, so if the Final compares with that game, everyone will be satisfied.

"United have talent in abundance, with Crerand, Setters, Quixall, Law and Charlton the famous names. But they haven't found that happy blend of skills and styles; they are individuals and they are a long way behind the great United sides of the past decade or so.

"I think, however, that if the United stars rise to the occasion, they have the genius to win the game."

It was time for the Manchester United players to stand up and be counted. Prove worthy of the transfer fees paid for them, the plaudits they were sometimes afforded and to convince the public, and their supporters, that they were indeed a team much more capable than the one that had stuttered through the past few months.

So, it was out onto a sun-kissed Wembley that Noel Cantwell lead his Manchester United team mates, kitted out in their red tracksuit tops with 'Manchester United' emblazoned in white on the back, like championship boxers heading into the ring. It was not an afternoon for nerves and the United side were all seasoned professionals with perhaps the exception of David Gaskell in goal, but he had weathered an F.A. Charity Shield tie against Manchester City at Maine Road as a mere unexperienced teenager, so Wembley should hold no fears. Perhaps if Leicester City had abandoned their defensive plans, or at least toned them down, and concentrated on the weakness, the one chink in the armour, that was the United 'keeper, the outcome may well have been different.

Gaskell was to drop the ball on a couple of occasions early in the game, inviting the white shirted Leicester front men to steal a shot at goal, but they were in a wasteful mood. In his 'News of the World' report, Frank Butler wrote of the 'keeper: "[He] was the most jittery man of the match. He must have given Matt Busby and his own colleagues heart failure. He handled the ball as though it were on fire, dropping the most innocent lobs and crosses."

The game as a whole was an open, exciting affair, a fitting ninety minutes for what was the Football Association's centenary year. Both sides made their own contribution, but there was, in all honesty, only going to be one winner on the day.

It was down to Denis Law to create the first real opening of the afternoon, crafting the ball through towards Quixall as the United inside-right moved forward, but it glided across the Wembley turf and just out of his reach.

Leicester, in response, switched the action quickly to the opposite end where Crerand and Dunne allowed Stringfellow the time and space to send an inviting ball across the face of the United goal, where Cantwell turned it away from danger at the expense of a corner. It was a warning that United heeded.

Crerand began to control the game, his interceptions and long probing passes were to become a memorable feature of the Final. One pass sent Giles scurrying away and, as his cross moved tantalisingly towards Law, it was only a timely intervention by Banks in the Leicester goal that averted the danger.

Gaskell failed to assert the same confidence as his opposite number as play again moved swiftly to the opposite end. Cross picked out Gibson with a simple pass, but as Gaskell dived for the resulting shot, he allowed the ball to bounce over him, but much to his relief Foulkes was on hand to clear.

David Herd scoring his second goal, United's third,
in the 1963 FA Cup Final with Denis Law watching on

Those two Leicester breakaways were their only contribution to the opening twenty minutes or so, as United pressed forward more often and began to look the more composed of the two sides. Their probing and attacking danger kept the Leicester defence constantly occupied and prevented much in the way of counter-attacks.

With the clock ticking towards the half-hour mark, the opening, and decisive goal materialised. A Charlton effort was saved by Banks, but the clearance was weak and only went as far as Crerand, who was soon pounding back towards the Leicester penalty area, where he squared the ball to Law in front of goal. Turning his back to goal, Law quickly spun round and guided the ball past a helpless Banks. It was classic Law. United were in front.

Five minutes later he came within inches of making it 2-0. Striding through the Leicester defence, beating three men with relative ease, moving the ball from right to left as if tied to his boot, he drew Banks from his goal before shooting. 'Goal' was on the lips of many, but suddenly McLintock appeared from out of nowhere to deflect the ball round the post for a corner.

Leicester City began the second half as if they had spent ten minutes being reprimanded on the headmaster's carpet and once again Gaskell dropped a cross and was anxiously looking for the ball as Cross somehow managed to squeeze it past the post.

Twelve minutes into the second half, the outcome was more or less decided. A Giles cross floated over the Leicester defence and fell to Charlton on the left. His low ground shot was partly stopped by Banks, but ran on to David Herd, who had little more to do than tap the ball into the vacant goal. On another day, Banks would have saved comfortably.

Two goals in front and confidence flowed through the United team as it had failed to do throughout the previous weeks and months. Law was here there and everywhere, pulling the Leicester defence in every direction. Crerand was at his arrogant best. These two alone caused enough problems for Leicester without taking their eight out-fieled team mates into consideration.

Leicester City by their own standards were disappointing, not having secured a victory since the semi-final helped little, but they should have picked up on the uncertainty of Gaskell in the United goal and had they done so, then they might have achieved more. They were also shorn of the creativity of the past, Sjoberg and Norman more than happy just to clear their lines than to look around for a possible attack-starting pass.

But Leicester plodded away as the red shirts swarmed across the green turf like bees seeking honey, and they were rewarded with a goal ten minutes from time. Gaskell was penalised for holding the ball for too long, and although the unnecessary free-kick was initially cleared, the ball found its way to McLintock, just outside the United penalty area. His shot for goal, rebounded off Setters, but he immediately returned it into the danger area where Keyworth flung himself forward to head into the bottom corner as Gaskell dived in vain.

Many could have been forgiven for thinking, here we go again, but the goal proved to be something of a wake-up call to United who had been looking more than content to simply play out the remainder of the ninety minutes with their slender advantage. The goal could also have revitalised Leicester, but coming to the conclusion that their early endeavour could prove to have been all for nothing, United decided on one final hurrah.

Charlton sent a raking pass through to Law on the right, the ball was then quickly diverted out to Herd on the left. Calmly, he lobbed it back into the middle of the Leicester penalty area where Law leaped like a salmon and headed the ball goalward. Banks, rooted to the spot, turned to his left, uncertain as to where the ball was going, but was relieved when it hit the post and rebounded into his arms. Law fell to the turf in despair.

Then with five minutes remaining, the destination of the F.A. Cup was put beyond doubt. A high cross from Giles saw Banks jump, but

**Noel Cantwell is presented with the FA Cup
by Her Majesty Queen Elizabeth II**

failing to grasp the ball, allowing it to fall to the feet of Herd who fired home. There was no way back for Leicester now.

"At last, we are back in the big-time" proclaimed a jubilant Matt Busby. "I had only one anxious moment. In the first ten minutes of the second-half I felt we were going away from it and Leicester coming in, but we regained our poise and there were no further worries.

"Our lads played really well and I thought Denis Law was magnificent. But it was a great team performance."

Unbeknown to many, Law played throughout the second half suffering from heat stroke and kept calling to the United bench for a wet sponge. "It was murderous out there" he was to say. "The heat was overpowering. I was completely whacked and thought I might pass out. That's why I kept douching my head and neck with cold water." When the final whistle went, Law was more than happy to simply receive his medal from the Queen, walk quietly round the pitch and disappear up the tunnel.

Of Law, United assistant manager Jimmy Murphy was to say: "You can have Pele – I will have him [Denis Law] every time.

"The £115,000 we paid for Law represents the biggest transfer fraud of all time. We paid farthings for a player who is the greatest I have ever seen; a player who can do the lot; a player who is a football team in himself."

Maurice Setters and United captain Noel Cantwell on the Cup winners' lap of honour following the victory over Leicester City

Peter Lorenzo, the 'Daily Herald' reporter who had back United to lift the F.A. Cup way back at the start of the season was to write: "At last the 'T' has fallen in the right place. Manchester UNTIED have become Manchester UNITED. Now I predict this big occasion team who came good so magnificently at Wembley will do well in the European Cup Winners Cup next season.

"They will do even better when Matt Busby, already the biggest spender in British Soccer, starts spending again."

He continued: "It would be stupid to ignore the obvious weaknesses in a side that touched wondrous heights in the 3-1 win against an incredibly listless Leicester team. If United are to seriously challenge Spurs, the European holders, and the formidable foes from overseas, Matt may have to splash out another £100,000.

"His top requirements, judged over the whole disappointing season, are a goalkeeper and a centre-forward. David Gaskell does not inspire confidence. David Herd, despite his two goals – his first in the Cup this season – lacks mobility and ball control to keep this potentially dynamic attack purring."

From a packed 100,000 Wembley, the scene swung to treble that amount on the streets of Manchester, with many of that 300,000 packed into Albert Square in front of the Town Hall. Four hundred were injured, around half of whom were children, as crash barriers were swept away as the crowds surged forward in a tidal wave of humanity. Warnings were given over loudspeakers as the open topped coach carrying the United players and officials slowly weaved its way towards the city centre.

The United party had left St Pancras Station in London that morning to the sound of the lady station announcer calling "three cheers for Manchester United", while the station master sported red and white flowers in his button-hole. No one denied Busby's team their accolades.

It had been a long, hard, often traumatic season, but it was not yet over, as United had further obligations to fill, a three-match tour in Italy. Most, if not all would have been more than happy to throw the boots into a cupboard and forget about the game for a couple of months, but it was the second week of June before they could finally relax, disappear on holiday and re-charge those batteries.

On that close-season tour, Juventus were beaten 1-0, AS Roma 3-2 and Livorno 2-0, a fitting end to a memorable season, one that could have been so, so different if it had not been for those momentous ten days in May.

CHAPTER SIX
THE UNITED PLAYERS AND SEASON STATS

This chapter records the playing careers of the Manchester United players who represented the club during the 1962-63 campaign in more detail, as well as what happened to them after leaving Old Trafford. We also run through the season team line-ups game by game with the match programme and attendance figures etc.

HARRY GREGG

Harry Gregg will be forever known as the hero of the Munich air disaster; but he was equally as brave as a goalkeeper and was one of the best to represent the club.

As a boy, he won five international caps with the Northern Ireland schoolboy side, before beginning his adult playing career with Claughey United, moving to Windsor Park Swifts, Linfield's reserve side, before joining Coleraine in May 1951.

Working as a joiner, he won an amateur cap against England in 1951-52 before signing professional forms at the age of nineteen, going on to represent the Irish League in March 1952.

Gregg left Coleraine for Doncaster Rovers on October 9th 1952, two days after the transfer was confirmed and he made his debut for them against Blackburn Rovers in January of the following year.

Like many debutants his name was not to appear in the match programme, the Doncaster issue for that January 24th fixture but nevertheless, he was to make an impression despite conceding three in a stirring 3-3 draw.

His displays caught the eye of Matt Busby, who was on the lookout for a commanding goalkeeper and he was signed from Doncaster Rovers for £23,500 in December 1957, making his debut against Leicester City at Old Trafford on December 21st.

Commanding he certainly was, the Northern Ireland international ruling his penalty area with an iron fist, giving the team a renewed confidence as they attempted to conquer both domestically and in Europe.

His deeds in the immediate aftermath of the Munich disaster are well documented, but in truth caused the heroic goalkeeper considerable embarrassment, as he was unable to face the relatives of the team mates who died for some considerable time.

Harry Gregg was monumental in the team rebuilding following the crash, but could do little to prevent the FA Cup Final defeat by Bolton three months later, where he was once again thrust into the spotlight being unceremoniously bundled into the back of the net by Bolton's Nat Lofthouse for their second goal.

But despite what he had gone through on that dismal Thursday afternoon in Munich in February 1958, he was back to his best between the sticks, being voted the best goalkeeper in the 1958 World Cup Finals in Sweden.

Although he was to win twenty-five caps for his country, domestic honours were to pass him by, due to injuries more than anything else, missing out on the 1963 FA Cup win and the 1964-65 league championship and upon the arrival of Alex Stepney in 1967, he decided that at thirty-four, he should move on and joined Stoke City.

He was to retire from playing at the end of the 1966-67 season.

Remaining in the game, he took over the managerial position with Shrewsbury Town in 1968, where a young Jim Holton came under his supervision. Remaining with Shrewsbury until November 1972 when he moved to Swansea City, resigning three years later to join Crewe Alexandra.

His time at Crewe came to an end in 1978 and his next port of call was back at Old Trafford as a goalkeeping coach under Dave Sexton, playing a huge part in bringing a young Gary Bailey up to first team standard.

When Sexton departed Old Trafford in 1981 so did Harry Gregg, taking up an assistant manager role under Lou Macari at Stoke City, but he was sacked with the former United player in April 1985, following a disagreement.

He then moved to Carlisle United, again as assistant manager, this time under Bob Stokoe, but stepped into the manager's chair during the 1986-87 season, but left following relegation to the Fourth Division at the end of that season.

May 2012 saw United travel to Ireland to play an Irish League Select XI in a testimonial for the hero of Munich, a more than well-deserved honour.

The name of Harry Gregg will always be remembered by Manchester United supporters, particularly those of a certain age, and it was with great sadness that they learned of the passing of the heroic goalkeeper on February 16th 2020.

DAVID GASKELL

David Gaskell was signed by Manchester United in 1956 from youth side Orrell St Luke's, having represented England at both schoolboy and youth level, having also represented Wigan and Lancashire Schoolboys.

Unlike many, he did not have to take the long journey through the United youth, 'A', 'B' and reserve sides before making his first team debut, as he received an unexpected call-up in the F.A. Charity Shield fixture against Manchester City at Maine Road in August 1956.

He had gone to simply watch the game from the stand, but following an injury to Ray Wood, a United official recalled seeing him entering the ground and he was sought out and sent on to replace temporary 'keeper Duncan Edwards between the sticks. Such was his performance, that many watching the game simply thought that Wood had returned to the fray.

His full debut did not come until fifteen months later, against Tottenham Hotspur on November 30th 1957.

Signing professional forms in 1957, he missed out on England under 23 honours through injury, and they continued to hamper his United career, but following the F.A. Cup Final against Leicester City he eventually represented England at that level during an end of season tour.

He was to constantly find himself in and out of the side, replaced first by Pat Dunne and then by Alex Stepney and in August 1967 there was talk of joining Leicester City, but the move fell through, as did one to play in America.

In 1967, he turned to playing rugby for a team in Wigan where he had business interests and he was given a free transfer by United in April 1967.

He joined non-league Wigan Athletic during 1968-69, making over three dozen appearances before returning to the Football League with Wrexham prior to the 1969-70 season.

Having failed to make a league appearance during the 1972-73 season, he was given a free transfer in May 1973 and had a brief spell in South African football before retiring.

BILL FOULKES

A former miner and no-nonsense defender who joined the club in March 1950 from Whiston Boys Club.

As a young professional, he continued to play on a part time basis, working down the mine during the day and training at night, continuing to do so following his first team debut against Liverpool at Anfield in December 1952. But after breaking into the side on a regular basis in September 1953, he decided to give up his day job and concentrate on his footballing career.

It proved to be a wise move, as bar three months out of the side in 1956, he remained a first-choice defender, either at full back or centre-half, until the late 1960's, winning one England cap in 1955, along with under 23 and Football League honours.

At club level he was to win four league championship medals, an FA Cup winner's medal, three FA Charity Shield plaques and a European Cup winner's medal in 1968. He was also to appear in two losing FA Cup Finals in 1957 and 1958.

Surviving the Munich disaster, he was appointed captain of the rebuilt side and continued to hold that role until he felt the pressure was becoming too much for him.

Undoubtedly, his finest hour in the red shirt came on May 15th 1968 in Madrid, when he abandoned his defensive duties as United, 3-2 down on aggregate against Real Madrid, fought to salvage their European Cup semi-final second leg tie. Meandering up field, he was to score a rare goal which took United into the Final and the fulfilment of so many dreams and on an emotional night at Wembley in the resulting final, he played his part in the historic 4-1 win over Benfica.

Towards the end of the sixties, however, age was beginning to tell and following a 4-1 defeat against Southampton in August 1969, he decided that he had played the last of his 688 games for the club and took up a role as youth coach. He was later to take on coaching and managerial roles in America with Chicago Sting, Tulsa Roughnecks and San Jose Earthquakes, in Norway with Stenjker, Lillestrom and Viking Stavanger, in Japan with Mazda and at home with Witney Town.

JIMMY NICHOLSON

Discovered by United scout Bob Harpur, whilst playing for Boyland Youth, the Northern Ireland schoolboy internationalist, and captain of the All-Ireland schoolboy side, joined United on amateur forms in May 1958 and before he had turned 16 had won Irish youth and under 23 caps.

Progressing through the United junior ranks, he made his first team debut on August 24th 1960 against Everton at Goodison Park., six months after signing professional and by the end of that 1960-61 season the talented half-back had made his full Northern Ireland international debut, going on to win fifty-one caps for his country.

Competition for places in the United side of the period was fierce, having to compete with the likes of Setters, Stiles and Lawton, injuries also causing more than a few problems, but it was the signing of Pat Crerand, that finally saw his first team appearances limited and in December 1964, he reluctantly left Manchester United and joined Huddersfield Town for something of a bargain fee of only £7,500.

An own goal on his Town debut was not the best of starts, but over a period of nine years, Jimmy Nicholson was to make over four hundred appearances for the Leeds Road side and in season 1969-70, as club captain, he played a major part in guiding Huddersfield to the Second Division Championship.

A knee injury curtailed his appearances and he moved to Bury in December 1973, where he spent two and a half years, helping the Gigg Lane side to promotion from the Fourth Division.

He was to see out his playing career at non-league level with Mossley and Stalybridge.

IAN MOIR

Ian Moir had been expected to sign for this home-town club Aberdeen, having trained with them in their Wednesday evening coaching schools, whilst also playing as a junior with a local Aberdeen Youth

League side Powis whilst also turning out for South United. But it was to be the red of Manchester United that he was to wear instead, having been seduced by the Old Trafford set-up and by Matt Busby who he considered "was like a father to all the youngsters" during a three-week trial. when he went south in October 1958.

Upon signing amateur forms for United as a 15-year-old in November 1958, he made rapid progress through the junior ranks, turning professional two years later in June 1960 and was soon producing some notable per-formances in the Central League side.

A rather indifferent start to United's1960-61 First Division forced Matt Busby to ring the changes for the trip to Bolton on October 1st, with Moir making a favourable debut in the 1-1 draw. But it wasn't until the final weeks of the 1960-61 season that the slimly built young-ster was to enjoy an extended first team run, playing in seven of the final twelve fixtures, scoring his first senior goal in the 1-1 home draw with Arsenal.

Season 1962-63 began favourably for him, but, like others in that strange season, he was to fall by the wayside, particularly after the return of Bobby Charlton who claimed his favoured number eleven shirt.

With the emergence of a certain George Best and the tendency of Busby to reshuffle the forward line, he more often than not found himself in and out of the first team picture and with the signing of John Connelly from Burnley in 1964, he was transferred to Blackpool for a fee of £30,000.

Following the Bloomfield Road sides relegation in 1966-67 he moved to Chester for a fee of £10,000 in May 1967 and a year later joined Wrexham for the first of two spells, a year with Shrewsbury sandwiched in between.

A brief sojourn in South Africa upon leaving Wrexham in 1975 was to bring down the curtain on his playing career.

NOBBY STILES

Once seen, never forgotten, could quite easily be a tag-line for Nobby Stiles, both on and off the pitch. Diminutive in stature, but what he lacked in inches he certainly made up for in grit and determination

as countless opponents will confirm, while away for the game, the bespectacled half-back looked more like an office manager or school teacher than an aggressive football-ing predator.

Collyhurst born and despite being on the small side, he captained Manchester Boys in 1956-57, stepping up into the Eng-land Schools side the following season, going on to win five caps at that level. His performances were noticed by numerous clubs, but any approaches were to little avail, as Nobby was a United supporter, idolising Eddie Colman, and once there was interest from Old Trafford, his football-ing destination was decided, joining the Old Trafford ground staff in September 1957.

In his early days at the club, often flitting between half-back and inside-forward, it was noticed that his tackles were often miss-timed, so Matt Busby sent him to an eye specialist, where it was found that an incident with a trolley bus some years previously had left him with impaired vision. Contact lenses immediately improving his game, although some might argue that his tackling was never to improve.

Having captained the United youth team, he made first team appearances in friendlies before his league debut at Bolton on Octo-ber 1st 1960. He made a big impact on the team, with his dislike of losing and his tough and aggressive approach to the game, but he was to be severely disappointed towards the end of the 1962-63 season, as having made thirty-one league appearances, he was omitted from United's cup final line up due to having picked up an injury prior to the Wembley show-piece.

Regaining his place the following season, he was soon knocking on the England international door, winning his first cap in 1965 and a year later he was dancing around Wembley holding aloft the World Cup, compensation indeed for missing out on United's visit in 1963.

League championship honours and the ultimate club success of the European Cup were also to come his way, but in the summer of 1971, he felt that the time was right to leave Old Trafford and he joined Mid-dlesbrough for £20,000.

Two years later, he could be found at Preston North End alongside Bobby Charlton, later taking on a coaching/assistant managers role before becoming manager. Leaving Preston in June 1981 he took up a coaching role with Vancouver Whitecaps alongside his brother-in-law Johnny Giles before returning to England to become assistant manager at West Bromwich Albion, again alongside Giles, becoming manager in his own right between October 1985 and February 1986.

He was later to return to United in a coaching capacity between 1989 and 1993, playing his part in the development of the likes of Giggs, Beckham, Scholes and the Neville's. Awarded an MBE in 2000, he passed away in October 2020.

DENNIS WALKER

One meagre First Division appearance was all Dennis Walker could manage in a Manchester United career that spanned almost four years.

A former captain of the Cheshire Schoolboy side and a trialist with the England Schools side, he joined the Old Trafford ground staff in March 1960 as an apprentice, signing professional forms just over two years later.

Beginning the season playing for United's 'A' team in the Lancashire League, he was given a taste of first team football against Bolton Wanderers in Cork and ended that 1962-63 season making his first team debut against Nottingham Forest in the final league match of the campaign.

Although he spent his early days as a half-back, he played mainly as an outside left in the Central League side and it was in that position, he was to make his debut. Had his stuck to that original position it is doubtful that his United career would have taken a different course and due to the experienced players holding both positions and the talent coming through the ranks, he left United and joined York City in April 1964, returning to his more natural half-back position and helping them to promotion from the Third Division and scoring twelve goals in his first fourteen games.

Two successive relegations followed and he was transferred to Cambridge United in the summer of 1968. At Cambridge, he was a member of the team that progressed from the Southern League to the Fourth Division in 1970. He was to spend the latter years of his career with Poole Town.

FRANK HAYDOCK

Although playing with Eccles and District Schools, it was with Blackpool that Frank Haydock took his first steps on the senior footballing ladder, joining the Seasiders as an amateur in June 1956. But a year later, he moved to United, again as an amateur, signing professional forms in December 1959.

Less than a year later, he was making his first team debut against Blackburn Rovers at Old Trafford on August 20th 1960, but despite having shown promise in the United Central League side, he found it difficult to dislodge Bill Foulkes from the centre-half spot and was to make only six appearances before joining Charlton Athletic in August 1963 for £10,000. Other clubs had shown an interest in taking him away from Old Trafford on numerous occasions previously, but United were always against letting him go.

December 1965 saw him on the move again, having made over eighty appearances for Charlton, joining Portsmouth, where he made over seventy appearances before signing for Southend United, his final League club.

Upon retiring he moved into the hotel business in Blackpool and could often be found playing in charity games against show biz XI's.

TONY DUNNE

A £5,000 fee took Tony Dunne from Shelbourne to United in April 1960, going on to give the club twelve years' service of consistency at the highest level, making him a candidate for any All-Time Great United XI.

Tony Dunne began his playing career in Dublin with local youth side Stella Maris before stepping into the senior game with Shelbourne in 1958. With Shelbourne he was to win the FAI Cup in 1960, but at that point he was already a Manchester United player.

He made his United debut against a matter of weeks after signing, coming on as substitute for Shay Brennan against Real Madrid, with his league debut coming against Burnley at Turf Moor on October 15th 1960.

An injury to Noel Cantwell in November 1961 saw him claim a regular place and except for missing a dozen or so games in the middle of the 1962-63 season, he was an automatic choice until 1973, switching between the two full back positions with ease.

Such were his performances for United, that he was soon to win international recognition, making his Republic of Ireland debut against Austria in April 1962, the first of thirty-three caps, having already represented his country at amateur level.

He was to win an FA Cup winners medal in 1963, League Championship medals in 1965 and 1967 and of course a European Cup winners medal in 1968. He was also voted Irish Footballer of the Year in 1969.

With United struggling during season 1972-73, he continued to give his usual 100% effort and commitment and it was to come as something of a shock when he was given a free transfer by Tommy Docherty in April 1973, especially when his experience would have been most beneficial to a struggling side.

Moving to Bolton Wanderers, Tony Dunne maintained his high standard of play in the Second Division as the Burnden Park side strode towards the Championship, as United were relegated.

Despite having left Old Trafford, he was awarded a testimonial match, against Manchester City, for his services to the club and a crowd of 17,859 turned up to show their gratitude and earn Dunne around £12,000. Tony Dunne was to remain at Bolton for six years, adding almost another 200 appearances to his career total.

In 1979, with his career drawing to a close, he moved to the States and joined Detroit Express before returning to Bolton to take up the role of assistant manager, going on to replace former United team mate Bill Foulkes as manager of Norwegian club Steinkjer for the 1982-83 season. Upon returning to Manchester became manager of a golf driving range in Altrincham.

SAMMY McMILLAN

Sammy McMillan was signed by Manchester United, as a sixteen-year-old amateur, in 1957, signing professional two years later. For the highly talented youngster, progress was swift, although at one point he considered walking away from the game and returning home. But he persevered and on November 4th 1961, he made his first team debut, playing outside left against Sheffield Wednesday away.

As Busby juggled his side in pursuit of a winning formula, McMillan also played in the following two games, scoring in the second

of those against, a 4-1 defeat at Ipswich Town. Back in the reserves despite his goal, McMillan continued to develop and towards the end of that season, re-appeared to play in eight of the final nine fixtures, during which time he scored five goals, with doubles against Leicester City and Sheffield United.

So many promising youngsters were around Old Trafford at this time, providing stiff competition for a first team place, there was little hope for Sammy McMillan securing a regular place in the side. His performances in the Central League did not, however, go unnoticed as he was given his international debut at the age of twenty-one, against England, at centre forward, a position completely alien to him, on 20 October 1962. A further cap against Scotland followed.

With first team opportunities obviously restricted, the possibilities of a move to Wrexham materialised and after some consideration, he decided to take the gamble, moving to the Welsh side on Christmas Eve 1963, for a fee of £8,000.

1967 saw him move to Southend United for a fee of £6,000, where he took on more of a mid-field role and two seasons later, he could be found with Chester, before seeing out his playing career with Stockport County and Owestry Town, where a back injury forced him to retire in 1972.

MARK PEARSON

Played for Derbyshire and England Boys before joining United straight from school in 1955, progressing into the United and England youth set up before turning professional in 1957.

His United debut was to come sooner than expected being called into the makeshift side to face Sheffield Wednesday in the F.A. Cup on February 19th 1958 in the aftermath of the Munich disaster.

A regular place was not something that he could tie down and he was to come in for some criticism for his rugged style of play, something that was often was put down more to his inexperience, as he did show that he had the makings of a good player and always made the most of the opportunities that he was given.

Those opportunities, however, soon became less frequent and he decided that a move was perhaps best and joined Sheffield Wednesday in October 1963 for a fee of £20,000.

After two years at Hillsborough, he was on the move again, joining Fulham, before finishing his league career at Halifax Town in 1968-69. He was later to be found in the non-league set-up with Bacup Borough.

ALBERT QUIXALL

Albert Quixall's footballing life began on the ground staff of Sheffield Wednesday, with the former England schoolboy making his debut for the Owls as a 17-year-old in February 1951. Within two years, following a dazzling display in an inter-league match, he was making his full England debut against Wales and in 1955-56 played a leading role in Wednesday's Second Division title triumph.

Somewhat strangely, his fifth international cap was to be his last, despite being only twenty-one.

Christened the 'Golden Boy of English Football' by the press, his ball-playing skills won him many admirers and in September 1958, seven months after he had captained Sheffield Wednesday against United at Old Trafford, in that memorable first game after Munich, Matt Busby paid what was then a record fee of £45,000 for his signature as he set about re-building his decimated team. Many of those who had perished at Munich were close friends of Quixall and it was thought that this was partly behind his decision to leave Sheffield Wednesday.

Following his move across the Pennines, he took a little while to settle despite a favourable debut against Tottenham Hotspur at Old Trafford on September 20th 1958, but he was soon turned in consistent performances up until 1961-62.

The 1962-63 season started badly for the talented inside-forward and at one point it looked as though he might leave Old Trafford for pastures new, but he soon regained his form with his goals proving important in the fight against relegation, scoring from the penalty spot in that all important game at Maine Road, while he was also to play his part in the 1963 FA Cup win.

An intelligent, creative inside forward, but could sometimes struggle to get into games, he once again found himself out of favour in 1963-64 and in September 1964 he was transferred to Third Division Oldham Athletic for £7,000.

Two years later he moved to Stockport County and later played at non-league level with Altrincham and Radcliffe Borough.

DAVID HERD

In the lower regions of non-league and amateur football, it is not unusual for father and son to line up alongside each other, but in the world of the professional game, it is certainly something of an irregular occurrence. But, on the final day of season 1950-51, Alec Herd (aged 39) and his seventeen-year-old son David, filled the inside forward positions for Stockport County in their home fixture against Hartlepool United, with the youngster marking his league debut with a goal.

A fee of £10,000 took him to Arsenal in August 1954 and he soon began scoring freely for the Londoners, finishing top scorer in 1958-59, 59-60 and 60-61, before joining United in the summer of 1961 for £35,000.

It had taken Busby a while to get his man, as previous approaches to Arsenal had failed, but once at Old Trafford, the Scottish international soon formed a fine partnership with Denis Law and on November 26th 1966, against Sunderland, he had the distinction of scoring against three different goalkeepers.

Season 1966-67 saw him score his 100th United goal, but later that season, a broken leg against Leicester City effectively brought an end to his Old Trafford career and in the close season of 1967-68 he joined Stoke City. He later played for Waterford in the Republic of Ireland before having a stint as manager of Lincoln City between March 1971 and December 1972.

David Herd was a typical old-school centre-forward, although he contributed as much to United's sixties success through giving more than able assistance to the 'Trinity', and the others, as he did through scoring goals.

SHAY BRENNAN

Brought up in Wythenshawe, South Manchester, Shay Brennan, upon leaving St John's school, began a joinery apprenticeship whilst at the same time played as an inside forward for the St John's Old Boys' team in the South Manchester and Wythenshawe League.

An eye-catching performance for a League representative XI against the Manchester Catholic League, caught the attention of both United and City scouts, but it was the representatives from the Maine Road club who were first to appear on the Brennan doorstep. Despite the offer of a place on the Manchester City ground staff, the United supporting youngster decided against signing, in the hope that a similar offer would come from United. A couple of days later, much to his relief, it did.

Signing for Manchester United in April 1955, Shay Brennan progressed through the lower levels of club football in the illustrious company of Duncan Edwards, Eddie Colman, Bobby Charlton and Wilf McGuinness, playing centre forward in the team that won the F. A. Youth Cup in season 1954-55.

At the time of the Munich Air Disaster, he was a nondescript third team player and during the afternoon prior to that memorable Sheffield Wednesday cup tie, he played table tennis with friends, completely unaware of Jimmy Murphy's plans to include him in the United starting line-up. "You play on the left wing", he was later to hear the genial Welshman say to his complete and utter disbelief.

"I had not appeared before a crowd of more than 20,000 before then" Shay later recalled, "and that was when I was a member of the United team which won the F. A. Youth Cup a few years earlier". Not only that, I had never played at Old Trafford before".

After the match, Shay was to say, "The two goals I scored in the 3-0 victory are forever etched in my memory. I scored the first direct from a corner kick, a rather lucky affair, as these shots invariably are.

"I tried for an in-swinger by hitting the flag kick with my right foot. The ball swung in beautifully under the floodlights and was suddenly wafted even further towards goal by a gust of wind and curled over the goalkeeper's head into the net.

"In the second half, the ball came through from our defence to Mark Pearson, who switched it quickly to me. I tried a shot, the ball rebounded off a defender and at the second attempt, I rammed it into the Wednesday net for number two."

In 1962, he was named in England's pool of forty for the 1962 World Cup, following two appearances for a F.A. XI. However, he failed to make the final squad, but three years later, he became the first player to be capped by the Republic of Ireland under the parentage ruling.

By the late sixties, Brennan's United first team League appearances were becoming fewer, with only sixteen in the Championship winning season of 1966-67 and thirteen in 1967-68. The European Cup run of that latter season saw him make only three appearances, which fortunately for him included the semi-finals and Final.

Following that European Cup win, his career was on a downward slope, with only thirteen starts made during 1968-69 and eight the following year.

At the end of 1969-70, he was given a free transfer by the club and upon Matt Busby's suggestion, became player-manager of League of Ireland side Waterford.

During season 1970-71, he was awarded a life pension by Manchester United for his loyal years of service and in August 1986, his former club played a Shamrock Rovers XI in a specially arranged testimonial match for him.

A place in either of the full back positions in the United All Time Great XI would unfortunately pass Shay Brennan by, but you would be hard pushed to find a more popular player at Manchester United during his time at the club.

NOEL CANTWELL

Noel Cantwell left the Republic of Ireland as a 20-year-old in 1952, joining West Ham United, stepping up from the juniors to the first team in his first season with remarkable ease. A year later, he was winning the first of his thirty-six Republic of Ireland international caps, against Luxembourg.

Season 1957-58 saw the Hammers lift the Second Division title and on a bigger stage, Cantwell's performances soon caught the attention of, Matt Busby, who was still in the process of team building following the Munich disaster, with the United manager paying £29,500 to prise him away from London's East End in November 1960.

He was quick to settle in the north of England and his arrival helped to strengthen the United defence that was in much need of some stability and following his United debut in a friendly against Bayern Munich on 21 November, he took over the left back position for the trip to Cardiff five days later. His presence doing little to prevent a 3-0 defeat at the hands of the Welshmen. Results, however, quickly improved with Cantwell becoming a rock in the sometimes frail defence.

After missing a few games through injury in early 1961-62, he returned to the side, but rather surprisingly at centre-forward, although the international footballer and cricketer soon showed his versatility by notching a couple of goals.

Appointed captain in 1962-63, and despite the continuing poor form at First Division level, United strode towards Wembley and the FA Cup Final, with Cantwell lifting the trophy following the 3-1 victory over Leicester City.

In January 1963, however, he lost his place in the starting line up to Tony Dunne, who was switched from right to left back and from then until April 1965, he was to make only four First Division appearances, with two of those coming at centre forward, scoring once.

Season 1965-66 added a further twenty-three League starts to his list of appearances, but by the start of the following season, it became obvious that his days at Old Trafford were numbered and despite not being a regular first team player, he could be depended upon when he was called into the side, but with those first team appearances few and far between he decided to hang up his boots early in season 1967-68, relinquish his position as Chairman of the PFA and take up the post of manager with Coventry City, whilst holding a similar post with the Republic of Ireland.

Leaving Coventry City in October 1972, he managed Peterborough United before going Stateside, returning to Peterborough in December 1986 as manager, before becoming the club's general manager.

BOBBY CHARLTON

Bobby Charlton is a name synonymous with that of Manchester United and his is a name known world-wide despite having hung up his boots more than four decades ago.

Born into a footballing family, with both uncles and brother involved in the game, he left his Ashington home upon leaving school in 1953, having won England schoolboy honours, moving to Manchester to join United, signing professional forms two years later, springing into

prominence with three United Youth Cup winning teams before making his debut against Charlton Athletic in October 1956, scoring twice in the 4-2 win. It was the beginning of a playing career that would span all corners of the world, lifting countless personal and team honours with both United and England.

Despite not commanding a regular place in that 196-57 season, he made enough appearances to claim a championship medal and ending that first season with an appearance in the FA Cup final, finishing on the losing side against Aston Villa.

Still not a regular the following season, he was, however, on that fateful trip to Belgrade, but escaped the carnage at Munich, returning to the fray a few weeks later, before winning his first full England cap in April 1958, scoring against Scotland at Hampden.

He kicked off the first post-Munich season with a hat-trick against Chelsea, scoring nine in the first seven games, finishing the season with twenty-nine, maintaining an excellent scoring rate throughout the sixties, whilst playing mainly at outside left, having moved wide from inside forward, as United won the league twice and the FA Cup once.

Sandwiched in between the two league titles in 1965 and 1967, he was named as Footballer of the Year and European Footballer of the Year in 1966, a year that saw him share in the success of England's World Cup triumph.

As the decade approached its end, Charlton was now captain of his beloved United, playing a more central role, but there was still one trophy that eluded him and his manager Matt Busby. A 4-3 aggregate win over Real Madrid in the 1968 European Cup semi-final took United to within 90 minutes from lifting the sought-after trophy.

Those 90 minutes were to stretch to 120, but on an emotional May night at Wembley, having scored United's first and fourth goals, he was to lift the European Cup high above his head after United had defeated Benfica 4-1.

The following year he was awarded the OBE for his services to football, winning his 100th cap against Northern Ireland at Wembley in April 1970, marking the occasion with his 48th England goal. Earning his 106th cap during the 1970 Mexico World Cup, he decided to call time on his international career following England's quarter final defeat by West Germany.

Awarded a testimonial by United in September 1972, during a season that also saw him set club record of 564 league appearances, he announced his retirement, bowing out against Verona in an Anglo-Italian Cup tie on 2 May 1973, having amassed an overall total of 758 appearances, scoring 249 goals. The former remaining unbroken until 2008, when Ryan Giggs brushed it aside.

Upon leaving United, he managed, and came out of retirement to play for Preston North End, finally hanging up his boots following three games with Waterford in the Republic of Ireland.

A spell as director and caretaker manager of Wigan Athletic in the early '80's preceded his return to Old Trafford as a director.

Awarded a knighthood in 1994, having added a CBE to his earlier OBE, Bobby Charlton was still a familiar face at Old Trafford and beyond prior to illness in 2020, but remained one of the most respected individuals in not simply British, but World football.

PHIL CHISNALL

Former Stretford and Lancashire Schools and England schoolboy international Phil Chisnall joined United as a 15-year-old amateur straight from school, progressing through the ranks and making his first team debut in December 1961 against Everton at Goodison Park. He was to score his first goal eight games later in a 2-0 win over Manchester City at Maine Road.

A run of sixteen games at the start of season 1963-64 earned him a place in the England under 23 side, but with Graham Moore joining United, he was to make only a further four appearances before moving to Liverpool in April 1964 for around £30,000.

At Anfield, things didn't go as planned and he was to make only eight appearances before moving to Southend United in 1967. He later played for Stockport County prior to retirement.

PAT CRERAND

The signing of Pat Crerand was what could be described by the well-used clique, 'the last piece of the jigsaw', as Busby completed his rebuilding programme following the demise of his team at Munich.

Born in the east end of Glasgow, Crerand joined his beloved Celtic from Duntocher Hiberian in August 1957.

The old adage of 'practise makes perfection' was particularly true in the case of the young Celtic player, as it was not an uncommon sight at Celtic Park to see Crerand attempting to knock over traffic cones from various distances, often seventy to eighty yards, as he honed up on his passing skills. He was soon to develop into one of the best half backs in Scotland after making his debut in the green and white hoops on October 4th 1958 in a First Division fixture against Queen of the South at Celtic Park.

As well as skilful, Crerand also possessed a fiery streak, which was seen in a half time flare up with trainer Sean Fallon, during a game with rivals Rangers, a confrontation that was to shorten the Scottish internationalists time at Parkhead. Two weeks later, he was trying on the red and white jersey of Manchester United for size, with Matt Busby quickly agreeing to pay a sum of £56,000 for the talented wing half.

With Britain under a blanket of snow and ice for weeks on end, Crerand's Manchester United debut came in a friendly against Bolton Wanderers in Cork, on February 13th 1963, with his talent clearly visible despite playing on a mud-covered pitch. His League debut coming ten days later at Blackpool.

His Scotland career, having won sixteen full caps, came to an end in 1966, following various confrontations with the Scottish selectors, but his country's loss was clearly United's gain, as he added League Championship and European Cup winners medals, in 1965, 1967 and 1968, to the F.A. Cup one of 1963. "When Crerand played well, United played well" soon became a common saying. Something that George Best was to back up when he said, "Paddy made the team tick, he always gave United the edge when it mattered".

As the League appearances became fewer at the beginning of the seventies, more time was taken up coaching the younger players at Old Trafford and he was eventually appointed reserve team manager.

With the appointment of Tommy Docherty as manager, Pat Crerand was appointed his assistant, but the relationship soured, with Crerand's position demeaned to watching United's next opponents.

Fed up with the non-day to day involvement, he quickly grasped the opportunity to become manager at Northampton Town in January 1976, quitting his £8,500 a year job with United. In later years he could still be found at Old Trafford, working for the club's MUTV channel.

DENIS LAW

In the 1990's, a Frenchman arrived at Old Trafford in a surprise transfer. The enigmatic talisman was soon to be hailed as 'the King' by countless adoring fans, but for those who had stood on the Old Trafford terraces during the sixties, he was but a mere pretender to the throne, as there was only, and would ever be, one 'King of Old Trafford'. His name was Denis Law.

If there was ever an unlikely looking footballer as a youngster, then it was the skinny, bespectacled, 5' 3" Aberdonian, but despite his physical appearance, Law had an inbuilt talent as a footballer and Archie Beattie, a scout with Huddersfield Town noted that special something and quickly recommended him to his brother Andy, then manager with the Yorkshire side. Impressing in a trial, Denis was signed on amateur forms in April 1955, earning £5 per week, with half of that going on food and rent.

Twenty months later, on December 24th 1956, he made his Huddersfield debut against Notts County, having a quiet game by his standards, but he now had one foot on the ladder and there was only one way he wanted to go.

Having gained Scotland international recognition, winning his first cap in October 1958, with the Scottish international manager, Matt Busby, already having tried to lure him to Old Trafford, he was soon the centre of attention and on March 15th 1960, Manchester City paid a record fee of £55,000 for his signature.

His performances at Maine Road, like they had been at Huddersfield, attracted much interest and with City constantly struggling, bigger club's felt that he could be easily prized away.

The inevitable happened in the summer of 1961 when Torino made City an unrefusable offer of £100,000 and he became the first in Britain to be transferred for a six-figure fee.

Life in Italy was far from enjoyable, with much controversy and near death in a car crash, so when there was a hint of interest from United, he was keen to return home.

Re-united with his former Scotland boss, Matt Busby having paid a British record fee of £115,000 to bring him home, he re-repaid the outlay with interest.

Scoring on his debut against West Bromwich Albion, the honours flowed like the goals, playing a major part in the 1963 FA Cup success, the club captaincy, European Footballer of the Year and two League championship medals in 1965 and 1967. But it was not all roses, as his fiery Scottish temperament, sometimes as quick as his lightening goal scoring reflexes, often had him in trouble with officials, bringing three lengthy suspensions between 1963 and 1967.

His daredevil performances also brought injuries and it was a knee injury that robbed him of an appearance in the 1968 European Cup Final.

Law bounced back, but by the beginning of the seventies, Manchester United were not the team who had taken the previous decade by storm as they were now on a downward slide.

Now in his thirties, Denis still had much to offer, but with the arrival of Tommy Docherty, his days as a Manchester United player were now numbered. On April 7th 1973, unbeknown to the 48,593 supporters inside Old Trafford for the match against Norwich City, they were watching his last match in the red of United.

At the end of that season, Docherty gave Law a free transfer, amid much controversy, and he returned to Maine Road for the start of the 1973-74 campaign, climaxing in what was to be a dramatic swansong.

Returning to Old Trafford to face a relegation threatened United, he scored the only goal of a game which came to a premature endue to a pitch invasion. Denis was to leave the pitch almost immediately after scoring. Despite what many believe, it was't the goal that relegated United.

In February 2002 he unveiled a 10' high bronze statue of himself under the Stretford End and six years later, in May 2008, he was immortalised again along with Best and Charlton on the Old Trafford forecourt.

NOBBY LAWTON

A product of Manchester and Lancashire Schools football, who joined the ground staff in 1956, turning professional in April 1958.

He made his debut against Luton Town two years later in April 1960, with his early appearances mostly at half-back, but was later also to appear as an inside forward.

Dropping out of the first team picture in 1962-63, following the signing of Pat Crerand, he joined Preston North End in March 1963 for a fee of around £22,000. Still only twenty-three, he found things more relaxed and began to enjoy his football more and captained the Preston side in the 1964 F.A. Cup Final against West Ham United.

1967 saw him move to Brighton and Hove Albion, as he was beginning to find the rigours of Second Division too much and he spent three seasons on the south coast before joining Lincoln City in 1971, where he spent a season and a half before retiring due to a knee injury.

MAURICE SETTERS

An outstanding, robust, hard tackling half-back who signed for his local league club Exeter City, after winning England schools honours, making his league debut in 1954. Eleven games and two seasons later, he joined West Bromwich Albion for £3,000 in January 1955 where he was to gain Army and England under 23 honours, representing the latter some sixteen times. Although playing mainly at half-back, he could also play a more defensive role, turning in some good performances at full-back prior to joining United in January 1960 for a fee of £30,000.

Setters added a physical side to United's game, captaining the side on occasions and leading by example with his no-frills, uncompromising play, as Matt Busby continued his re-building work following Munich.

Like many during that 1962-6 season, with United's performances considered inconsistent at best, he found himself in and out of the side, but managed to secure a place in the side for the 1963 F.A. Cup Final success.

In 1964, Setters lost his number six shirt to Nobby Stiles and with his days at Old Trafford now numbered, although still having much to offer, Stoke City paid United £30,000 in November 1964 for his signature.

At Stoke, he soon became a firm favourite, as he was at his next club, Coventry City, who he joined in November 1967. Three years later, he was with Charlton Athletic, before moving into management with Doncaster Rovers which was followed by various positions with Sheffield Wednesday, Rotherham united and Newcastle United, before becoming Jack Charlton's right-hand man with the Republic of Ireland.

JOHNNY GILES

A Republic of Ireland Schoolboy international who joined United from Home Farm in July 1956, making his debut three years later against

Tottenham Hotspur on September 12th 1959 gaining full international honours that same season.

He began as an inside-forward, but was moved to the wing with considerable success until suffering a broken leg during 1960-61. He soon recovered, going on to win an FA Cup medal in 1963, but was surprisingly allowed to leave the club in August of that year, joining Leeds United for £37,500. A transfer that was considered a huge mistake.

This was probably proved correct as Giles continued to flourish at Elland Road, playing a huge part in the Elland Road clubs success in the sixties and going on to appear in five F.A. Cup Finals.

Having played over 600 games for Leeds he joined West Bromwich Albion, first as player-manager, guiding them back to the First Division, whilst holding a similar position with the Republic of Ireland. He then went on to manage Shamrock Rovers, Philadelphia Fury and Vancouver Whitecaps before returning to West Bromwich Albion.

8TH AUGUST 1962 -
HAMPDEN PARK –
FRIENDLY – 80,000
GLASGOW SELECT 2 MANCHESTER UNITED 4
UNITED – GASKELL, BRENNAN, DUNNE, STILES,
FOULKES, SETTERS, GILES, QUIXALL, HERD, LAW,
MOIR
SCORERS - MOIR 2, SETTERS, HERD.
GLASGOW SELECT – NIVEN, MACKAY, CALDOW,
CRERAND, MCNEILL, BAXTER, HENDERSON,
MCMILLAN, HUGHES, DIVERS, WILSON.
SCORERS - DIVERS, MCMILLAN.

18TH AUGUST 1962 - OLD TRAFFORD –
DIV. 1 - 51,685
**MANCHESTER UNITED 2 WEST BROMWICH
ALBION 2**
UNITED – GASKELL, BRENNAN, DUNNE, STILES,
FOULKES, SETTERS, GILES, QUIXALL, HERD, LAW,
MOIR.
SCORERS – HERD, LAW.
WEST BROMWICH ALBION – MILLINGTON,
HOWE, G. WILLIAMS, S. WILLIAMS, JONES, DURY,
JACKSON, BURNSIDE, SMITH, KEVAN, CLARKE.
SCORERS – KEVAN, SMITH.

2ND AUGUST 1962 - GOODISON PARK –
DIV. 1 - 69,501
EVERTON 3 MANCHESTER UNITED 1
UNITED – GASKELL, BRENNAN, DUNNE, STILES,
FOULKES, SETTERS, GILES, PEARSON, HERD, LAW,
MOIR.
SCORER - MOIR
EVERTON – WEST, PARKER, THOMSON, GABRIEL,
LABONE, HARRIS, STEVENS, BINGHAM, VERNON.
YOUNG, VEALL.
SCORERS – YOUNG 2, PARKER

25TH AUGST 1962 – HIGHBURY –
DIV. 1 - 62,308
ARSENAL 1 MANCHESTER UNITED 3
UNITED – GASKELL, BRENNAN, DUNNE, NICHOL-
SON, FOULKES, LAWTON, GILES, CHISNALL, HERD,
LAW, MOIR.
SCORERS – HERD 2, CHISNALL.
ARSENAL – MCKECHNIE, MAGILL, MCCULLOUGH,
CLAMP, BROWN, SNEDDON, ARMSTRONG, BARN-
WELL, STRONG, EASTHAM, SKIRTON.
SCORER – CLAMP.

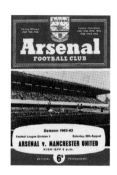

29TH AUGUST 1962 – OLD TRAFFORD –
DIV. 1 – 63,437
MANCHESTER UNITED 0 EVERTON 1
UNITED - GASKELL, BRENNAN, DUNNE, NICHOL-
SON, FOULKES, LAWTON, GILES, CHISNALL, HERD,
LAW, MOIR.
EVERTON - WEST, PARKER, THOMSON, GABRIEL,
LABONE, HARRIS, STEVENS, BINGHAM, VERNON.
YOUNG, MORRISSEY.
SCORER – VERNON [PEN].

1ST SEPTEMBER 1962 – OLD TRAFFORD –
DIV. 1 – 39,847
MANCHESTER UNITED 2 BIRMINGHAM CITY 0
UNITED - GASKELL, BRENNAN, DUNNE, NICHOL-
SON, FOULKES, LAWTON, GILES, CHISNALL, HERD,
LAW, MOIR.
SCORERS – GILES, HERD.
BIRMINGHAM CITY – SCHOFIELD, LYNN, SISSONS,
HENNESSEY, SMITH, BEARD, HELLAWELL, BLOOM-
FIELD, HARRIS, LEEK, AULD.

5TH SEPTEMBER 1962 – BURNDEN PARK –
DIV. 1 – 44,859
BOLTON WANDERERS 3 MANCHESTER UNITED 0
UNITED - GASKELL, BRENNAN, DUNNE, NICHOL-
SON, FOULKES, LAWTON, GILES, QUIXALL, HERD,
LAW, MOIR.
BOLTON WANDERERS – HOPKINSON, HARTLE,
FARRIMOND, THRELFALL, EDWARDS, RIMMER,
HOLDEN, HILL, DAVIES, MCGARRY, PILKINGTON.
SCORERS – DAVIES, PILKINGTON [PEN], HILL.

8TH SEPTEMBER 1962 – BRISBANE ROAD –
DIV. 1 – 24,902
LEYTON ORIENT 1 MANCHESTER UNITED 0
UNITED - GASKELL, BRENNAN, DUNNE, NICHOL-
SON, FOULKES, LAWTON, MOIR, SETTERS, HERD,
LAW, MCMILLAN.
LEYTON ORIENT – GEORGE, CHARLTON. LEWIS,
LUCAS, BISHOP, LEA, DEELEY, BOLLAND, DUN-
MORE, GRAHAM, MCDONALD.
SCORER – MCDONALD.

**12TH SEPTEMBER 1962 – OLD TRAFFORD –
DIV. 1 – 37,721**
MANCHESTER UNITED 3 BOLTON WANDERERS 0
UNITED - GASKELL, BRENNAN, DUNNE, STILES,
FOULKES, SETTERS, GILES, LAWTON, HERD, LAW,
CANTWELL.
SCORERS – HERD 2, CANTWELL.
BOLTON WANDERERS – HOPKINSON, HARTLE,
COOPER, THRELFALL, EDWARDS, HATTON, HILL,
HOLDEN, DAVIES, DEAKIN, PILKINGTON.

**15TH SEPTEMBER 1962 – OLD TRAFFORD –
DIV. 1 – 49,193**
MANCHESTER UNITED 2 MANCHESTER CITY 3
UNITED - GASKELL, BRENNAN, DUNNE, STILES,
FOULKES, NICHOLSON, GILES, LAWTON, HERD,
LAW, CANTWELL.
SCORERS – LAW 2.
MANCHESTER CITY – TRAUTMANN. BETTS, SEAR,
KENNEDY, LEIVERS, CHADWICK, YOUNG, DOBING,
HARLEY, HAYES, WAGSTAFFE.
SCORERS – DOBING [PEN]. HAYES, HARLEY.

**19TH SEPTEMBER 1962 – BERNABEU STADIUM –
FRIENDLY – 80,000**
REAL MADRID 0 MANCHESTER UNITED 2
UNITED - GASKELL, BRENNAN, DUNNE, STILES,
FOULKES, LAWTON, GILES, PEARSON, HERD, LAW,
MOIR.
SCORERS – PEARSON, HERD.
REAL MADRID – VINCENTE, RIVILLA [SUB. ISIDRO],
SANTAMARIA, MIERA [SUB. CASADO], MULLER,
ZARRAGA [SUB. ZOCO], AMANCIO [SUB. FELIX
RUIZ], EVARISTO [SUB. FELO], DI STEFANO, MEN-
DOZA [SUB. YANKO DAUCIK], GENTO [SUB. RUIZ].

**22ND SEPTEMBER 1962 – OLD TRAFFORD –
DIV. 1 – 45,954**
MANCHESTER UNITED 2 BURNLEY 5
UNITED - GASKELL, BRENNAN, DUNNE, STILES,
FOULKES, LAWTON, GILES, LAW, HERD, PEARSON,
MOIR.
SCORERS – STILES, LAW.
BURNLEY – BLACKLAW, ANGUS, ELDER, WALKER,
TALBUT, MILLER, CONNELLY, POINTER, LOCH-
HEAD, MCILROY, HARRIS.
SCORERS – CONNELLY 3, LOCHHEAD, MCILROY.

**25TH SEPTEMBER 1962 – OLD TRAFFORD –
FRIENDLY – 47,532**
MANCHESTER UNITED 2 BENFICA 2
UNITED – GREGG, BRENNAN, DUNNE, STILES,
FOULKES, LAWTON, GILES, LAW, QUIXALL, CHIS-
NALL [SUB. MOIR], MCMILLAN.
SCORERS – LAW, QUIXALL [PEN].
BENFICA – BARROCA, JACINTO, CRUZ, CAVEM,
RAUL, HUMBERTO, AUGUSTO, [SUB. SILVA], EUSE-
BIO, AGUAS [SUB. TORRES], COLUNA, SIMOES.
SCORERS – EUSEBIO 2.

**29TH SEPTEMBER 1962 – HILLSBOROUGH –
DIV. 1 40,520**
SHEFFIELD WED 1 MANCHESTER UNITED 0
UNITED – GREGG, BRENNAN, DUNNE, STILES,
FOULKES, LAWTON, GILES, LAW, QUIXALL, CHIS-
NALL, MCMILLAN.
SHEFFIELD WEDNESDAY – SPRINGETT, HORROBIN,
MEGSON, EUSTAGE, SWAN, KAY, WILKINSON,
YOUNG, LAYNE, DOBSON, HOLLIDAY.
SCORER – KAY.

**6TH OCTOBER 1962 – BLOOMFIELD ROAD –
DIV. 1 – 33,242**
BLACKPOOL 2 MANCHESTER UNITED 2
UNITED – GREGG, BRENNAN, DUNNE, STILES,
FOULKES, NICHOLSON, GILES, LAW, HERD,
LAWTON, MCMILLAN,
SCORER – HERD 2.
BLACKPOOL – WAITERS, ARMFIELD, MARTIN,
CRAWFORD, GRATRIX, DURIE, WATT, MCPHEE,
CHARNLEY, PARRY, HORNE.
SCORERS - MCPHEE, CHARNLEY.

**13TH OCTOBER 1962 – OLD TRAFFORD –
DIV. 1 – 42,252**
MANCHESTER UNITED 0 BLACKBURN ROVERS 3
UNITED – GREGG, BRENNAN, DUNNE, STILES,
FOULKES, NICHOLSON, GILES, LAW, HERD, CHARL-
TON, MCMILLAN,
BLACKBURN ROVERS – ELSE, BRAY, NEWTON,
CLAYTON, WOODS, MCGRATH, RATCLIFFE, LAW-
THER, PICKERING, DOUGLAS, HARRISON.
SCORERS – MCGRATH, HARRISON, LAWTHER.

**20TH OCTOBER 1962 – WHITE HART LANE –
DIV. 1 – 51,314
TOTTENHAM HOTSPUR 6 MANCHESTER UNITED 2**
UNITED – GREGG, BRENNAN, CANTWELL, STILES,
FOULKES, SETTERS, GILES, QUIXALL, HERD, LAW,
CHARLTON.
SCORERS – HERD, QUIXALL [PEN].
TOTTENHAM HOTSPUR – BROWN, BAKER, HENRY,
BLANCHFLOWER, NORMAN, MACKAY, MEDWIN,
WHITE, ALLEN, GREAVES, JONES.
SCORERS – GREAVES 3, MEDWIN 2, JONES.

**27TH OCTOBER 1962 – OLD TRAFFORD –
DIV. 1 – 29,904
MANCHESTER UNITED 3 WEST HAM UNITED 1**
UNITED – GREGG, BRENNAN, CANTWELL, STILES,
FOULKES, SETTERS, GILES, QUIXALL, HERD, LAW,
CHARLTON.
SCORERS – QUIXALL 2, LAW.
WEST HAM UNITED – LESLIE, BURKETT, LYALL,
PETERS, BROWN, MOORE, BRABROOK, WOOS-
NAM, SEALEY, BYRNE, MUSGROVE.
SCORER – MUSGROVE.

**29TH OCTOBER – OLD TRAFFORD –
FRIENDLY – 15,035
MANCHESTER UNITED 3 FIRST VIENNA 1**
UNITED – GASKELL, BRENNAN, CANTWELL,
STILES, FOULKES, SETTERS, GILES, QUIXALL, HERD,
LAW, CHARLTON [SUB. DUNNE].
SCORERS – CHARLTON, HERD, OG.
FIRST VIENNA – SCHMIED, KOZICH, WEBORA,
LIENNER, DIRNBERGER, KOLLER, LAHNER,
PICHLER, VISOLINOVIC, WIEGER, SCHIEHL.
SCORER – KOLLER [PEN].

**3RD NOVEMBER 1962 – PORTMAN ROAD –
DIV. 1 – 18,483
IPSWICH TOWN 3 MANCHESTER UNITED 5**
UNITED – GREGG, BRENNAN, CANTWELL, STILES,
FOULKES, SETTERS, GILES, QUIXALL, HERD, LAW,
CHARLTON.
SCORERS – LAW 4, HERD.
IPSWICH TOWN – HALL, CARBERRY, MALCOLM,
BAXTER, NELSON. PICKETT, STEPHENSON,
MORAN, CRAWFORD, BLACKWOOD, LEADBETTER.
SCORERS – BLACKWOOD 2, CRAWFORD.

10TH NOVEMBER 1962 – OLD TRAFFOD –
DIV. 1 – 43,810
MANCHESTER UNITED 3 LIVERPOOL 3
UNITED – GREGG, BRENNAN, CANTWELL, STILES,
FOULKES, SETTERS, GILES, QUIXALL, HERD, LAW,
CHARLTON.
SCORERS – HERD, QUIXALL [PEN], GILES.
LIVERPOOL – LAWRENCE, BYRNE, MORAN,
MILNE, YEATS, STEVENSON, CALLAGHAN, HUNT,
ST JOHN, MELIA, A'COURT.
SCORERS – ST JOHN, MELIA, MORAN.

17TH NOVEMBER 1963 – MOLINEUX –
DIV. 1 – 27,305
WOLVES 2 MANCHESTER UNITED 3
UNITED – GREGG, BRENNAN, CANTWELL, STILES,
FOULKES, SETTERS, GILES, QUIXALL, HERD, LAW,
CHARLTON.
SCORERS - LAW 2, HERD.
WOLVERHAMPTON WANDERERS – DAVIES,
SHOWELL, THOMPSON, KIRKHAM, WOODFIELD,
FLOWERS, WHARTON, CROWE, STOBART, BROAD-
BENT, HINTON.
SCORER – STOBART 2.

24TH NOVEMBER 1962 – OLD TRAFFORD –
DIV. 1 - 36,852
MANCHESTER UNITED 2 ASTON VILLA 2
UNITED – GREGG, BRENNAN, CANTWELL, STILES,
FOULKES, SETTERS, GILES, QUIXALL, HERD, LAW,
CHARLTON.
SCORER – QUIXALL 2 [1 PEN].
ASTON VILLA – SIDEBOTTOM, FRASER, AITKEN,
CROWE, SLEEUWENHOEK, TINDALL, MACEWAN,
BAKER, DOUGAN, O'NEILL, BURROWS.
SCORERS – DOUGAN, OG.

1ST DECEMBER 1962 – BRAMALL LANE –
DIV. 1 - 25,173
SHEFFIELD UNITED 1 MANCHESTER UNITED 1
UNITED – GREGG, BRENNAN, CANTWELL, STILES,
FOULKES, SETTERS, GILES, QUIXALL, HERD,
LAWTON, CHARLTON.
SCORER – CHARLTON.
SHEFFIELD UNITED – HODKINSON, COLDWELL,
G. SHAW, RICHARDSON, J. SHAW, SUMMERS,
ALLCHURCH, KETTLEBROUGH, SHIELS, HODGSON,
SIMPSON.
SCORER – SIMPSON [PEN].

8TH DECEMBER 1962 – OLD TRAFFORD –
DIV. 1 – 27,496
MANCHESTER UNITED 5 NOTTINGHAM FOREST 1
UNITED – GREGG, BRENNAN, CANTWELL,
NICHOLSON, FOULKES, LAWTON, GILES, QUIXALL,
HERD, LAW, CHARLTON.
SCORERS – HERD 2, CHARLTON, GILES, LAW.
NOTTINGHAM FOREST – ARMSTRONG, WILSON,
GRAY, WHITEFOOT, MCKINLAY, PALMER, HOCKEY,
ADDISON, JULIENS, QUIGLEY, LE FLEM.
SCORER – ADDISON.

15TH DECEMBER 1962 – THE HAWTHORNS –
DIV. 1 – 18,113
WEST BROM 3 MANCHESTER UNITED 0
UNITED – GREGG, BRENNAN, CANTWELL, STILES,
FOULKES, NICHOLSON, GILES, QUIXALL, HERD,
LAW, MOIR.
WEST BROM – POTTER, HOWE, S. WILLIAMS,
CRAM, JONES, DRURY, JACKSON, FENTON, SMITH,
KEVAN, CLARKE.
SCORERS – CRAM, SMITH, JACKSON.

22ND DECEMBER 1962 – OLD TRAFFORD –
DIV. 1 – 22,559
MANCHESTER UNITED 0 ARSENAL 1 -
ABANDONED – 56TH MINUTE.
UNITED – GREGG, BRENNAN, CANTWELL, STILES,
FOULKES, SETTERS, GILES, QUIXALL, HERD, LAW,
CHARLTON.
ARSENAL – MCCLELLAND, MAGULL,
MCCULLOUGH, BARNWELL, NEILL, SNEDDON,
MACLEOD, STRONG, BAKER, EASTHAM, ARM-
STRONG.
SCORER – BARNWELL.

26TH DECEMBER 1962 – CRAVEN COTTAGE –
DIV. 1 - 23,928
FULHAM 0 MANCHESTER UNITED 1
UNITED – GREGG, BRENNAN, CANTWELL, STILES,
FOULKES, SETTERS, GILES, QUIXALL, HERD, LAW,
CHARLTON.
SCORER – CHARLTON.
FULHAM – MACEDO, COHEN, LANGLEY, MUL-
LERY, KEETCH, WATSON, LEGGAT, COOK, BROWN,
ROBSON, STRATTON.

2ND FEBRUARY 1963 – GLENMALURE PARK, DUBLIN – FRIENDLY – 18,000

MANCHESTER UNITED 2 COVENTRY CITY 2

UNITED – GREGG, BRENNAN, CANTWELL, STILES, FOULKES, SETTERS, GILES, QUIXALL, HERD, LAW, CHARLTON.

SCORERS – QUIXALL, CHARLTON.

COVENTRY CITY – WEESON, SILLETT, KEARNS, HILL, CURTIS, FARMER, HUMPHRIES, HALE, BLY, WHITEHOUSE, REES.

SCORERS – FARMER, WHITEHOUSE.

13TH FEBRUARY 1963 – FLOWERS LODGE, CORK – FRIENDLY – 6,000

MANCHESTER UNITED 4 BOLTON WANDERERS 2

UNITED – GREGG, BRENNAN, CANTWELL, CRE-RAND, FOULKES, SETTERS, GILES, QUIXALL, HERD, LAW, WALKER.

SCORERS – CRERAND, QUIXALL [PEN], LAW, GILES.

BOLTON WANDERERS – HOPKINSON, HARTLE, FARRIMOND, STANLEY, EDWARDS, RIMMER, LEE, HILL, DAVIES, DEAKIN, BUTLER.

SCORERS – LEE [1 PEN].

19TH FEBRUARY 1963 – DUBLIN – FRIENDLY – 20,000

DUBLIN SELECT 0 MANCHESTER UNITED 4

UNITED – GREGG, BRENNAN, CANTWELL, CRE-RAND, FOULKES, SETTERS, GILES, QUIXALL, HERD, LAW, CHARLTON.

SCORERS – HERD 2, LAW, CHARLTON.

DUBLIN SELECT – DUNNE, KEOGH, BROWNE, DALTON, CAHILL, NOLAN, O'NEILL, MOONEY, BAILHAM, TYRELL, BOYCE.

SUBSTITUTE - BYRNE.

23RD FEBRUARY 1963 – OLD TRAFFORD – DIV. 1 – 33,182

MANCHESTER UNITED 1 BLACKPOOL 1

UNITED – GREGG, BRENNAN, CANTWELL, CRE-RAND, FOULKES, SETTERS, GILES, QUIXALL, HERD, CHISNALL, CHARLTON.

SCORER – HERD

BLACKPOOL – WAITERS, ARMFIELD, MARTIN, MCPHEE, GRATRIX, DURIE, HILL, QUINN, NAPIER, CHARNLEY, HORNE.

SCORER – CHARNLEY [PEN]

2ND MARCH 1963 – EWOOD PARK –
DIV. 1 -27,924
BLACKBURN ROVERS 2 MANCHESTER UNITED 2
UNITED – GREGG, BRENNAN, CANTWELL, CRE-
RAND, FOULKES, SETTERS, GILES, QUIXALL, HERD,
LAW, CHARLTON.
SCORERS – LAW, CHARLTON
BLACKBURN ROVERS – ELSE, BRAY, NEWTON,
CLAYTON, WOODS, MCGRATH, FERGUSON,
DOUGLAS, PICKERING, BYRON, HARRISON.
SCORERS – BYRON. PICKERING.

4TH MARCH 1963 – OLD TRAFFORD –
FA CUP 3RD ROUND – 47,703
MANCHESTER UNITED 5 HUDDERSFIELD TOWN 0
UNITED – GREGG, BRENNAN, CANTWELL, STILES,
FOULKES, SETTERS, GILES, QUIXALL, HERD, LAW,
CHARLTON.
SCORERS – LAW 3, QUIXALL, GILES.
HUDDERSFIELD TOWN – WOOD, ATKINS, PARKER,
BETTANY, TAYLOR, DINSDALE, MCHALE, WHITE,
STOKES, MASSIE, O'GRADY.

9TH MARCH 1963 – OLD TRAFFORD –
DIV. 1 – 53,416
MANCHESTER UNITED 0 TOTTENHAM HOTSPUR 2
UNITED – GREGG, BRENNAN, CANTWELL, CRE-
RAND, FOULKES, STILES, GILES, QUIXALL, HERD,
LAW, CHARLTON.
TOTTENHAM HOTSPUR – BROWN, HOPKINS,
HENRY, MARCHI, NORMAN, MACKAY, SAUL,
WHITE, SMITH, GREAVES, JONES.
SCORERS – JONES, SAUL.

11TH MARCH 1963 – OLD TRAFFORD –
FA CUP 4TH ROUND – 52,265
MANCHESTER UNITED 1 ASTON VILLA 0
UNITED – GREGG, BRENNAN, CANTWELL, STILES,
FOULKES, SETTERS, GILES, QUIXALL, HERD, LAW,
CHARLTON.
SCORER – QUIXALL
ASTON VILLA – SIDEBOTTOM, FRASER, AITKEN,
TINDALL, CROWE, DEAKIN, MACEWAN, WYLIE,
THOMSON, WOOSNAM, BURROWS.

16TH MARCH – OLD TRAFFORD –
FA CUP 5TH ROUND – 48,298
MANCHESTER UNITED 2 CHELSEA 1
UNITED – GREGG, BRENNAN, CANTWELL, STILES,
FOULKES, SETTERS, GILES, QUIXALL, HERD, LAW,
CHARLTON.
SCORERS – LAW, QUIXALL.
CHELSEA – BONETTI, SHELLITO, MCCREADIE,
VENABLES, MORTIMORE, UPTON, MURRAY, TAM-
BLING, MOORE, SORRELL, BLUNSTONE
SCORER – SORRELL.

18TH MARCH 1963 – UPTON PARK –
DIV. 1 – 28,950
WEST HAM UNITED 3 MANCHESTER UNITED 1
UNITED – GREGG, BRENNAN, CANTWELL, CRE-
RAND, FOULKES, SETTERS, GILES, STILES, HERD,
LAW, CHARLTON.
SCORER – HERD.
WEST HAM UNITED – RHODES, KIRKUP, BURKETT,
BOVINGTON, BROWN, MOORE, BRABROOK,
BOYCE, SEALEY, HURST, SCOTT.
SCORERS – BROWN, SEALY, OG [BRENNAN].

23RD MARCH – OLD TRAFFORD –
DIV. 1 – 32,782
MANCHESTER UNITED 0 IPSWICH TOWN 1
UNITED – GREGG, BRENNAN, CANTWELL, CRE-
RAND, FOULKES, SETTERS, GILES, QUIXALL, HERD,
LAW, CHARLTON.
IPSWICH TOWN – BAILEY, CARBERRY, COMPTON,
BAXTER, NELSON, ELSWORTHY, STEPHENSON,
BLACKWOOD, CRAWFORD, PHILLIPS, LEADBETTER.
SCORER – LEADBETTER.

30TH MARCH 1963 – HIGHFIELD ROAD –
FA CUP 6TH ROUND – 44,000
COVENTRY CITY 1 MANCHESTER UNITED 3
UNITED – GREGG, BRENNAN, DUNNE, CRERAND,
FOULKES, SETTERS, GILES, QUIXALL, HERD, LAW,
CHARLTON.
SCORERS – CHARLTON 2, QUIXALL.
COVENTRY CITY – WEESON, SILLETT, KEARNS,
HILL, CURTIS, BRUCK, HUMPHRIES, BARR, BLY,
WHITEHOUSE, REES.
SCORER – BLY.

1ST APRIL 1963 - OLD TRAFFORD –
DIV. 1 – 28,124
MANCHESTER UNITED 0 FULHAM 2
UNITED – GREGG, BRENNAN, DUNNE, CRERAND,
FOULKES, SETTERS, GILES, CHISNALL, QUIXALL,
LAW, CHARLTON.
FULHAM – MACEDO, COHEN, LANGLEY, MULLERY,
KEETCH, ROBSON, KEY, LEGGAT, COOK, BROWN,
O'CONNELL.
SCORERS – O'CONNELL, LEGGAT.

9TH APRIL 1963 – VILLA PARK –
DIV. 1 - 26,867
ASTON VILLA 1 MANCHESTER UNITED2
UNITED – GREGG, BRENNAN, CANTWELL, CRE-
RAND, FOULKES, SETTERS, GILES, STILES, HERD,
QUIXALL, CHARLTON.
SCORERS – SETTERS, CHARTON.
ASTON VILLA – GAVAN, FRASER, AITKEN, CROWE,
SLEEUWENHOEK, TINDALL, BAKER, THOMSON,
DOUGAN, WOOSNAM, BURROWS.
SCORER – THOMSON.

13TH APRIL 1963 – ANFIELD –
DIV 1 – 51,529
LIVERPOOL 1 MANCHESTER UNITED 0
UNITED – GREGG, BRENNAN, DUNNE, CRERAND,
FOULKES, SETTERS, GILES, STILES, QUIXALL, LAW,
CHARLTON.
LIVERPOOL – LAWRENCE, JONES, MORAN, MILNE,
YEATS, STEVENSON, CALLAGHAN, HUNT, ST JOHN,
MELIA, ARROWSMITH.
SCORER – ST JOHN.

15TH APRIL 1963 – OLD TRAFFORD –
DIV. 1 – 50,005
MANCHESTER UNITED 2 LEICESTER CITY 2
UNITED – GREGG, BRENNAN, DUNNE, CRERAND,
FOULKES, SETTERS, QUIXALL, STILES, HERD, LAW,
CHARLTON.
SCORERS – HERD, CHARLTON.
LEICESTER CITY – BANKS, SJOBERG, NORMAN,
MCLINTOCK, KING, APPLETON, RILEY, CROSS,
KEYWORTH, GIBSON, CHEESBROUGH.
SCORERS – CROSS, NORMAN.

16TH APRIL 1963 – FILBERT STREET –
DIV. 1 – 37,002
LEICESTER CITY 4 MANCHESTER UNITED 3
UNITED – GREGG, BRENNAN, DUNNE, CRERAND,
FOULKES, SETTERS, QUIXALL, STILES, HERD, LAW,
CHARLTON.
SCORER – LAW 3
LEICESTER CITY - BANKS, SJOBERG, NORMAN,
CROSS, KING, APPLETON, RILEY, HEATH, KEY-
WORTH, MCLINTOCK, GIBSON.
SCORERS – KEYWORTH 3, HEATH.

20TH APRIL 1963 – OLD TRAFFORD –
DIV. 1 - 31,179
MANCHESTER UNITED 1 SHEFFIELD UNITED 1
UNITED – GREGG, BRENNAN, DUNNE, CRERAND,
FOULKES, SETTERS, QUIXALL, STILES, HERD, LAW,
CHARLTON.
SCORER – LAW.
SHEFFIELD UNITED – HODGKINSON, COLDWELL,
G. SHAW, RICHARDSON, J. SHAW, SUMMERS,
ALLCHURCH, WAGSTAFF, PACE, JONES, HARTLE.
SCORER – HARTLE.

22ND APRIL 1963 – OLD TRAFFORD –
DIV. 1 – 36,147
MANCHESTER UNITED 2 WOLVES 1
UNITED – GASKELL, BRENNAN, DUNNE, CRE-
RAND, FOULKES, SETTERS, QUIXALL, STILES,
HERD, LAW, CHARLTON.
SCORERS – HERD, LAW.
WOLVERHAMPTON WANDERERS – DAVIES,
SHOWELL, THOMSON, KIRKMAN, WOODFIELD,
GOODWIN, CROWE, MURRAY, STOBART, BROAD-
BENT, WHARTON.
SCORER – OG [DUNNE].

27TH APRIL 1963 – VILLA PARK –
FA CUP SEMI-FINAL – 68,312.
MANCHESTER UNITED 1 SOUTHAMPTON 0
UNITED – GASKELL, DUNNE, CANTWELL, CRE-
RAND, FOULKES, SETTERS, GILES, STILES, HERD,
LAW, CHARLTON.
SCORER – LAW.
SOUTHAMPTON – REYNOLDS, WILLIAMS,
TRAYNOR, WIMSHURST, KNAPP, HUXFORD, PAINE,
O'BRIEN, KIRBY, BURNSIDE, SYDENHAM.

1ST MAY 1963 – OLD TRAFFORD –
DIV. 1 – 31,878
MANCHESTER UNITED 1 SHEFFIELD WED 3
UNITED – GASKELL, BRENNAN, CANTWELL,
CRERAND, FOULKES, SETTERS, QUIXALL, STILES,
HERD, LAW, CHARLTON.
SCORER – SETTERS.
SHEFFIELD WEDNESDAY – SPRINGETT, JOHN-
SON, MEGSON, MCAENEARNEY, SWAN, YOUNG,
FINNEY, QUINN, LAYNE, FANTHAM, DOBSON.
SCORERS – FINNEY, QUINN, MEGSON.

4TH MAY 1963 – TURF MOOR –
DIV. 1 – 30,266
BURNLEY 0 MANCHESTER UNITED 1
UNITED – GASKELL, DUNNE, CANTWELL, CRE-
RAND, FOULKES, SETTERS, GILES, STILES, QUIX-
ALL, LAW, CHARLTON.
SCORER – LAW.
BURNLEY – BLACKLAW, ANGUS, ELDER, O'NEILL,
TALBUT, MILLER, CONNELLY, ROBSON, LOCHHEAD,
SIMPSON, HARRIS.

6TH MAY 1963 – OLD TRAFFORD –
DIV. 1 – 35,999
MANCHESTER UNITED 2 ARSENAL 3
UNITED – GASKELL, DUNNE, CANTWELL, CRE-
RAND, FOULKES, SETTERS, GILES, STILES, QUIX-
ALL, LAW, CHARLTON.
SCORER – LAW 2.
ARSENAL – MCCLELLAND, MAGILL, CLARK,
BARNWELL, BROWN, MCCULLOUGH, MACLEOD,
STRONG, BAKER, SAMMELS, SKIRTON.
SCORERS – BAKER, STRONG, SKIRTON.

10TH MAY 1963 – ST. ANDREWS –
DIV. 1 – 21,814
BIRMINGHAM CIT 2 MANCHESTER UNITED 1
UNITED – GASKELL, DUNNE, CANTWELL, CRE-
RAND, FOULKES, STILES, QUIXALL, GILES, HERD,
LAW, CHARLTON.
SCORER – LAW.
BIRMINGHAM CITY – WITHERS, LYNN, GREEN,
HENNESSEY, SMITH, BEARD, HELLAWELL, BLOOM-
FIELD, HARRIS, LEEK, AULD.
SCORERS – BLOOMFIELD, LEEK.

15TH MAY 1963 – MAINE ROAD –
DIV. 1 – 52,424
MANCHESTER CITY 1 MANCHESTER UNITED 1
UNITED – GASKELL, DUNNE, CANTWELL, CRE-
RAND, FOULKES, STILES, QUIXALL, GILES, HERD,
LAW, CHARLTON.
SCORER – QUIXALL [PEN].
MANCHESTER CITY – DOWD, KENNEDY, SEAR,
OAKES, LEIVERS, GRAY, YOUNG, DOBING, HARLEY,
HAYES, WAGSTAFFE.
SCORER – HARLEY.

18TH MAY 1963 – OLD TRAFFORD –
DIV. 1 – 32,759
MANCHESTER UNITED 3 LEYTON ORIENT 1
UNITED – GASKELL, DUNNE, CANTWELL, CRE-
RAND, FOULKES, SETTERS, QUIXALL, GILES, HERD,
LAW, CHARLTON.
SCORERS – LAW, CHARLTON, OG [S. CHARLTON].
LEYTON ORIENT – GEORGE, S. CHARLTON,
TAYLOR, LUCAS, BISHOP, LEA, MASON, GIBBS,
DUNMORE, BOLLAND, MUSGROVE.
SCORER – DUNMORE.

20TH MAY 1963 – CITY GROUND –
DIV. 1 – 16,130
NOTTINGHAM FOREST 3 MANCHESTER UNITED 2
UNITED – GASKELL, DUNNE, CANTWELL, CRE-
RAND, HAYDOCK, BRENNAN, QUIXALL, STILES,
HERD, GILES, WALKER.
SCORER – GILES, HERD.
NOTTINGHAM FOREST – GRUMMITT, BAIRD,
MOCHAN, WHITEFOOT, MCKINLAY, WINFIELD,
HOCKEY, ADDISON, JULIANS, QUIGLEY, LE FLEM.
SCORERS – ADDISON, MOCHAN, JULIANS.

25TH MAY 1963 – WEMBLEY –
FA CUP FINAL – 99,604
LEICESTER CITY 1 MANCHESTER UNITED 3
UNITED – GASKELL, DUNNE, CANTWELL, CRE-
RAND, FOULKES, SETTERS, GILES, QUIXALL, HERD,
LAW, CHARLTON.
SCORERS – HERD 2, LAW.
LEICESTER CITY - BANKS, SJOBERG, NORMAN,
MCLINTOCK, KING, APPLETON, RILEY, CROSS,
KEYWORTH, GIBSON, STRINGFELLOW.
SCORER – KEYWORTH.

29TH MAY 1963 – FRIENDLY – 20,000
JUVENTUS 0 MANCHESTER UNITED 1
UNITED – GREGG, DUNNE, CANTWELL, CRERAND,
FOULKES, SETTERS, GILES, CHISNALL, HERD, LAW.
MCMILLAN.
SCORER – MCMILLAN.
JUVENTUS – MATTREL [SUB. ANZOLIN], EMOLI,
CASTANO, SALVADORE, LEONCINI, DEL SOL,
SACCO, PATTAGLIA, MIRANDA, SICILIANO [SUB.
ZIGONI], STACCHINI [SUB. ROSSI].

1ST JUNE 1963 – FRIENDLY – 20,000
AS ROMA 2 MANCHESTER UNITED 3
UNITED – GREGG, DUNNE, CANTWELL, CRERAND,
FOULKES, SETTERS, GILES, CHISNALL, HERD, LAW,
MCMILLAN.
SCORERS – MCMILLAN, LAW, GILES.
AS ROMA – MATTEUCCI, FONTANA, BERGMARK,
PESTRIN, LOSI, JONSSON, LEONARDI, LOJACONO,
J. CHARLES, ANGELILLO, MANFREDINI.
SCORERS – ANGELILLO 2.

Law's decider
A goal eight minutes from time by Denis Law gave Manchester United a 3—2 win a friendly match with Roma in Rome last night.
Howitt scored a hat-trick to help Stoke City to a 5—0 win over Hapoel in Tel Aviv.

6TH JUNE 1963 – LIVORNO - FRIENDLY – 15,000
LEGHORN 0 MANCHESTER UNITED
UNITED - GREGG, DUNNE, CANTWELL, STILES,
FOULKES, LAWTON, GILES, CHISNALL, HERD, LAW,
MCMILLAN.
SCORERS – HERD, CHISNALL.
LEGHORN – UNKNOWN.

Manchester United Win
Manchester United, the English cup-holders, beat Leghorn F.C. 2-0 in a friendly soccer match at Leghorn, Italy, last night. John Chisnall (eighth minute) and Dave Herd (57th) scored for United.

FOOTBALL ASSOCIATION CHALLENGE CUP
SEASON 1962-1963

* * *

Celebration

Dinner & Dance

of the
MANCHESTER UNITED
FOOTBALL CLUB

* * *

FINAL TIE

Manchester United

versus

Leicester City

* * *

Lancaster Room, Savoy Hotel, Strand, London
25th MAY, 1963